Attims

Why Marxism?

WHY MARXISM

?

The Continuing Success of

a Failed Theory

ROBERT G. WESSON

———

Basic Books, Inc., Publishers

NEW YORK

Library of Congress Cataloging in Publication Data

Wesson, Robert G.
  Why Marxism?

  Includes bibliographical references and index.
  1. Socialism. 2. Communism. I. Title.
HX36.W44   335.4   75-9138
ISBN 0-465-09188-1

CONTENTS

PREFACE

IT IS CUSTOMARY, in presenting a new book on such a well-worn subject as Marxism, to offer the reader some explanation as to why it is considered necessary to add yet another treatment of the subject. Briefly, the answer is that this book is not so much about Marxism as about why so many books have been written about it. This is not to be understood by analysis of the doctrines, an endless and baffling task to which little attention is given here, but by study of the uses of Marxism for various people, parties, and revolutionary movements which came into command of great states; that is, of Marxism as a serious kind of political poetry.

Marxists will not care to see the question put in this way, because it implies that adherence to the doctrines is to be understood not because they reveal the truth but because they fulfill more or less irrational political and psychological needs. It is not intended thereby necessarily to impugn either the intelligence or sincerity of many genuine believers. Some, no doubt, have taken their Marxism at least as cynically as many advertising copy writers take their work, but it may be assumed that dedicated idealists have been very numerous in both East and West.

In this study there is no claim of originality for any piece of information; and ideas are owed to many writers, as indicated by footnotes. Professor Adam B. Ulam and Dr. Milorad Drachkovitch saw the manuscript, and I am very grateful for their comments, especially the numerous and detailed suggestions offered by the latter. Both, however, will undoubtedly find enough to disagree with in this book—perhaps no one will like everything in it. A large debt is also owed to the unfailing assistance at all stages of Deborah T. Wesson.

Robert G. Wesson
Santa Barbara, California
September, 1975

vi

Why Marxism?

INTRODUCTION

THE LIVING Karl Marx was a dismal failure. He passed most of his life in poverty, dependent on the charity of the capitalist Friedrich Engels. His writings were never sufficiently in demand to earn a living. He had great difficulty in finishing anything, and the bulk of what he wrote he never saw in print. His revolutionary activities came to nothing, and capitalist Europe was more tranquil and stable when he left the scene than when he came on it. The radical organizations with which he was associated broke up in a few years, or he broke them up in disgust. He quarreled violently with virtually all the leaders of the socialist and revolutionary movements of his day. The working class of England, where he lived in exile, paid him little heed and soon forgot him. Engels prepared a flattering eulogy for his burial, but only nine persons were there to hear it.

The dead Marx has come into unexampled success. Marxism is the basis of official ideologies governing about a third of the world's population, and millions of people in non-Marxist countries voluntarily subscribe to political parties and to an ideology supported by Marxist (or Marxist-Leninist) states. Marxism-Leninism is the only worldwide political movement, with Communist parties in all countries where not suppressed by force.

Even more remarkable than this political success has been

3

Marxism's appeal to other millions who accept no party discipline, who are under no compulsion, and who do not stand to gain materially by accepting a Marxist outlook. A large part of the world's intelligentsia and university students, especially outside the English-speaking countries, look on Karl Marx as a towering authority, a supergenius. Indeed, in recent years, the stature and importance of non-Communist Marxism have grown, especially in Europe. The empirical-minded British were long unimpressed by Marxist theorizing, but in the 1970s Marxists have become powerful in the trade unions and Labour Party. Even in the decidedly anti-Communist United States, Marxist and near-Marxist studies prospered mightily in the early 1970s, especially in the elite institutions. The amount of writing on the ideas attributed to Marx far exceeds that dedicated to any other person whose claim to authority is based solely on his pen. No other nonreligious works have been so widely discussed and analyzed as those of Marx.

This enormous gap between contemporary and latter-day appraisal badly needs explanation. The obvious answer, and the one which Marxists must give, is that Marx discovered great truths which humanity has come only belatedly to appreciate—still inadequately, in the opinion of converts. But truth is single, and there is no agreement among Marxists as to what the truth of Marxism is. There are as many interpretations of Marxian ideas as there are of the Bible, and writers frequently offer yet another "true" meaning. Marxists disagree bitterly among themselves, one school denying to another the right to call itself Marxist.

Marx himself left no very definite theory for his successors to pick up and prove right. His serious and mature work was mostly in economics, a science then in its infancy; it is improbable that someone working over a hundred years ago and using the concepts of his age could have made revelations of much scientific utility (aside from possible inspirational value) for modern sophisticated economic analysis. It is often said that Marx's big contribution was historical materialism, but he never gave a systematic exposition of his theory. Some Marxists would reject the mature works as irrelevant and fasten onto the early manuscripts. But it is doubtful whether these youthful compositions offer significant original insights in social studies, whatever their poetic appeal.

Thus, if one looks to the works of Karl Marx, it is difficult to see how they could provide an appropriate interpretation of twentieth-century facts. The ideas which inspired Marx were evoked pri-

4

marily by the dislocations and tensions of the Industrial Revolution. Theories devised in response to the transition from a semifeudal agricultural to a capitalist-industrial order are not likely to be very applicable to the quite different problems of transition from modern industrial to what has been called postindustrial society. It is understandable that Marxism appeals, albeit illogically, to developing countries suffering the traumas of early industrialization. But Western intellectuals have to find in Marxism a significance beyond what the originator intended.

Marx spoke to the nineteenth century, and little in his corpus would seem to have been written for the ages. Most of his works are polemical. The most eloquent and most quoted, the *Communist Manifesto,* was indeed a manifesto, a vibrantly unobjective call to action; even *Capital* is largely a protracted damnation. His ideas were those of his day. The labor theory of value, the basis of the economic analysis which was developed to give substance to his theory of history and revolution, was common doctrine (mostly from Ricardo) in the first half of the nineteenth century but was already becoming obsolete in Marx's lifetime. The materialistic interpretation of history was more original, but independent Marxists nowadays hardly take it seriously except in a very general way. The only reality to which the supposedly universal analysis may be fairly comfortably applied is the transition from feudalism to capitalism in Europe—the experience for which Marx wrote. Moreover, inconsistencies abound. Perhaps fortunately for the popularity of Marxism, one can cite texts to show that Marx was authoritarian or democratic, that he believed absolutely in revolution or allowed a gradualist approach to socialism, that he was humanitarian or esteemed the deprived only for their utility to the cause, that he was a materialist or an idealist, that he was deterministic or voluntaristic.

The usefulness of a scientific theory lies in its predictive power; but, as is often pointed out, the predictions made or implied by Marx have nearly all been falsified by history. The claim for the moral authority of the proletariat was based on the assumption—rather gratuitous even at the time—that it would grow to include a large majority of the people. Nowhere has this even approximately come true; as a class the factory workers passed their apogee in Marx's lifetime. Their proportion of the population has since declined in leading industrial nations, and their wages have not sunk to subsistence levels, as Marx's theories required. The middle classes, whom Marx marked for extinction, perversely increased with industrial maturity. Economic crises did not become ever worse, and the expected revolution failed to come in the industrial countries. Marx and Engels practically gave up on it in their later years.

For such reasons, it was becoming obvious by the time of World War I that Marxism was outworn. Practically everything had turned out contrary to expectations, and the idea that the workers would seize power in the most advanced industrial countries was increasingly insubstantial and, for most people, undesirable. The events of 1914 showed up the futility of international Marxism, incorporated in the Second International; workers followed the call to national (not class) solidarity. As the war was coming to an end, revolution in the name of Marx came not in an advanced capitalist state but in relatively backward, largely preindustrial Russia. The results of the effort to establish a Marxist-based socialism were an eloquent refutation of the expectations of abundance, happiness, and freedom which Marxists had long nurtured. Not until 1928 did Russia recover its prewar standard of living, and its industrial workers have remained considerably less free than they were under tsarist rule.

Subsequent experiences would seem to have been more than ample, in a logical universe, to complete the discrediting of the Marxist approach. The Soviet system, without private property, engendered the most murderous tyranny since Genghis Khan's. Even the ideal of equality, which had somewhat softened the rigors of the Leninist era, was set aside as Stalin raised up a new privileged ruling class. When the capitalist order cracked in the industrialized West, this led not to rule by the proletariat but to fascist dictatorship. And the supposedly socialist Soviet state's cynical and aggressive foreign policy—including the partition of Poland with Hitler, the swallowing up of small states, and the war against Finland—demonstrated that socialization did not bring pacifism.

The record of recent years has piled up ever more contradictions to the basic ideas of Marxism. The Soviet Union and other states claiming inspiration from Marx have shown themselves to possess no magic recipe for prosperity; to the contrary, they have evinced increasing dependence on technological importation from supposedly backward capitalist states. Violent dissension between Russia and China laid to rest the idea that the abolition of private ownership of means of production would suffice to ensure universal harmony. Far from being a revolutionary's dream, the Soviet Union appeared more and more a stiff, staid, bureaucratic, elitist society.

Introduction

Moreover, the concerns of the world have changed. The misery of the industrial proletariat was a real problem in Marx's day. But since then, and especially since World War II, the woes of factory workers have tended to recede as a major social question. To some extent, especially in less developed countries, factory workers form practically a privileged class; the horrors of poverty and deprivation lie elsewhere. Today, the gap between rich and poor nations is more grievous than that between capitalists and workers of the industrial countries. New problems, about which Marxism had nothing to say at all, have piled up: the threat of nuclear war, disequilibria in international trade and finance, population problems, energy and resource concerns, dangers to the environment, and other difficulties that arise when technological outruns institutional progress. In this new world, the *Communist Manifesto* should be only a footnote to the history of early industrialization.

Yet Marxism rolls on as though confirmed by all that has occurred, gathering strength as it becomes less and less relevant to the changing age. It has grown partly because more and more ideas have been tacked onto it, albeit with limited relation to logical consistency. Lenin attached an analysis of imperialism, with the result that anti-imperialism to a large extent took the place of anticapitalism. Peasant revolution was brought into a Marxist-proletarian framework, qualifying revolutionary movements in preindustrial countries as Marxist. Authoritarian organizational and governmental principles were built into the Marxist-Leninist canon. Many thinkers also used the amorphous mass of Marx's and Engels's lucubrations as a taking-off place for various kinds of theory building in economics and sociology, and even in anthropology and psychology. Marxism thus outgrew the limited and time-bound testament of the founder, thereby saving itself from obsolescence. It has also been singularly fortunate in its ability to build upon success, deriving intellectual strength from political utility and vice versa, pyramiding humble beginnings as a doctrine of leftist discontent into massive strength as an official or unofficial ideology of many countries and groups. Its believers have made it important, and its importance has brought new believers.

Just how this has come about is a complex story, part of the confused and tumultuous history of the past hundred years. It can never be fully understood; it certainly has large elements of the personal and accidental. But it is the purpose of this book to trace some of its major aspects, the stages by which Marxism found growing importance and acceptance, from Engels's reformulation of the master's thought, through social democracy and the Russian Revolution, to the bitterness of the Third World and the New Left.

This story is embedded in the history of the maturing and spreading industrial revolution and its effects, especially on those who have felt left behind. *Why Marxism?* Why one hears so much today about an expatriate nineteenth-century German scholar, who scribbled in a cloud of cigar smoke while his family scrimped to pay the butcher, whose writings are arid, often unreadable, and very dated, is one of the key questions of our time.

CHAPTER

I

Marx's Marxism

ORIGINS

THE USES and emphases of Marxism have continually evolved, and emphasis has shifted in various directions: revolution, reform, workers' benefits, peasant discontent, state-sponsored industrialization, anti-Westernism, national liberation. But at the heart of Marxism has been an abiding theme of protest against Western-style industrialization and against one or another of its putative effects—oppression, inequality, dehumanization, destruction of human values, and the degradation of people, within the state through class oppression, externally through the subjugation of nations to colonial or semicolonial status. This, and no theory or article of doctrine, is the consistent core of Marxism.

Marxism was a human response to rapid, poorly understood, and threatening change. The contemporary world sees itself as peculiarly beset by changes arising from technological innovation, but the onslaught of modernization a century and a half ago in Western Europe was perhaps even more traumatic because it meant the uprooting of a previously rather stable social order. By 1779 displaced weavers were rioting and destroying mills in some British towns. First in England, then on the continent—in Belgium, France, and, by the mid-nineteenth century, in Marx's Germany—

the traditional order was visibly crumbling before the onrush of the strange new ways of seeking wealth through machinery that came to be lumped together as "capitalism." The stirrings of the new industrial way of life as Karl Marx (born 1818) was coming to maturity evoked a unique ferment of proposals for fundamental social change. It was a time of blossoming for socialist theories—those of Saint-Simon, Fourier, Proudhon, Blanqui, and Bakunin. Marxism was merely the most sophisticated and thoroughgoing—and the most favored by history.

From the viewpoint of the beneficiaries, it was an age of golden progress. There was a host of new devices and useful applications. The steam engine was perfected, coke was applied to the smelting of iron, and iron and steel rapidly became a major industry in England. Innovations in textile manufacturing increased the output of weavers and spinners a hundredfold, and cloth of better quality than all but the finest handwoven fabrics could now be woven with a tiny fraction of the preindustrial labor input. The overall effect could only be a large growth of the national product.

There were also social gains. New factory towns gave employment to the surplus labor force which had been growing in the countryside, and previously pauperized vagrants were recruited for the looms and mills. The new capitalists—a very small group—formed a more productive, less parasitic upper class than the nobles and landholders; indeed, they were usually hardworking, sometimes greedy but often ascetic and devoted entrepreneurs, not infrequently of humble origins.

Yet the Industrial Revolution evoked an outcry of pain and resentment. Indignant conservatives deplored factory chimneys, the desecration of the landscape, and the chaos of laissez-faire; socialist thinkers like Marx theorized about a sweeter life. The new industrial towns were built without experience or order; conditions in them often became shameful, and population growth ate up much of the growth in productivity. Factories were constructed, in that careless age, with little regard for pleasure or health. The new system of labor was tedious and grinding; if hours of work were no longer than peasants had to put in during harvest season, the repetitious and unnatural character of factory work made it much more exhausting. Whether or not hardships were greater than those of previous ages, they were new hardships and so to be protested.

The capitalists were also resented because they were new. However parasitic feudal lords may have been, they were accepted by age-old tradition, and there was a certain mutuality of feudal relations. But the new capitalists seemed to have power without responsibility. They were literally nouveaux riches, elbowing aside the respected authorities and grasping for political power corresponding to their new wealth. Inequality may have been no greater, but it was more conspicuous and more grating. Relations between upper and lower classes were no longer dictated by custom but were reduced to the crass cash nexus decried by Marx. Factory workers were subjected to a new insecurity; drawn away from a familiar environment to the confusion of the city, regarded by the factory owner not as people but as "hands," they were unprotected by custom or government and forbidden to organize in self-defense. The peasant forced into a slummy new industrial town by enclosures of the fields, mechanization of agriculture on large estates, or rural overcrowding may have increased his money income, but his life was probably less pleasant. In the new towns, peasant life and culture were degraded, brutalized, and made anomic; craftsmen were deprived of their livelihood, and the machine appeared as destroyer of old virtues, cultural traditions, and the human relations of the traditional order.

The socialist outcry may consequently be understood as a sort of poor man's conservatism, essentially retrospective, looking back to the stability and security of guild-regulated production. Indignation was directed not only against unfair treatment of the workers but against commercialization and the erosion of old values of social solidarity. As the *Communist Manifesto* put it in 1848, "The bourgeoisie, wherever it has got the upper hand, has put an end to all feudal, patriarchal, idyllic relations," leaving "no other nexus between man and man than naked self-interest, than callous 'cash-payment.'" Consequently, "the bourgeoisie has stripped of its halo every occupation hitherto honored and looked up to with reverent awe. It has converted the physician, the lawyer, the priest, the poet, the man of science into its paid wage laborers." Further, "all that is solid melts into air, all that is holy is profaned." [1]

In the works of the so-called "utopian" socialists as well as of the "scientific" Marx and Engels, socialism looked to a restoration of solidarity and intimacy in society. Cooperation would replace the heightened or newly irritating conflict of classes. The virtues of the idealized simpler past would be restored; mankind would learn to live as a harmonious family, enjoying the fruits of the bountiful earth, with luxury for none but enough for all.

11

Even if industrialization had not produced social dislocation and friction, many voices would probably have been raised against inequality and injustice, because these were also times of increasing education, popular journalism, scholarly inquiry, and consequently of growing social awareness. It may be that the commonly accepted picture of the deteriorating conditions of wage earners in the early nineteenth century is mostly the result of greater attention and publicity.[2] The misery of the new proletariat was an affront to ripening ideals of human decency and justice, and the new injustice was not to be ignored as the old had been.

Radical protest and reform proposals took on special meaning because of the political event which opened modern times, the French Revolution.[3] In the search for alternatives, many, including Marx, found this historical model supremely inspiring. The simple people of Paris had asserted their claim to humane values, equality, and the rights of man. The embattled multitude assaulted the Bastille and brought back the fleeing king to face revolutionary justice; organized in the Paris Commune, they fought off the bitter onslaughts of reactionaries of France and all Europe. It was a rebirth of the world, a great new dawning of humanity and justice. For the first time in history, revolution became an ideal; insurrection of the people against their masters took on an aura of right and freedom.

The political atmosphere of Marx's youth was dominated by the French Revolution, and much of his thought may be interpreted as an effort to find out why it had failed.[4] During 1843–1844, Marx collected a large amount of material on its history and institutions, and even in the 1870s and 1880s Engels was still looking back to the precedents of 1789–1793. In our own century, the Russian Revolution was permeated with the idea that it was the sequel to the French Revolution and had to follow its outlines and details.[5] As Lenin said, "We Bolsheviks are the Jacobins of the twentieth century." [6]

If the British provided an economic analysis for the new day, the French furnished most of the revolutionary doctrine. In both England and France, many ideas later to be called "Marxian" were in the air.[7] Many writers denounced the enrichment of the few, the pauperization of the masses, and the enslavement of man by machinery.[8] The idea of social class as an active force in history came to the fore in the historiography of the French Revolution. Saint-Simon, for example, felt that, since the French Revolution had liberated the bourgeoisie, the next task was the liberation of the proletariat.[9] He looked to the eventual withering of the state into a merely administrative apparatus. "To each according to his need" was borrowed from the Bible by Babeuf and Étienne Cabet.

Indeed, there was a direct line through Babeuf's followers, from his Conspiracy of Equals to Marx's Communist League.[10] The French communists talked of adding economic equality to political equality (which was yet far from being attained) and of recovering the true nature of man by abolishing private property. Fourier, raising a theme later important for Marxism, sought to abolish the antithesis between town and country—a bit of nostalgia for the simpler life. Jean-Paul Marat furnished the vibrant Marxian catchwords, "The proletarians have nothing to lose but their chains" and "The workers have no country." [11]

In England, the Chartists, who viewed history as class struggle and believed capitalism was degenerating into monopoly, gave an example of organization of the laboring masses that caused shivers in genteel society from roughly 1838 to 1850. Numerous writers, including William Cobbett, anticipated Marxian ideas in their violent protests against the abuses of industrialization and the selfishness of the ruling classes.[12] And Robert Owen, who introduced (or at least popularized) the word "socialism," did much to propagate the idea that the woes of society could be eliminated by community of goods. In sum, as the modern age was dawning economically, culturally, and politically, discontent from the disruptions of industrialization combined with the effects of the French Revolution to produce a unique outburst of radical thinking. It seemed (at least to a small layer of intellectuals) that justice might be achieved by persuading the people to take action; a new revolution might signal the final liberation of mankind.

THE YOUNG MARX

TO FASHION his philosophy of protest, Marx had only to take up, flesh out, and mold together many of the ideas in the air. His special contribution was to put the socialist cry of pain into Hegelian terms, using his philosophic tools for a root-and-branch attack on the social order. Marx was, like Engels, a Young Hegelian; that is, he belonged to a group of German intellectuals who wished to convert

Hegelianism from a support for the established order into a weapon against it—a fairly easy task because the Prussian monarchy was far from embodying a philosophical ideal. Like Hegel, Marx sought a single comprehensive explanation for all reality. He retained, in essence, the Hegelian thesis that the ultimately real is the absolutely rational; like Hegel, he looked to the restoration of order and community by the realization of the ideal. As a communist, Marx continued to believe that history had meaning in its inevitable progress toward this goal; moreover, since in the Hegelian framework everything is accessible to understanding, the world could be transformed. Marx wished to bring the process of realization of the historical Absolute into a material, hence supposedly sounder frame.

Marx was a rebel well before he took up the proletarian cause or communism, and he remained a rebel all his life. But his rebelliousness evolved as he progressed from insurgent philosophy student to mature scholar of capitalist economies. His first passion was atheism, an attack on the established faith of Prussia. Then, as he was reaching toward the themes of historical materialism and a political program based on the proletariat, he grasped "alienation" as a weapon with which to attack the new industrial order. The concept goes back to the Calvinist doctrine of the soul alienating itself from God. Hegel took it up; and Ludwig Feuerbach, a Young Hegelian, used it against the established order. Religion, he said, is based on a projection of human qualities; man invents his deity and makes himself subject to his own invention, thereby "alienating" (almost in the legal sense of "alienating" property) his own nature. Marx, as was his wont, gave the idea a more material cast. Not only is religion to be done away with, he wrote, but "the immediate task is to unmask human alienation in its secular form, now that it has been unmasked in its sacred form." [13]

Marx wrote loosely and variously of alienation, but his main thrust was to attribute it to economic relations—that is, to industrial capitalism: man is alienated because his work is sold. Human self-realization comes through productive work; when one has to turn over the fruits of one's labor to others, one is, in Marx's definition, "alienated." "Through estranged, alienated labour, then, the worker produces the relationship to this labour of a man alien to labour and standing outside it. The relationship of the worker to labour engenders the relationship to it of the capitalist. . . . *Private property* is thus the product, the result, the necessary consequence of *alienated labour,* of the external relation of the worker to nature and to himself." [14] This alienation derives not from the monotony of factory work but from the necessity of selling one's labor and contributing to another's product. If people had to pick poppies in perfumed meadows for the market, their labor would apparently still be alienated. In effect, the protest against alienation is a protest against the basic institution of market production, against wage work, and, incidentally, against being driven to do what Marx could never bring himself to do—to earn a regular living as a cog in the social order.

The Marxian protest against alienation was a metaphysical way of lamenting the loss of the supposed former unity of society, wherein man was a rounded being and the craftsman supposedly worked at his own pace at the trade of his choice with his own tools. Thus, the *Communist Manifesto* promised to combine agriculture and industry at a time when they were being sharply wrenched apart. Marx had written a few years earlier that

> as long . . . as activity is not voluntarily, but naturally, divided, man's own act becomes an alien power opposed to him, which enslaves him instead of being controlled by him . . . whereas in communist society, where nobody has one exclusive sphere of activity but each can become accomplished in any branch he wishes, production as a whole is regulated by society, thus making it possible for me to do one thing today and another tomorrow, to hunt in the morning, fish in the afternoon, rear cattle in the evening, criticize after dinner, in accordance with my inclination, without ever becoming hunter, fisherman, shepherd or critic. [15]

The naïveté of this nostalgic daydream is striking. But the idea has had a remarkable appeal for many modern readers, especially students and intellectuals in relatively affluent countries. "Alienation" bespeaks hatred of what we all hate at times, the slavery of employment and having to do work significant for others but not for oneself. For those who feel they are spending their lives (especially their youth) in meaningless tasks, lost in the tensions and complexities of urban existence, it is some consolation that Marx wrote about alienation and loss of humanness, however special his emphases. [16] Unhappily, Marx offered no analysis or immediate help for the loss of purpose and intimacy in the large, atomized society. His answer was, in effect, deeply pessimistic. Alienation could disappear only when people worked for the fun of it and, contrary to the trends of all civilized history, the division of labor had been superseded.

The extent to which the protest against alienation represents the "real" Marx has been much disputed. Particularly in the 1960s it was taken up eagerly by the New Left, which was mostly repelled by the more systematic analysis of classical Marxism. György Lukács had brought out this "humanist" side of Marx even before the *Economic and Philosophical Manuscripts of 1844*, the principal source in the Marxian corpus, was published in 1932. Others, such as Robert C. Tucker,[17] have argued that Marx never gave it up. It is at least undeniable that the dislike for occupational specialization remained near the center of Marx's and Engels's thinking. The idea that specialization is slavery is a recurrent theme, and the oppression of the workers is frequently perceived as much in the division of labor as in the cheating of the workers of the values they produce. Indeed, it can be argued that for Marx the purpose of the revolution was as much to end specialization as to achieve distributive justice.[18] On the other hand, a Leninist Marxist such as Louis Althusser contends that there was a complete break between the immature and mature Marx. Soviet Marxism, of course, has no room whatever for the concept of alienation.

HISTORICAL MATERIALISM

WHATEVER the appeal of alienation and Marxist "humanism" for Western intellectuals, Marx would today be unremembered if he had stopped writing in 1844. The rather widely shared conviction that society needed overturning, bolstered by somewhat novel philosophizing about redemption from the unhappiness of capitalism, would never have made Marxism a powerful system. Alienation is a romantic, individualistic, slightly abstruse concept of negative value for political mobilization. Probably for this reason, Marx and Engels left the early manuscripts, as they put it, to the "gnawing criticism of mice." They poured scorn on talk of humanism (repudiating it, for example, in the *Communist Manifesto*), and they turned, after 1844, to the more aggressive theories which went into classical Marxism.

Marx's stronger assault on capitalistic modernization was based on the theory that the new industrial society was only a transient stage of history, doomed to be superseded by a new form which would restore paradisiacal virtues. Putting the Hegelian dialectic in material terms, Marx observed that the structure of society was being changed by industrialization and proceeded to generalize from this fact. Thus, the development of technology and consequent changes in the means of production brought forth the new capitalist ruling class and everything associated with it; further development would inevitably cause a new ruling class to replace the despised capitalists. The interpretation was made more convincing by extending it into the past and showing how earlier stages of society had been dominated by ruling classes which controlled more primitive means of production, both in the land-based feudal society and in the slave-based society of antiquity. With his talent for system building, Marx further generalized that economic motives furnished the key to all history. Engels stated the basic idea in his graveside eulogy:

> As Darwin discovered the law of evolution in organic nature, so Marx discovered the law of evolution in human history: the simple fact, previously hidden under ideological growths, that human beings must first of all eat, drink, shelter and clothe themselves before they can turn their attention to politics, science, art, and religion; that therefore the production of the immediate material means of life and thereby the given stage of economic development of a people or of a period form the basis on which State institutions, the legal principles, the art, and even the religious ideas of the people in question have developed and out of which they must be explained, instead of exactly the contrary, as was previously attempted.[19]

The axiom is thus that people must first of all satisfy material needs. Hence the economic side of life, above all the production of goods, is primary in human society, and social relations are determined by the means of production. These, and relations to them, are the "infrastructure"; everything else forms a "superstructure" of culture, art, religion, laws, government, and so forth, made to serve the needs of production and the class which controls and profits by it. As Marx wrote, "It is not the consciousness of men that determines their being, but, on the contrary, their social being determines their consciousness." [20] This was a striking insight for an age accustomed to thinking of history in terms of kings and battles. However, historical materialism entwines two disparate ideas: first, that economic motivations are, consciously or unconsciously, dominant; and second, that history is made by technical invention. Marx was unclear as to how far social change was brought about by technological change, or how far social change came of itself or in conjunction with changes in relations to means of production, that is, of the class order. The relations of infrastructure to superstructure,

17

and what belonged to which, were also unclear; Marx and Engels were inclined, especially later in their lives, to concede that institutions might affect production as well as vice versa. Yet it was most attractive to postulate that history had an economic foundation and was consequently understandable, for in that case the end of capitalism could be scientifically predicted.

The economic understanding of history was also useful because it supported (although it did not require) the inference that history is class struggle. Since society is built on the means of production, control over them is the central issue; therefore the owning class is in perpetual conflict with the dissatisfied and at least potentially rebellious laboring class. Thus, seemingly political conflicts are in reality economic and class conflicts. To the superficial view it seems that history recounts much more conflict of nations and empires than of classes, but in the Marxist view one has only to see through the mystifications created by the beneficiaries of the established order to discern the economic reality of the Hegelian conflict. It was hence justified to call for violent revolution, which only made explicit and overt the social conflict ordinarily covered up by the ruling class.

Since technology changes gradually, it might be assumed that social change would also proceed, at least ordinarily, by very small steps. But Marx and Engels thought (except insofar as they retreated late in life) in terms of violent revolution. To support this view, they periodized history according to class rule in a rather simple way. First, in the tribal society of prehistory, when men were hunters and gatherers, there were no important means of production, no surplus to be expropriated, and therefore no ruling class and no state to support it. This Eden of primitive communism, before the sin of private property and greed came into the world, served not only as the logical starting point but also as the moral outline for the brotherly communist society of the future.

In the Marxist scheme, the transition to livestock raising and primitive agriculture evoked private property and the state. It became useful to keep the prisoners of the increasingly frequent wars, and antique society was consequently characterized by slaveholding and the use of slaves as living tools, the primary means of production. The real picture is less than clear, however, because in the varied societies of antiquity there were many gradations of freedom and bondage; in Athens, for example, slaves and freemen filled many of the same occupations.[21] The requirement that prefeudal civilizations be uniformly based on slavery has caused Marxist historians much difficulty, and Marx himself was troubled by its implications. He once asked why the art produced by the (supposedly) slave-based Greek states should still have value and could only conjecture that it was because the Greeks represented the childhood of society and everyone loves a child.[22]

The movement to the next stage, feudalism, also caused trouble, because (at least in Europe, the area of Marx's concern) it was associated much more with the breakup of the Roman Empire than with economic change. Moreover, it was accompanied not by an improvement in the means of production but by the economic decline of the Dark Ages, for which the Marxist scheme had no place.[23] Feudalism, however, was characterized as an agricultural society dominated by a landholding class and serfdom, a better marked era than the previous one, although it stretched over more than a thousand years and included quite diverse societies even within Western Europe.

It was the development of capitalism out of feudalism that Marx studied most and that fitted best into his general historical scheme. Improved means of production raised new classes of owners within or alongside the feudal order, as towns and commercial and manufacturing interests gradually gained wealth. Economic power then led to a drive for political power, and the new ruling class of capitalists or "bourgeoisie" (from an old word for townspeople) came to power. Here again, however, there were troublesome ambiguities. In most of Europe, serfdom disappeared long before anything like capitalism triumphed, even centuries earlier. Engels admitted, for example, that the Norwegians had never been serfs but were free peasants and petty bourgeois centuries before modern industry emerged.[24] With their preference for revolutionary change, Marx and his followers saw the mid-seventeenth-century English and late-eighteenth-century French revolutions as marking the advent of the bourgeoisie to power. On the other hand, the basic protest was against mechanical industry, and it was a famous aphorism of Marx that "the handmill gives you a society with the feudal lord; the steam-mill a society with the industrial capitalist." [25] Aside from the fact that there were handmills in antiquity, the Industrial Revolution began in England a century after its "bourgeois" revolution, and in *Capital* (published 1867) Marx spoke of England as the only fully capitalist country.[26] Industrialization was not conspicuous in France until the 1830s, nearly half a century after the French Revolution. The general picture was plausible in Marx's day, however, because of the obvious conflict between the claims of the rising industrial classes and the inherited prerogatives of feudal or semifeudal powers.

Having made the bourgeois capitalist order the new dispensation, replacing outworn feudalism, Marx might conceivably have hailed it and wished it success. Instead, he fervently attacked industrial capitalism, then in swaddling clothes, as morally wrong, wholly dominated by monetary considerations and greed. Under capitalism even marriage, according to the *Communist Manifesto*, is merely a business arrangement and the bourgeois wife an instrument of production. Although feudal lords had lived a parasitic existence for centuries, the newly emergent capitalists were already worn out; in the *Communist Manifesto* we learn that "the bourgeoisie is unfit any longer to be the ruling class in society." It was a newborn monstrosity. And whereas feudalism was permitted gradually to grow into capitalism without catastrophe, for capitalism Marx foresaw concentration, the enslavement and increasing misery of the many, and violent breakdown. The laws of class struggle proved, to the satisfaction of the young Marx, that reform was impossible.

The rationale of the historical schema was the projected supersession of capitalism and the emergence of man from the enslavement of past class society to the freedom of the classless society. The proletariat, as the class without property, could not emancipate itself without abolishing classes: "the bourgeois relations of production are the last antagonistic forms of the social process of production." [27] Since the state was primarily a class instrument, "with the introduction of the socialist order of society the state will dissolve itself and disappear." [28] Further, "the society which organizes production anew on the basis of free and equal association of the producers will put the whole State machinery where it will then belong—into the museum of antiquities, next the spinning wheel and the bronze axe." [29] With no class struggle, there would be no more politics; without private property, greed and envy would die away. Law would be replaced by morality. The anarchists' utopia of universal peace, brotherhood, and prosperity would be attained by a natural process.

It is not clear how seriously Marx took this glowing vision. Perhaps it was something like an advertising claim, the promise of a prophet who knew he could never be called to account. But it had plausibility. A thousand thinkers and prophets have blamed some or all of society's woes on money and private wealth; and thousands of others, sophisticated as well as naïve, have pondered the beauties of the simpler life without gold and all its complications. The utopia was the more acceptable because Marx made no effort to lay out how it should be organized so that men would joyfully collect garbage instead of fishing by sylvan streams, and so forth. Everyone was invited to fill in details according to his own fancy.

There were serious shortcomings to the historical sequence. Marxism has always been troubled by the contradiction between the automatic denouement through the dialectics of capitalism and the need for the proletariat purposefully to make a revolution. In practice, however, it was a fairly workable compromise to say (as Marx did in the preface to *Capital*), "One cannot alter at will the economic reality—one can only shorten the birthpangs." History creates the opportunity, but it is up to people to hurry it along. Psychologically, there was no contradiction; people will gladly work and sacrifice for a victory they consider inevitable.

More difficult for the Marxist movement was the related question of how far the succession of forms should be seen as universally applicable, a question which became acute once Marxism spread beyond the Western European countries for which it was intended. In *A Contribution to the Critique of Political Economy*, Marx had stated that "no social order ever disappears before all the productive forces for which there is room in it have been developed. . . ." [30] Likewise, in his preface to *Capital* he held that less developed countries must follow the path of the leader, England; he spoke of "these tendencies working with iron necessity towards inevitable results." [31] But Marx also recognized a type of economy incongruous with his schema, the Asiatic-despotic, characterized by self-contained village communities, lack of private property in land, and state-managed irrigation works. The static Asiatic mode did not fit alongside the dynamic European sequence of ancient-feudal-capitalist; unlike Europe, Asia was not propelled ever onward by invention and class struggle. Yet if the historical pattern was inevitable, it should be universal; and in the writings of Marx and Engels it seems ordinarily to be understood as something inherent in society.

CRITIQUE OF CAPITALISM

HISTORICAL MATERIALISM told the discontented that their sufferings under capitalism would pass and their day of glory would come with the sureness of a universal dispensation. But the theory was somewhat abstract and remote; by itself, it was not gripping enough to serve as a revolutionary credo. Hence, after the 1848 wave of liberal revolution receded, leaving only limited successes for "bourgeois" democracy and none for communism, Marx sought to bolster and make politically more cogent his thesis of the doom of the capitalist order by elaborating a critique of its economic mainsprings. It was natural that he should undertake this because after August 1849, he lived as an expatriate in London, where the study of economics was far more advanced than anywhere else and the available materials far more abundant.

Marx's years of poring over papers in the British Museum culminated in the publication in 1867 of the first of several projected volumes of *Capital*, his last major opus and the work which above all made his reputation as a scholar. The basic idea was the already old labor theory of value, which may be traced to John Locke, who rested the idea of personal property on the labor put into something. It was developed in classic form by David Ricardo (1772–1823). In the 1820s and 1830s, socialists generally took for granted that the wage earner was the creator of value and that capital was essentially nonproductive. Marx, however, drew conclusions beyond his predecessors. He left out the contributions to value of land rent, organization, entrepreneurship, and technology, although he could not have been unaware of them, and made the ordinary worker the sole creator of value. On occasion he conceded differences in the value of labor because of skills, but in *Capital* he stated uncautiously: "A working-day of given length always creates the same amount of value, no matter how the productiveness of labor, and, with it, the mass of the product, and the price of each single commodity produced may vary." [32] But if the labor theory of value was an oversimplification, the main point remained: the workers received less than evident justice seemed to require, and the cheating of the worker was attributable not to the greed or evil disposition of the employer (which might improve) but to the capitalist economy itself, which was to be changed by revolution.

Marx took over Ricardo's Iron Law of Wages, according to

22

which laborers were a commodity whose price was fixed by the cost of production. If workers were paid more than necessary for their subsistence and reproduction, they would multiply and increase the supply of labor, thereby lowering its price. This logic was pushed to the dialectically pleasing contention that wages actually decrease as production increases. Thus "the worker becomes all the poorer the more wealth he produces, the more his production increases in range and power. The worker becomes an ever cheaper commodity the more commodities he creates. With the *increasing value* of the world of things proceeds in direct proportion the *devaluation* of the world of men. Labor produces not only commodities: it produces itself and the worker as a *commodity*—and does so in the proportion in which it produces commodities generally." [33]

The owner, having control over the means of production, could appropriate the difference between subsistence wages—the cost of production of labor—and the selling price of goods. Taking little note of nonlabor costs, Marx called this difference "surplus value"—that is, value surplus to the worker's minimal needs for existence and reproduction. This idea, again, was current at the time; but Marx drew extreme conclusions. One was that, since profit comes from the surplus value of labor, laborsaving machinery must reduce profits. The broader conclusion was that wages, which even in Marx's day were generally somewhat over a bare subsistence level, should tend to sink with the growth of industrialization. It was an old thesis; Ricardo and others had written of the immiseration of the workers. Marx and Engels said in the *Communist Manifesto:* "Nay, more, in proportion as the use of machinery and division of labor increases, in the same proportion the burden of toil also increases, whether by prolongation of the working hours, by increase of the work exacted in a given time, or by increased speed of the machinery, etc." [34] Nearly twenty years later, when *Capital* was published, there was substantial evidence that reality was not so gloomy, but Marx returned to the theme that productivity could not raise wages. He gave a long list of reasons for supposing that the conditions of the workers could only deteriorate, without citing evidence that they actually did.[35] Instead, he turned apocalyptic rhetoric against capital "dripping with blood" and sentenced it to shattering revolution.

A few more logic-blocks completed the structured doom of the hated order. The middle classes must be ground down into the proletariat by competition and the oppression of the big owners, who would become richer and fewer. Because of the impoverishment of nearly everyone, demand for goods would fall; rates of profit would decline because it would be impossible to invest suitably the capital piled up in the hands of the few; and crises would become more frequent and more severe. The overgrown edifice of capitalist society would collapse. On its ruins the workers, disciplined by the factory but propertyless and hence uncorrupted, would erect the perfect, classless socialist society.

Marx's economics is the part of his theoretical construction which subsequent critics have treated most harshly; "the revelation of the secret of capitalist production," as Engels put it, is no longer taken seriously by many. Marxist activists ignore it except in its general tenor (as did Lenin), taking only the slogans. Even Marxist economists have made little or no use of the endless subtleties of value and price, profit, rent, labor power, and wages. That all value is created by labor is, of course, unrealistic; labor without capital is almost as useless as capital without labor. Not only did Marx find the contributions of nonmanual laborers, managers, merchants, and bankers of no value; he also saw the production of goods for sale as the whole of economics, to the neglect of transportation and commerce (supposedly nonproductive) and of the services which loom ever larger in modern economies. It would have been most remarkable if Marx had been able to contribute much to scientific economics, for he had no training in it and no contact with the economists of his day. He disliked the whole business and referred to it contemptuously; thus, he called his work on *Capital* "the whole shit (*Scheisse*)." [36]

Yet Engels's characterization of *Capital* as the workers' Bible was apt. It is inspirational and filled with moral purpose. The more readable part is the lengthy description of the misery of the British workers. True, the theory is tedious, abstract, and supported by hypothetical, not factual, examples. Marx, however, having postulated that capitalism would be superseded by the historical sequence, built a massive argument to show that it was so superlatively evil and so riven by contradictions that it could not last long. Thus Marx added a moral cause to the certainty of victory for the virtuous discontented. Standing over the cradle of capitalism, Marx foretold the early demise of the husky but rather ugly child so emphatically and elaborately that the world took note.

REVOLUTIONISM

MARX was not content to denigrate the capitalistic order and to argue its doom; almost everything he wrote was informed by the idea of revolution, the first passion of what Lenin called his "revolutionary soul." The whole system supported a preconceived end, the overthrow of the possessors. This proclivity for revolution was the chief difference between Marx and other socialists; therein lies much of the appeal of his personality and his doctrines. Marx took delight in violence and exhorted his party to take the lead in "popular vengeance." [37] In this spirit, he explicitly rejected "All men are brothers" as the slogan of the Communist League. "The last word of social science," he said, "will always be, '*Le combat ou la mort; la lutte sanguinaire ou le néant.*' " [38] Struggle, Marx once told an American journalist, was the ultimate reality.[39]

Even after the failure of the revolutionary impulse of the 1840s, when Marx withdrew from revolutionary conspiracy and sought instead to give his expectations a systematic basis, both he and Engels continued to look expectantly for the *Dies Irae* (as they called it) when the mighty would be cast down. In 1853, Marx stated flatly, ". . . on the Continent the revolution is imminent and will immediately assume a socialist character." [40] In 1854 they viewed the Crimean War as a prelude to revolution. In December 1857, Marx was disturbed by the idea that the revolution might come before he could finish his *Capital;* in 1859 he was placing hopes in the Austro-French conflict over Italy. Reading the signs to suit themselves, Marx and Engels continued to see revolution around the corner every few years.

Abrupt and violent change was by no means dictated by their theory of history or by the analysis of capitalism given in *Capital;* indeed, it does not really fit the dialectical scheme of forces working out their contradictions to generate the new condition. The only logical justification given for it was the reluctance of a possessing class to surrender its privileges peacefully. But many a ruling class has in fact gradually, albeit involuntarily, lost supremacy. Transitions from antique to feudal and from feudal to capitalist society were hardly marked by sudden shifts of power. The beginning of feudalism was quite undatable. The Industrial Revolution came to the continent long after the French Revolution, and feudal elements persisted in Germany for decades after it had become a leading industrial country. The argument that technical change must bring with it political ("class") change was plausible, but history has usually shown change to be gradual, complex, and evolutionary rather than sudden, simple, and revolutionary.

Marx, however, was quite willing to sacrifice theoretical consistency for hopes of revolution. Thus, far from really counting on the proletariat, the only class capable of making the new order, Marx and Engels hoped in 1848 for a communist revolution in unindustrialized Germany. In 1852 they had great expectations for a then very backward Italy, and at various times they looked to tenant farmers in Ireland, serfs in Russia, or slaves in America to initiate the overthrow of capitalism. Marx even hoped in 1853 that the Taiping Rebellion in China would set the world afire. He embraced the revolutionary Paris Commune of 1871 as a "Dictatorship of the Proletariat," although it was more "petty bourgeois" than proletarian.

Politically even more significant was Marx's readiness to surrender the generality of his laws of historical development and encourage the Russian Populists to strive to leap directly from backwardness into socialism, accepting the traditional village commune, with its customs of land sharing, as the potential germ of postcapitalist socialism. Preference for revolution over theory led him to support the activist Russians who were trying to tear down the regime by violence over the Russian Marxists who were trying to apply his ideas of historical materialism as best they could.

Marx's urge to annihilate the established order was doubtless fortified by personal circumstances. Barred from an academic career in Prussia because of his anti-authoritarian opinions, Marx gained precocious celebrity at age 24 as editor of the *Rheinische Zeitung,* only to be forced out after a few months. In 1849 he found himself an impoverished and unnoticed refugee in London with a noble-born wife and a growing family, unable to find employment worthy of his doctorate, with few hopes save for the revolution which might rescue him from poverty and obscurity, possibly to summon him to power and glory.

APPEAL OF THE MESSAGE

MARX was inconsistent in almost everything except his detestation for the regnant "bourgeois" order, but this consistency was the essence of his strength. He put together an intellectual battering ram against the new Western industrial capitalism, which was then, and still is, upsetting the world. He decried the wage system and equated the division of labor with slavery. He constructed an impressive historical schema to show that capitalism had to be superseded by a more virtuous order, socialism growing into communism. He decried the sufferings of the working classes, elaborated a theory to prove that they were inherent in the system of private ownership, and found reasons for believing that this evil order must break down. Not least, he postulated and advocated the revolution which would bring about the downfall of the new possessing classes. No one else made a case half so appealing for those who were sick of the crudities, ugliness, inequality, and haughtiness of capitalist-dominated industrial society.

Marx had other advantages also. He was the first to equip socialist passion with scientific language, giving timeless and somewhat retrospective longings a cloak of modern progressiveness. Speaking with utter self-righteousness and the conviction of absolute truth, he moved others with his indignation at the sufferings of the oppressed and the pride of the oppressors. He was an artist of verbal manipulation, sometimes carried away by his own conceits. For example, ". . . as philosophy finds its *material* weapons in the proletariat, so the proletariat discovers its *intellectual* weapons in philosophy. . . . *Philosophy* is the *head* of this emancipation [of man], and the *proletariat* is its *heart*. Philosophy cannot realise itself without abolishing the proletariat, and the proletariat cannot emancipate itself without realising philosophy." [41] His figures were often vivid, as in "the forest of uplifted arms demanding work becomes ever thicker, while the arms themselves ever thinner." [42]

While promising to make all things understandable, Marx was obscure, only relatively less so in his mature philosophy than in his juvenile poeticizing. But if one speaks like an oracle, one's words may be taken as a revelation. Like Hegel, Marx seems to owe something of his influence to his unintelligibility.[43] According to an eminent socialist, the prestige of *Capital* owes much to "its indigestible length, its hermetic style, its ostentatious erudition, and its algebraical mysticism." [44] Also adding to the interest in Marx is the fact that one can argue endlessly over what the master meant; it is possible to counter any criticism or any interpretation with words of Marx. The message is rich; one can find democracy or authoritarianism, individualism or reintegration into the social whole, determinism or voluntarism, materialism or idealism, freedom or discipline, all within the Marxist intellectual universe. The fuzzy sentences can be read as poetry. As Sidney Hook noted, "No program of action was so foreign that it could not be brought under Marxian formulas." [45]

"Long before me," Marx once wrote, "bourgeois historians had described the historical development of this class struggle and bourgeois economists the economic anatomy of the classes. What I did that was new was to prove: 1) that the *existence of classes* is only bound up with *particular historical phases in the development of production,* 2) that the class struggle necessarily leads to the *dictatorship of the proletariat,* 3) that this dictatorship itself only constitutes the transition to the *abolition of all classes* and to a *classless society.*"[46] These alleged discoveries are all problematic, and Marx, when he wrote this in 1850, had not even tried to prove them. But he offered a grand simplification of the overly complex human universe, or at least the message that such a simplification was possible. Society is complex and pyramidal; Marx would have it simple and two-layered. Therein lay his basic error and his basic appeal.

Marx did insist on a number of important realities, however. It was a considerable achievement to stress the significance of technology for human institutions at a time when this was little appreciated. It was insightful to put economics into history and to suggest to a smug civilization how ideology covers advantages and how attitudes are determined by interests. Marx was by no means the only strong critic of industrial society in his day, but he was perhaps the most trenchant.

Yet the attraction of Marxism lies not in its intellectual content but in the fact that Marx fashioned, as none before or since, a "metaphysics of revolution," [47] calling upon people to take an active role in bringing about the inevitable paradise. Man was to be his own redeemer, aided by the daemon of history. "Since, however, for socialist man, *the whole of what is called world history* is nothing but the creation of man by human labour, and the emergence of nature for man, he, therefore, has the evident and irrefutable proof of his self-creation, of his own origins." [48] Our woes are not with ourselves but with our institutions, and these are to be set aright.[49]

Marxism is more to be felt than understood. In almost any discussion of Marxist issues, the real arguments are likely to be emotional or political, touching ideals and values. For some, the essence of Marxism is not theory but approach or method. As Howard

Sherman put it, "It follows that there is no such thing as a single, definitive, correct interpretation of Marx; there is only the Marxist way of doing things." [50] And György Lukács expressed the view that the validity of the method would stand firm even if all factual assertions of Marxism were confuted.[51]

This was not, of course, the view of Marx and Engels, who claimed to be saying something about the real world. A method of inquiry is hardly to be judged except by the validity of its results. In any case, it is even harder to define Marxist method than Marxist theory. For some, the method seems to mean little more than an injunction to act on behalf of a set of "holy things"—the working classes, emancipation from the tyranny of money, and, above all, the creation of a new Eden by revolution in any non–Marxist–Leninist state. Some writers emphasize the unity of theory and praxis, with the former serving the latter. This apparently means that revolutionary action validates the theory; human action lends truth to the abstract scheme. Insofar as the Marxist "method" is not merely political attitude and action, it may be seen as emphasis on the interrelatedness of things (an implication of the dialectic), conflict, and social change in a "progressive" direction. Neither Marx nor his followers have excelled in clarifying the interrelatedness of events, even while overstressing a single aspect of causation, the economic. Few deny the importance of conflict; and nothing could be more obvious than change, accelerating since long before Marx. If Marxism is only method, it becomes a phantom.

It may be concluded that Marxism is more revelation than theory, a surrogate faith for an age losing its religion. Marx had the self-assurance of a prophet who has talked with God, and his way of oversimplifying issues through convoluted argument befits a dogma.[52] He was a poet, prophet, and moralist speaking as a philosopher and economist; his doctrine is not to be tested against mere facts but to be received as ethical-religious truth.[53] His categories and concepts are not to be concretely defined but directly apprehended by the spirit. Marxists, unlike Darwinians, claim orthodoxy as a virtue. Marx's hatred of traditional religions was bitter beyond the requirements of his theory (in Marx's view, not only was religion "the opium of the people," but the priest was also the moral equivalent of the hangman in upholding class rule), and it suggests the hatred of the new dispensation for the old.

Proudhon, a more moderate man, once exhorted Marx, "Let us not conduct ourselves like apostles of a new religion." [54] But Marx, like many of his followers, was fervently intolerant, and this was his strength. He may be seen as the founder of a new type of Christianity.[55] Marx gave the Word for salvation: as he said, "the philosophers have only *interpreted* the world in various ways; the point, however, is to *change* it." [56] *Capital* became a bible, no more read than the Scriptures, used for apt quotations and left to the interpretation of scholars, but important because it was there, a massive testimony to the revelation that labor is presently exploited but will be victorious in the future.[57] Marx was to lead the Chosen People out of slavery to the New Jerusalem.[58] The ways of this world (bourgeois society) were evil, and the philistines and men of money would be damned. Class-consciousness was a spiritual grace. The savior-proletariat would by its sufferings redeem mankind and bring the Kingdom of Heaven on earth, wherein, as foretold by the Old Testament prophets, pain would cease, warfare vanish, and the lion lie down with the lamb. Although he scornfully rejected utopianism, Marx was, like many a communistic-chiliastic prophet, the greatest of utopians.[59] Looking backward to a simpler age as well as forward to a brave new world, he heralded with difficult syllogism and arcane language the chastisement of sinners and the inevitable consummation of good.

CHAPTER
II

Engels's Marxism
and Social Democracy

THE NONSUCCESS OF MARX

THE IDEAS loosely woven together by Marx had potentially enormous appeal and utility, as the world has learned. But he was elevated to a major authority only after his death, and sanctified only after a major revolution made in his name converted him into a state philosopher. His writings came to be widely known and cited because a Marxist movement grew up; they did not themselves generate that movement.[1] The works which later became canonical were not in much demand in the times for which they were written. Except for the *Communist Manifesto*, they were heavy and pedantic, and even the *Manifesto* made no splash when issued in 1848; a second edition did not appear until the 1870s. Volume 1 of *Das Kapital* sold only 200 copies when first published in 1867. The 10,000 copies of a French edition issued in 1872–1875 were not sold out for 25 years,[2] and an English edition did not appear until 1887.

Many of Marx's works failed to come out in his lifetime, either because he had great trouble finishing manuscripts, a difficulty which appeared in his youth and became practically a kind of paralysis in his later maturity, or because they did not seem salable. *The German Ideology* (on which Engels collaborated) lay in manuscript form from 1846 to 1902. Engels in 1888 extracted *Theses on Feuerbach* from a manuscript of 1845. The *Critique of Political Economy* waited from 1859 to 1899. The *Critique of the Gotha Program*, Marx's rather petulant criticism of the German socialists' 1875 party statement, was not taken seriously by those to whom it was addressed,[3] and was first published by Engels in 1891. It thereupon became one of Marx's more cited works. The *Economic and Philosophical Manuscripts* of 1844 were hidden until 1932, and Marx's *Grundrisse der Kritik der politischen Ökonomie* was only put out (by the Russians) during World War II. Engels had similar experiences. His *Communist Catechism* of 1847 waited until 1914. His attack on Dühring was practically excluded from the main German Social Democratic publication in 1877;[4] it came out in French in 1912 and in English in 1935.

These publication dates testify to the growing importance of Marxism after 1875 and in this century, as events made old, unfinished manuscripts newly relevant to a world very different from that for which they were composed. Even Engels, a dedicated promoter of Marxism, was skeptical of their value. Of his *Outlines of a Critique of Political Economy* he conceded in a letter, ". . . I know only too well that it is now quite superannuated and full not only of mistakes but actual howlers." Of the old newspaper articles, many of which have been reprinted in recent years, he commented, "The majority of them are of no interest today."[5] He did not spare even his most celebrated work, *Anti-Dühring*, confessing that "the semi-Hegelian language of a good many passages of my old book is not only untranslatable but has lost the greater part of its meaning even in German."[6]

Marx was no more successful as a revolutionary leader. He was no orator, displayed no charisma, and disliked public appearances, preferring to work behind the scenes.[7] Ferdinand Lassalle and Pierre Proudhon were better known than Marx in their lifetimes. The Communist League, for which Marx and Engels drew up the strident *Manifesto*, had a short and feeble life. When the International Workingmen's Association was founded (1864), Marx was drawn in to draft its articles because of his literary skills; as corresponding secretary for Germany he was influential, usually behind the scenes, but he never really dominated it. In 1872 it was split by the Bakuninist controversy. Marx won out and the followers of

Bakunin were expelled, but by that time Marx had either become tired of the organization or found it insufficiently malleable. He destroyed it with a tactic similar to one used on the Communist League: the headquarters were shifted to an unsuitable spot (in this case, New York) where it soon broke up. Thereafter Marx actually opposed an international organization and had no organized following.

Nor could Marx be called a man of the people. Although theoretically endowing the proletariat with all virtue, he remained aloof from flesh and blood workers. He seems never to have stepped inside a factory or to have visited a workers' settlement; for information he relied on the reports published by the "bourgeois" regime. Especially in his youth, Marx undoubtedly had a real concern for social justice. But it is probably justified to say that "neither Marx nor Engels was interested in the poor as such." [8] Indeed, they often derided the riffraff and dregs of humanity, as in the *Communist Manifesto:* ". . . the social scum, that passively rotting mass thrown off by the lowest layers of old society. . . ." [9] Correspondingly, Marx cared little for the popular verdict. "The applause of the masses: popularity—was to Marx a proof of being in the wrong." [10] The proletariat was an instrument with which to remake society regardless of the effects on real workers. A German socialist, Gottschalk, said of the Marxists in 1849, "They are not in earnest about the salvation of the oppressed. The distress of the workers, the hunger of the poor, have only a scientific doctrinaire interest for them." [11] In 1847, Engels thought it necessary to welcome the potato blight, which brought starvation to millions, because it shook the established order,[12] and in 1850 he practically opposed the ten-hour workday bill.[13] Marx later extolled this law. However, he preferred that children be exploited, in the hope that they would become better revolutionaries:

> A general prohibition of child labor is incompatible with the existence of large-scale industry and hence an empty, pious wish. Its realization—if it were possible—would be reactionary, since, with a strict regulation of the working time according to the different age groups and other safety measures for the protection of children, an early combination of productive labor with education is one of the most potent means for the transformation of present-day society.[14]

Similarly, he opposed the emancipation of the serfs in Russia on grounds that it would strengthen the autocratic state.[15] Nor were his writings, studded as they were with classical allusions and quotations from various foreign languages, addressed to the common folk.

Marx was also harsh in personal relations. He was only 24 when he began to attack former friends or collaborators, such as Ludwig Feuerbach and Bruno Bauer, to whom he owed much; Arnold Ruge, his coeditor of the *Deutsch-Französische Jahrbücher;* and Moses Hess, who introduced him to communism. In 1846, in a group of 18 members, he initiated the practice of party purges with an assault on the well-intentioned but naïve Wilhelm Weitling. Somewhat later, Engels wrote, "What have we to do with a Party that is nothing more than a herd of asses, and that swears by us because its members look upon us as equals?" [16] Such pioneers of socialism (and usually would-be friends) as Proudhon, Lassalle, Hyndman, and Bakunin felt Marx's burning wrath, more because of envy or a lack of deference than because of doctrinal differences. Sooner or later he quarreled with everyone who had any claim to independent views, displaying more bitterness toward errant socialists than toward capitalist exploiters.

In a sense, the high point of his career came in 1848, when he had real hopes of a radical revolution in Germany, perhaps led by himself. Thereafter, only flickers of hope lighted the years; after the breakup of the Communist League in 1850, Marx was engaged in a gradual ideological retreat. In part, this may be attributed to the simple erosion of youthful radicalism. It was also attributable to the fact that the Industrial Revolution was maturing; Britain was leaving behind the shock of transition, with the new classes adjusting to new ways. Thus, Marx noted in 1852 the talk of wide extension of suffrage (which became reality in 1867): "Its inevitable result here is the political supremacy of the working class." [17] His inaugural address for the First International was essentially reformist, as he acknowledged the strength of capitalism and hailed the gains achieved through legislation, especially the ten-hour workday. And in the third volume of *Capital* he gave up the prediction of falling rates of profit, watered down the theory of surplus value, and recognized that managers, not capitalists, stood at "the soul of our industrial system." [18]

The Paris Commune reawakened some of the chiliastic fires, but its failure closed the era of popular revolutions in France, and the outlook became less hopeful than ever for Marx. Having liquidated the International, he published almost nothing more. He studied intensively, continuing to fill notebooks and pile up manuscripts, but he must have been unsure of his ideas. Perhaps for this reason he left the latter volumes of his cherished work, *Capital,* in great disorder; they did not fit the way the industrial economy was behaving before his eyes. In Marx's last important contribution, his *Critique of the Gotha Program,* he rejected numerous ideas with which he had once been associated—for example, that society was becoming divided between bourgeoisie and workers, that "labor is the source of all wealth and all value," and that labor was entitled to the full product. History was marching in the wrong direction.

In the last few years of his life, Marx was an urbane retired gentleman no longer anticipating revolution in the industrialized West, where he vaguely expected that something like "socialism" would come about by peaceful and democratic processes. What hopes he still had for violent change he laid on precapitalist Russia, where there was a promising upsurge of terrorism.[19] This was no great promise; Marx foresaw only that revolution in Russia would bring a democratic republic to Germany.[20] Yet for the Russian Populists he was willing to renounce the logical essence of his theories. In 1881, in a letter to the Russian revolutionary heroine Vera Zasulich, Marx limited the application of his "historic inevitability" to Western Europe and took the peasant community to be "the mainspring of Russia's social regeneration." [21] But if the Marxian outline of history was only a historical sketch (and a suprahistorical philosophical theory was a delusion), and if the renewal of society could come not from the new class of industrial workers but from traditional peasant institutions, then little was left of a lifetime of theorizing. In the same year, he turned his back on the once-glorified Paris Commune, stating that it was not and could not have been socialist.[22] The elderly Marx practically renounced Marxism.

THE SECOND BIRTH OF MARXISM

WHILE Marx was withdrawing into retirement and relaxing his ideas, a new Marxism was germinating and becoming an orthodoxy. This was partly because Marx was less active, so that his political ineffectuality and shifting positions were more easily forgotten. Outlasting the other greats of radicalism, such as Proudhon (d. 1865) and Lassalle (d. 1864), Marx became a respected (and after his death revered) figure, essentially above partisanship.

The Paris Commune may have hurt the radical movement, but

it was helpful to the reputation of Marx. True, he had little to do with it—few communards even knew his name [23]—but alarmed conservatives across Europe saw in it the hand of the International and of its mastermind, Marx; and they felt their suspicions confirmed by his lurid defense of the commune after its bloody suppression. Marx's reputation as an exponent of socialism, based largely on *Capital* and the reissued *Communist Manifesto,* waxed in the 1870s and 1880s; his followers began taking his statements more seriously and making more of them than had the master himself. Marx had in practice encouraged dogmatic use of his notions by his own exaggeration and rhetoric, but by the late 1870s the aging Marx would dismiss his followers' vulgarization of his teachings with the comment, "All I know is that I am not a Marxist." [24]

Marxism was nourished, cultivated, and expanded by a series of able men, including principally Engels; Engels's junior German friends, Bernstein and Kautsky; and the father of Russian Marxism, Plekhanov. These were seconded by such political leaders as Bebel and Liebknecht in Germany, Victor Adler in Austria, Jules Guesde in France, and V. I. Lenin in Russia.

Of these, Engels deserves the title of Foster Father of Marxism. Rarely, if ever, has a man owed so much to another as Marx owed to Engels. Less literary and subtle than Marx, Engels was a capable businessman whose acumen in the extraction of surplus value enabled him to support Marx and his family through many years, latterly in aristocratic comfort. Despite the drain of Marx's needs, Engels accumulated a large fortune. Unlike Marx, Engels actually mingled with proletarians and knew their life-styles at first hand, but it is typical of the Marxist approach that Engels never, so far as history relates, made a move to improve the condition of his workers.[25] The workingmen of the International were understandably suspicious of this industrialist who talked of revolution.

Engels not only sent Marx the money he pleaded for but took time from his other duties to compose long articles that appeared under Marx's name. There was no obvious need for Engels to subordinate himself; he lacked neither ideas nor writing ability. Yet Engels ghosted articles for Marx not only in the New York *Tribune* (over a hundred) but in a German paper; between 1851 and 1859 none of Engels's numerous writings appeared over his own name.[26] Why Engels should have been content to spend his life promoting Marx—he even assumed the paternity of Marx's illegitimate son— remains mysterious.

Engels's Marxism and Social Democracy

No less important was Engels's service during the years he survived Marx, 1883–1895, the blossoming years of Marxism. He, more than anyone else, was the maker of Marxism up to the Russian Revolution. After his retirement from business in 1869, his sole occupation was to promote the creed, and after Marx's death he dedicated himself to the literary heritage. He began the posthumous publication of Marx's manuscripts, which has continued almost to this day. He labored more than a decade over the second and third volumes of *Capital,* which became to an unknown degree his own creation or at least systematization.

Writing prolifically in the last decades of his life, Engels reshaped Marxist doctrine, interpreting and elaborating the teachings, making them stronger, more compelling, and more suitable for the politics of the day. In part, he broadened Marx's retreat from less defensible positions. He conceded that the workers may receive more than subsistence wages.[27] He several times allowed that other than economic factors played a part in history, giving reproduction and sex-related matters equal or even greater weight than production "as a determining factor," at least among primitive peoples.[28] Moreover, he conceded that "the state also is an economic power," which could go with or against economic development.[29] Engels apologized for having overstressed the economic basis: "Marx and I are ourselves partly to blame for the fact that younger writers sometimes lay more stress on the economy than is due to it. We had to emphasize this main principle in opposition to our adversaries, who denied it, and we had not always the time, the place, or the opportunity to allow the other elements involved in the interaction to come into their rights."[30]

It was also realism for Engels largely to surrender the emphasis on violent revolution which lay at the heart of Marx's thinking. Instead, Engels held out hope for the political instruments which were bringing obvious benefits to the masses. In 1885 he commented, "Since 1848 the English Parliament has undoubtedly been the most revolutionary body in the world and the next elections will open a new epoch, even if this does not reveal itself very quickly. There will be workers in Parliament, in increasing numbers and each one worse than the last. . . ."[31] By 1895 he was prepared to accept revision on a broad front, finding legal methods better than illegal, admitting the strength of capitalism, and conceding that the kind of uprising which he and Marx had so long awaited was obsolete in the face of new military technology. The

37

one-time would-be dashing general of revolution had almost become a Social-Democratic reformer.[32]

Engels was also the chief popularizer and "vulgarizer" of the thought of Marx. He wrote more simply and less figuratively; at the same time, Engels (with the assistance chiefly of Kautsky and Plekhanov) made Marxism more scientific-technical. He wanted to round it out into a modern, reasonably consistent, all-embracing world view. In an age of high prestige for science, Engels developed "scientific socialism" on the Marxian foundation. A French socialist paper wrote of him upon his death:

> Engels, no one will deny, was, with St. Simon, Fourier, and Marx, one of the least disputable fathers of the Socialist doctrine. It was under his influence, owing to his pen, that it has assumed the character of rigour and scientific precision which we love in it.[33]

Marx and Engels used "utopian" as a brand of folly; theirs was the only "true" socialism. Engels even claimed, at the end of his life, to have done away with more speculative approaches: "This conception [historical materialism] puts an end to philosophy on the historical field, just as the dialectic conception of nature makes all natural philosophy unnatural and impossible." [34]

This "scientific" approach meant emphasizing and broadening economic causation and linking it with the dialectic applied to nature. Engels extended principles of historical materialism back into prehistory, to the hypothetical beginnings of human society, depicting an idyllic "gentile" society, the detailed evolutionary stages of which he outlined on scanty evidence.[35] He endowed matter with something like purpose, in what has been called "a caricature of Marx's thinking." [36] Materialism supported the economic interpretation of politics and the belief that all the ills of society would be remedied by a reordering of economic relations. Engels made the course of history more straightforward, and the coming of socialism more inevitable. The progress of science, for example, was based on economics: "If society has a technical need, that helps science forward more than ten universities. . . . We have known anything reasonable about electricity only since its technical applicability was discovered." Further, "if a Napoleon had been lacking, another would have filled the place. . . ." [37] Through Engels's work it became the common sentiment that "Karl Marx expresses the great fact that socialism is built on the dicta of science." [38] With its clearcut categories, law of historical sequence, and certainty of progress toward socialism, Marxism as propounded by Engels gave revolutionary zeal something of the character of geometry.

Marxism thus became the chief intellectual framework of European socialism, ripened from a nice dream to a supposedly scientific certainty. Marxism stood out over its competitors in several ways. Unlike gentler socialisms, it called for and rationalized political struggle of any intensity, and it was correspondingly appropriate for a time when wage earners were becoming politically important. It told an important and organizable sector of the population that it was the salt of the earth, that it produced all wealth and deserved much more of it. Marxism did not lay its wager on specific schemes such as cooperatives, credit institutions for workers, or model communities, all of which might be tried and found deficient; its goal was fittingly distant and difficult to discredit. Compared to plans for immediate utopias, such as those of Fourier and Cabet, Marxism seemed rational and sensible. Marx's refusal to say much about the future society saved him from the silly details of just how households would be organized, or even how the laundries of the future would operate, matters which occupied the utopian planners. Marx's utopia was not to become outdated.

Marx's supremacy also owes much to the weakness of the competition. There were overstatements and absurdities in Marx's works, but such men as Saint-Simon, Fourier, and Proudhon were guilty of at least as many. Proudhon, for example, was abusive and anti-Semitic (as was Marx); he was also intolerant of anything not French, extolled war as a bringer of justice, and believed in the inferiority of women and various races.[39] Lassalle disqualified himself by spending many years helping a certain Countess Hatzfeldt obtain a divorce and by his inclination to compromise with Bismarck. But if Lassalle had not thrown away his life at age 39 in a duel over a girl, Marx's chances for dominating the German socialist movement—the only one where he had much basis for influence—would have been poor.

Marx, on the other hand, was the only eminent socialist with a higher education and title of "Dr."; consequently, he was the intellectual to whom other socialists might turn to draft a document or edit a paper. As the decades passed, moreover, no new competition arose. The first part of the nineteenth century was a unique time for socialist theory building; the French Revolution filled the air, the Industrial Revolution was new, and emotional reactions were fresh. Subsequent thinkers (Mosca, Pareto, Sombart, Michels, etc.) may have been more realistic analysts of society than Marx was, but their very realism prevented them from promising salvation on this earth.

The immodesty of Marx's claims stood him in good stead; it was still better that Engels spoke of him from the day of his burial as "the greatest living thinker." It only helped Marxism that Engels took it more seriously and literally than the originator did, becoming more pontifical as heir than the prophet had been. Other devoted adherents, such as Liebknecht and Guesde, also did their share to sanctify the master. To propagate the theories, the young Marxists started a journal in 1883; Marx became the only socialist theoretician to have, so to speak, a platform of his own.

Marx thus became a sort of father figure of socialism, submerging his onetime rivals. The socialist movement was semireligious in tone; as it grew in the last decades of the nineteenth century, it gloried in its apostles, symbols, holy day, red banner, martyrs, and heroic myths—as that of the Paris Commune, cultivated by Marx. It needed its Bible, its prophet, and its authoritative philosophy. In the first part of the nineteenth century, when socialism was vibrant with new thought, there was less call for such a figure. Later, it was felt necessary to have an intellectual support, someone to cite for respectability, a thinker who could claim to have put all "bourgeois" thinkers in the shade with a grand structure of economy, history, sociology, and philosophy beyond the grasp of ordinary men. Marx was the most acceptable, partly because he admitted diverse interpretations and prescribed no definite course of action. Men of diverse views, ardent for revolution or happy to watch capitalism prepare the way for its own downfall, united only by the desire for change at the expense of present-day possessors, could gather in his name. It did not hurt but helped that he spoke not to workers but to revolutionary agitators and discontented intellectuals, who assumed the duty of interpreting and propagating the word.

As Marx became the chief symbol of socialism, it became impermissible—treason to the workers—to attack him. Marxism became a bandwagon; men whose ideas and temperament were much closer to Bakunin, Blanqui, or Proudhon came to call themselves Marxist because this was the proper thing for socialists to be.

WESTERN SOCIAL DEMOCRACY

THE ADVANCE of Marxism in the years that elapsed between the death of Marx and that of Engels may be gauged by contrasting the dismal funeral of Marx, at which nine people heard Engels lament "the passing of this Titan," and the obsequies at Engels's cremation, attended by French, Russians, Poles, Austrians, Netherlanders, Germans, and Italians, among others, and including a half dozen socialist deputies to various parliaments and sundry notables.[40] In twelve years, Marxism had grown from almost nothing to a major force in European politics.

Primarily, however, the movement was German. In 1874 the German Social Democratic party became politically significant by winning nine seats in the Reichstag. By 1890, despite the spread of socialist politics to many countries, perhaps five-sixths of socialist voters were still German.[41] There were several reasons why the Germans were especially disposed to accept Marxism. Marx and Engels spoke to them as Germans and in their own language; during the formative years, Engels worked with and through Germans, the theorists Kautsky and Bernstein and the dedicated followers Liebknecht and Bebel. Marx's doctrine was steeped in German philosophy, and for this reason Marx had long felt that Germany was more ready than other countries for a communist revolution. After the founding of the Second Reich in 1871, industrialization proceeded very rapidly; and by 1890, Germany was surpassing the old industrial leader, England. A large and relatively educated (hence self-aware) working class emerged which did not fit into the old semifeudal society. The dissonance between economic and political development was exasperating, for power continued to rest mostly with a hereditary king-emperor and a conservative military-bureaucratic elite.

Nonetheless, it was Lassalle who, with no help from Marx and Engels, made socialism a mass movement. After Lassalle's death, German Marxists and Lassalleans were close enough together to amalgamate in a single party in 1875. With the lapse of Bismarck's antisocialist laws in 1890, the Social Democratic Party (as the socialists called themselves, avoiding the old name of "communist" to dissociate themselves from the Paris Commune) leaped into prominence with 1.5 million votes. In 1891 the party became nominally fully Marxist, with the Erfurt Program authored by Engels and Kautsky.

The Germans thus became the chief exponents of Marxism in the decades preceding World War I. But Kautsky and his followers, although firm in dogma, were elastic in action and proposed nothing contrary to the legalistic order of the *Rechtstaat*. Although the German workers acquired an interest in German prosperity, the party was still excluded from power. It was thus encouraged to assume irresponsible Marxist verbal positions. Since, moreover, the German Social Democrats saw their backward, militaristic, class-bound state as typically capitalist, their first aspiration was democracy, which seemed equivalent to a classless society. To call for equal rights for workers was revolutionary enough.

Although France was actually the first country to have a Marxist labor party, begun in the early 1800s by Jules Guesde and Marx's son-in-law, Paul Lafargue, Marxism did not make much progress there. French socialism and the French labor movement had a native revolutionary heritage in Proudhon, Saint-Simon, and Blanqui, and the French felt less need for Marxist doctrine. Guesde and Lafargue were unable to draw more than a small fraction of French radicals to their side. The French trade unions, much smaller than the German, were syndicalist in orientation and preferred the idea of the strike as a class weapon, à la Sorel. The same was true in Italy and Spain, where syndicalism and anarchism continued to be stronger than Marxism.

In England after midcentury, opinion moved away from Marx as democratization progressed; Chartism died out, and trade unionism seemed more rewarding to English workers than revolution mongering. The Fabian movement, begun in 1883, with its philosophy of gradual amelioration by enlightenment, was more to British taste. The Fabians assumed that the intellectuals were the real managers of society in any case, so the desired change, a vaguely defined socialism, could be effected by converting *them*. A British socialist (Labour) party arose in the 1890s but did not become a major political power until World War I.

Still, except for England, Marxism was spreading as a generalized doctrinal force. By 1910, socialists claimed 17 percent of the members of parliament in Austria, 11 percent in Germany, 42 percent in Russian-held Finland, 21 percent in Belgium, 21 percent in Denmark, and smaller percentages in all the democratic countries of Europe.[42] The parties were generally built on the trade unions (for which Marx had little use), but the leaders were almost everywhere of more or less bourgeois origin. The workers, desirous of improving their lot and possibly their class status, were seldom such devoted and doctrinaire socialists as were discontented intellectuals, desirous of improving society.

In sum, Marxism in these decades was spreading and prospering mightily. But there was a cost. It was in practice a reformist Marxism, not the revolutionary creed of 1848 and the *Communist Manifesto*. The Marxists had become orderly collectivists, daily engaged in striving for small advantages of the sort which Marx once regarded as impossible and which *were* impossible under the logic of his system.

MARXISM IN RUSSIA

ALTHOUGH prior to World War I the chief home of Marxism was Germany, the land of Marx and Engels, the historical role of that doctrine was to be far more fateful in Russia. Yet its very existence in Russia was anomalous. Marx had expressly said that "new, higher relations of production never appear before the material conditions of their existence have matured within the womb of the old society itself." To believe otherwise would deny economic causation and admit other, principally political, factors to a dominant role. Marx, moreover, specifically denied Russia a revolutionary role. Bakunin, he had objected, "wants the European social revolution, founded on the economic basis of capitalist production, to take place at the level of the Russian or Slav agricultural and pastoral people. *Will*, not economic conditions, is the foundation of his social revolution." [43]

Yet politics overruled theoretical consistency. In the 1870s and 1880s, Marx and Engels were looking rather desperately for signs of a revolution to brighten their declining years; and Russia, where agitation of the intelligentsia was becoming ever more intense, seemed to be the most promising area of all. In 1877, Marx had this comment on the expected defeat of Russia in its war with Turkey: "This time the revolution begins in the East, hitherto the unbroken bulwark and reserve army of counter-revolution." [44] Marx and Engels admired the Russian Populists, who were actively conspiring and assassinating, and were even willing to sacrifice doctrinal sense by accepting the Populists' beloved peasant commune as a potential starting point for communist development. They were only concerned that the revolution come. Engels wrote: "In my opinion the most important thing is that Russia be given a push, that the revolution break out. Whether this faction or that faction gives the signal, whether it happens under this flag or that matters little to me." [45]

In seeking to give Russia a push, Marx and Engels in effect seized a great truth about their doctrine: no matter what it seemed to say, it was much better suited for early than mature industrialization, and better fitted to the political needs of relatively backward countries than of relatively advanced ones. Russia in the last decades of the nineteenth century was just embarking on large-scale industrialization; its manufacturing output tripled between 1877 and 1897.[46] As elsewhere, the effects included social, economic, and political malaise. Incipient capitalism was rather ugly, visibly exploitative, and crude, bringing unhappiness to many. The workers were not very numerous (about 1 percent of the population in 1900, slightly more than the nobility), but they were concentrated in large cities and treated like the British workers of a century earlier. Handicrafts suffered, and peasants lost a winter livelihood. The newly rich capitalists were resented as intruders who fattened greedily on the sweat of the poor, and they were the more resented because very many were non-Russian, visible reminders of Russia's inability to industrialize on its own.

Russia, like many non-Western countries today, was also more hospitable to radicalism because the tsarist government permitted practically no political participation. Those who perceived the necessity for change could only scheme and dream, and their dreams often had no foundation in the real life from which the dreamers were excluded. There consequently developed in Russia a peculiar non-Marxian class, the intelligentsia—a class then novel, although something like it has since grown up in the less developed countries—whose Western-style education had left them sufficiently educated to see Russia's defects but not to appreciate their own limitations. They were mostly students, writers, and, in due course, revolutionary political leaders; they bitterly resented their futility, found their society deeply wrong, and passionately hoped to change it. The underlying preoccupation of their endless discussions was Russia's relations with the West, a West they had to look up to because of its technological superiority but which they hated for the same reason. Since religion was the creature of the detested state and symbolized intellectual backwardness, they were irreligious. Yet, as Herzen observed, "having discarded positive religion, we have retained all the habits of religion, and having lost paradise in heaven we believe in the coming paradise on earth, and boast about it." [47] Convinced of the overwhelming greatness of Russia, whatever its present poverty and humiliations, they could only foresee for it a glorious destiny. "Let us," said Belinsky, "envy our grandchildren and great-grandchildren who are destined to see Russia in 1940—standing at the head of the educated world, laying down laws in science and art, and receiving the tribute of respect from the whole of enlightened humanity." [48] The way to make Russia great and happy could only be by revolution to remake the state. Revolution became practically an ersatz religion.

Yet the intelligentsia had no clear idea how the revolution might come. At one time, such men as Belinsky and Herzen vaguely hoped that a good tsar would arise to cast down the evil nobles and save the people, establishing perhaps a species of monarchic communism. But the democratic mentality of the West was filtering in and mixing with the old equalitarian (or pseudo-equalitarian) ethos of the empire, [49] and the conviction grew that regeneration could come only from the common people. The logical conclusion was that the revolution was to be made by enlightening the peasants, the true and virtuous nine-tenths of the population. In this conviction, many a young idealist went out as a missionary to the dark countryside, especially in the 1870s. But the peasants failed to respond, less because they were averse to protest than because they lived in a different world from these intellectuals of middle- or often upper-class origin.

Perhaps a long educational campaign might have succeeded eventually, but these young radicals wanted quick results. Rebuffed, they began rethinking tactics. They continued to idealize the people, but they decided the revolution would have to be made by the enlightened few who really wanted it; in practice, they became elitist. Democracy would come only after the revolution made it possible to reeducate the people.

New themes and new ways had to be found to achieve the necessary and inevitable regeneration of Russia. Looking for a quick road to happiness, the intelligentsia preferred to read the most advanced—that is, most radical—Western thinkers. In the middle years of the nineteenth century they mulled over such writers as Saint-Simon, Fourier, and Proudhon; and in due course Marx came to their attention. The first translation of *Capital* was into Russian in 1872, fifteen years before the first English version. The Russian translation was put out in an edition of 3,000 copies, and 900 were sold in six weeks.[50] Several other works by Marx subsequently sold better in Russia, despite its small number of educated persons, than anywhere else, even in Germany. Marxism seeped in via Engels and German social democracy—Germany was by far the strongest intellectual influence on Russia—and the upsurge of Marxism in Germany was reflected in its general acceptance in Russia in the 1890s.[51]

The time was right. Reliance on the peasants had seemingly failed, but a new industrial working class was rising. Although very small proportionately, the factory proletariat was more reachable, more organizable, less ignorant, and altogether more promising than the peasantry as a revolutionary class. Just as capitalism was growing enough to become irksome, the Russians were presented with a teaching which promised that it would be superseded by something infinitely better. Those who were depressed by the seemingly hopeless struggle could console themselves with the certainty of victory. As a Populist exclaimed on reading *Capital*, "The knowledge that we feeble individuals were backed by a mighty historical process filled one with ecstasy and established such a firm foundation for the individual's activities that, it seemed, all the hardships of the struggle could be overcome." [52]

Marxism appealed for numerous other reasons, which were, for the most part, similar to those that more recently have made it the favorite ideology of intellectuals in less developed countries. It was a way of damning the West in terms of modern Western ideals. It seemed like a scientific creed that should help Russia catch up with the West; as the latest mode of Western thought, it should be the best. For those who stood in awe of modern science and longed to grasp for themselves its power but had no real idea of scientific fact and method, Marxism offered practically a new faith, with answers to the problems of history, ethics, and philosophy as well as economics and politics. It was a happy discovery for intellectuals who were atheists not from scientific conviction but from political principle that their atheism implied, in Marxism, "scientific socialism."

Marxism was relevant for Russia because revolution was relevant: "As the anonymous bearer of Russian history, and of world history, the Russian wanted nothing less than paradise on earth and he heard a promise of this paradise in the tremors of the revolution." [53] That the Marxist revolution would destroy the developing bourgeois or capitalist order was also excellent. The intelligentsia scorned middle-class commercialism and saw capitalism as immoral and unjust not only because it was new and intrusive, as it had been in England and Germany, but because the spirit of the system was foreign to Russia, as were many of its practitioners. It was easy to believe that destroying this alien growth would restore the simple happiness of the old days on a theoretically higher level—the basic promise of Marx's thought. It was the timeless peasant dream of a land of milk and honey, with no taxes or conscription, brought up to date.

The Populist worship of the common people was easily turned into the exaltation of the proletariat. The Marxist analysis of society as class-ruled was more convincing in Russia (although the classes of tsardom were politically as well as economically based) than in freer, more capitalistic, and less stratified countries. The idea of law as the command of a selfish elite was correspondingly more credible, and the conclusion that happiness would be achieved by abolition of classes was more persuasive. Indeed, in Russia this ideal was embedded in peasant tradition and long antedated Marx; the idealization of the peasant commune was easily transmuted into the idealization of Marxist communism.

Nor was it an accident that the young Marx's consistent ruthlessness appealed to Russian émigrés in Paris.[54] If Marx was intolerant and prone to exaggeration, so were they. If Marxism was scholastic and a little detached from concrete reality, this too suited them, as they knew industrial society only from books. The dialectic—the unity of opposites and negation of the negation—well fitted their commingling of passion and logic. If Marxism was basically moralistic, the leading trait of the Russian intelligentsia was a moral approach to social and political problems.[55] That Marxism was internationalist and antinationalist appealed to the universalism of the multinational empire; it potentially offered a new and better basis for integration of the peoples under the tsar. Not least, Marxism appealed to placeless intellectuals, for it implicitly promised authority to the educated elite which would have to replace both traditional ruling powers and the newer capitalists.

For such reasons, many an educated young Russian came, especially in the 1890s, to believe in Marxism with the fervor of

Russian messianism, the passion of a religious people without a heavenly God. It was easy to be Marxist because the authorities were not much alarmed by it; it seemed too dry and academic to threaten much, more anticapitalist than antitsarist; and conservatives who disliked industrialization and the West in general might even half welcome it. The university youth was gripped by it, and many who were not fully converted were much influenced. The radical "establishment" was strong enough that a critical Marxist, Peter Struve, at one time had difficulty in getting his writings published. As Lenin wrote of the mid-1890s, "Marxist books were published one after another, Marxist journals and newspapers were founded, nearly everyone became a Marxist, Marxists were flattered, Marxists were courted, and the publishers rejoiced in the ready sale of Marxist literature." [56]

Out of this diffuse Marxist movement there arose a Marxist party. Georgy Plekhanov (1856–1918), a onetime Populist who emigrated in 1880 and was converted in France to thoroughgoing Marxism, in 1883 started the first Russian Marxist organization, the tiny Liberation of Labor group, in Geneva. Only in 1903, however, was the Russian Social-Democratic Labor Party properly organized at its Second Congress in Brussels and London (the first, in 1898 inside Russia, was a failure). Although there were multiple programs and many shades of belief, most Russian political Marxists tended, at least for a few years, to hold together; and they had some common traits which set them off from the Western Social Democrats. For one thing, they were remarkably young, a veritable youth movement; as late as the 1905 congress, the oldest person present was 35. (It was ordinarily held that revolutionaries were played out after age 30.[57]) Whereas Western Marxist parties had some connection with real workers, the Russians' concept of the workers was largely abstract, and when workers were recruited the Russian Marxist leadership was reluctant to bring them into positions of authority.[58] Unlike Western Marxist parties, the Russian Social Democrats were not much disposed to moderation. No trade unions acted as a moderating force. Agitation for reform was almost as much subject to repression as advocacy of revolution; smallness of membership encouraged ideological narrowness and intolerance, a characteristic heightened by Lenin but not peculiar to his group. Russian Marxists were given to violent language and cared little for "bourgeois objectivity," which is still an object of Soviet contempt. They had little feeling for democracy; even the moderate and scholarly Plekhanov in 1903 indicated that results of elections need not be respected unless convenient.[59]

The Russian Marxist movement and the party were, however, divided into moderates versus activists, anti-elitists versus elitists. Some took the position that in view of the immaturity of capitalism in Russia, the only sensible course was to work for economic gains (the "Economists") and organize for better times. The leading exponent of this reformist view, a view more consistent with Marxism as generally understood in the West at this time, was Plekhanov, who, after Engels and with Kautsky, was a prime mover in the making of post-Marxian Marxism. He was a thorough historical determinist; the term "dialectical materialism" was his coinage. For him, history was made by class forces, not by great men; and the sequence of social orders was fixed. This meant, in his view, that the Russian proletariat was to save Russia by bringing it into the mainstream of Western socialism. However, it was necessary to wait patiently for capitalism to grow and ripen in Russia—unless revolution in the West advanced revolution in Russia and abbreviated the capitalist stage. He warned that a premature revolutionary coup would bring not socialism but an Oriental-style caste despotism, "a political abortion, like the ancient empires of China or Persia, that is, a revived tsarist despotism resting on a communist base." [60]

This more cautious approach is commonly associated with the Mensheviks, the faction which at the 1903 congress took a slightly less elitist attitude than did Lenin's Bolshevik group.

Lenin was the preeminent spokesman of those who derided caution, reformism, and such downgrading of revolutionary action. However, much of the sense of activism was expressed by Trotsky, who did not affiliate with Lenin until 1917. He wanted the proletarian revolution to come on the heels of the bourgeois. As he wrote in relation to the semirevolution of 1905, "The theory of permanent revolution makes clear that in the backward bourgeois nations of our time, the democratic tasks fall to the dictatorship of the proletariat, and that this dictatorship makes the carrying out of socialist tasks its primary objective. . . ." [61]

Thus, in Russia, Marxism took another step away from the teachings of Marx, turning into a creed for a less developed country irritated by modernization and by its strained relations with Western civilization.

LENIN AND THE PARTY

FOUNDED in 1903, the Russian Social Democratic Party immediately split into two main factions because such a split was inherent in its nature. It was torn, like the parties of Western Europe, between those of more revolutionary temperament and those more prepared to look to the logic of history and progress to prepare the new social order. The split was also a replay of the old, mid-nineteenth century division in the Russian intelligentsia between the Westernizers, who wished Russia to evolve in the wake of Western Europe, and the Slavophiles, who were more insistent on the special Russian destiny.

Lenin himself was the center of conflict. He began his seminal programmatic work of 1902, *What Is to Be Done?*, with an assault on the efforts to make the party "a democratic party of social reform," and throughout the remainder of the prewar period his chief preoccupation was to combat what he considered backsliding and cowardice in Russian Marxism. Although he was not very successful—his group was usually in the minority—from our perspective he seems to represent the more truly Russian position, the ideas closer to Russian political reality and traditions.

Philosophic differences between Lenin's Bolsheviks and the Mensheviks were not deep or clear-cut, and both factions claimed to be the best of Marxists. But the Mensheviks sacrificed much of the revolutionary spirit of Marxism to the Marxist logic of historical inevitability. If the coming revolution was to be bourgeois-capitalist, the Marxists and the proletariat could at best hope to influence the resultant bourgeois regime, while awaiting the maturation of Russian capitalism. In other words, the Marxists would act as a reformist party.

Lenin, on the other hand, sacrificed much of the belief in the inevitability of social change through technological development to the Marxist revolutionary spirit. For Lenin, the whole approach of economic analysis was secondary; he was attracted by the idea of "class war, relentless and thorough-going, aiming at the final destruction of the enemy." [62] If some modification of literal Marxism was necessary, Lenin, even while claiming to be the strictest adherent of the master, was not disturbed. As he wrote in 1899, "We think that an independent elaboration of Marx's theory is especially essential for Russian socialists; for this theory provides only general *guiding* principles, which in *particular* are applied . . . [differently in different countries]." [63] Lenin's argument was that he was taking the position Marx would have taken in the situation.

The result of applied Leninism, the building of a supposedly Marxist socialist state in largely preindustrial Russia, turned Marxism upside down and reversed the relation of politics to economics; a political movement led to economic development. But before 1917, Lenin not only did not claim to be able to build socialism on the Russian foundation—this was not explicit policy until Stalin's "Socialism in One Country" in 1924—but he also did his best to fit Russia into the Marxist picture. Like other Russian Marxists, he emphasized and exaggerated similarities between Russia and the West. He recognized that the Russian factory proletariat was small, but he noted that it was politically important beyond its size because it was concentrated in the main cities and in large factories; there it was accessible and relatively class-conscious, in accordance with Marx's ideas of the preparation of the proletariat for its role.

Lenin also saved Marxist appearances by finding capitalism in the countryside. He lumped landowners with capitalists as exploiters of a proletariat of sorts, not only the large landholders, who had only about a tenth of the arable land on the eve of the revolution, but the better-off peasants able to accumulate a little livestock beyond their immediate needs and to hire a few helpers. On the other hand, the poorer peasants, at least those who had to hire out their labor, became an exploited proletariat. Lenin encountered a problem here, however. According to the sense of Marxism, he could only promise the peasants nationalization of the land, a program which appealed to the peasantry much less than did the simple redivision of land promised by the competing Socialist Revolutionary Party. For this reason and because the Bolsheviks were city-bound people, Lenin's party achieved little strength in the countryside. But Lenin recognized the potential of peasant jacqueries (he was willing to try to harness any discontent, Marxist-oriented or not, including those of religious dissidents and restive minority nationalities), and he came to power in 1917 partly by virtue of his willingness to compromise his Marxist principles and promise land to the peasants.

Lenin's crucial amendment of Marxism, however, was to assign the prime role in the making of the revolution to the revolutionary party instead of the proletarian class. This was implied by bringing in the peasants and others as agents of revolution; to guide the sundry forces it was clearly necessary to have a sort of general staff standing over them. The shortage of proletarians also made it requisite to assign a special role to the party. Since they were few, they could not in any case provide a broad basis for support, and their weakness was to be compensated for by the dedication and zeal of the organized few. Worse, as Lenin recognized, the workers were not acquiring revolutionary class feeling but were being seduced by the lure of a few more kopecks. But he did not conclude, with the revisionists, that party ideology should be revised to conform to reality. Instead, rejecting the Marxist principle of consciousness arising from material existence, he urged that the party, armed with Marxist teachings, undertake to educate and guide the workers. The bourgeois-led party did not have to follow the urges of the workers, but should instead lead them where they ought to wish to go, to revolution and socialism.

This was not necessarily opposed to Marxist teaching. While Marxist theory regarded proletarian consciousness as the result of the proletarian condition, the Fathers of Socialism (whose nonproletarian origins were pointed out by Lenin) had spoken and acted as though the workers were to be educated to their role. In the Communist Manifesto they gave a formulation of the role of the party not radically different from Lenin's: "The Communists, therefore, are on the one hand, practically, the most advanced and resolute section of the working-class parties of every country, that section which pushes forward all others; on the other hand, theoretically, they have over the great mass of the proletariat the advantage of clearly understanding the line of march, the conditions, and the ultimate general results of the proletarian movement." [64] Marx's party at this time was even more nonproletarian than Lenin's sixty years later. It was taken for granted that the intellectuals should give their superior knowledge to the workers.

Lenin's theory was fairly well in accord with Social Democratic practice. Bebel was for a long time practically king of the German party, and Kautsky admitted that the proletariat needed bourgeois guidance toward socialism.[65] The Mensheviks also saw themselves, bourgeois intellectuals, as natural leaders of the proletariat. The difference lay in Lenin's franker acceptance of the responsibilities of superior knowledge and in the Mensheviks' presumably greater willingness to surrender power to true proletarians where these should be able to take over.

Lenin's assignment of a leadership role to the party had several consequences. Party members were to be special characters—heroes, so to speak, standing over the masses in the tradition of conspiratorial Populism. Membership had to be restricted to the dedicated and faithful, and it was essential that all members possess the true doctrine. The party had to be dogmatic because its title to authority was not consent but the possession of truth.

The leadership role of the party also excluded democracy within it; unity was too precious and too fragile. Lenin claimed that the conditions of repression under which the party operated within Russia prevented democracy, but the real reason was elitism. Elections for higher party posts being ordinarily not feasible, the leadership became a self-selected, self-perpetuating little oligarchy—the narrower, the more purely bourgeois, and the more isolated from its following because it lived in exile. Democratic procedures became in Bolshevism what they have remained in Soviet practice, a facade for appearances and a means of "strengthening ties with the masses." In this, too, Lenin was close to the practice of the young Marx and Engels. Membership in the Communist League of 1848–1850 entailed full submission to party rules and decisions, as befitted the staff of revolution.[66]

The leadership role of the party and the making of revolution in an unindustrialized country also excluded democracy *after* the revolution. Lenin, while not forswearing democracy as a long-term goal, insisted that the immediate aim of revolutionary action was not democracy but dictatorship of the proletariat.

Dictatorship of the proletariat was an old idea; Babeuf and Blanqui, as well as the Russian Populists, had thought in terms of a group seizing total power to usher in the new order. Lenin pointed to Marx's uses of the term, which were not numerous but were fairly emphatic. For example, in his letter to J. Weydemeyer, Marx emphasized the thesis that "the class struggle necessarily leads to the *dictatorship of the proletariat*." [67] But it was never clear whether this meant what dictatorship usually means (arbitrary rule by a dictator or perhaps a very small group), or merely the unlimited domination of a class which was itself to be the majority, "the immense majority" according to the *Communist Manifesto*.

Much, if not all, of what came to be known as Leninism was thus presaged in the writings and the approach of Marx. But Lenin picked out what suited him and created a new kind of party, one designed to exercise total leadership over the masses and organized internally around a single group of leaders—the most effective machine for the concentration of authority yet invented. This required ideology in a new sense; loyalty was all-important, and to be loyal meant believing in the prescribed manner. Marx, as interpreted by the leader, became an oracle as never before. This conception also required firmness of party structure; Lenin was much more of a party organizer than any of his competitors, and he could treat party workers in Russia simply as his "agents." [68] As Krupskaya wrote of *What Is to Be Done?*, "It [the party] put forward a complete organizational plan in which everybody could find a place, could become a cog in the revolutionary machine. . . .[69]

In Lenin's party, Marxism became the ideology not of a workers' movement but of a leadership movement like those of Mao, Castro, and others rather less concerned with the will of the people and more with their own glory.

THE SUBSIDENCE OF MARXISM

LENIN'S MOVEMENT contained in embryo a new grandeur for Marxism, but for most of the years up to the revolution of 1917 this promise was very faint. Social Democratic Marxism, the second phase, came to a peak in the 1890s, thereafter declining until rejuvenated by World War I.

The fact is that after 1875, conditions were becoming less favorable for the Marxist approach, even in the Engels-revised version. Welfare legislation and state intervention on behalf of the less fortunate were expanding from small beginnings. Bismarck's social insurance laws of the 1880s conspicuously made the workers beneficiaries of the state. The scramble for overseas colonies, which could plausibly be given a Marxist interpretation and which gave the Marxists a good cause, climaxed in the 1880s and thereafter receded. Moreover, as ordinary workers in industrial countries secured the vote and began to use it, with Engels's full approval, they sought more democracy and reforms within the constitutional system. Indeed, in swelling and attracting many voters, the socialist parties became deradicalized. To appeal widely, they had to adopt policies attractive not only to factory workers but also to the "petty bourgeoisie"—craftsmen, small shopkeepers, teachers, and so forth. The socialist parties grew bigger, more cumbersome, and less frightening. Engels candidly recognized this fact when, in his last work, the preface to the 1895 edition of Marx's pamphlet on the Paris Commune, he conceded that "history showed we were wrong," postponing the revolution to the dim future.[70]

Ideological confusion was the result. Some Marxists tried practically to deny the evidence; others sought explanations for the supposedly temporary failure of events to take the predicted turn. Still others took the less comforting view that if facts contradicted theory, so much the worse for the theory. The theory, then, was to be revised, since it could not be frankly discarded; and there arose a tendency within Social Democratic Marxism known to this day as Revisionism.

The leading exponent of Revisionism was Eduard Bernstein (1850–1932). A fervent revolutionary in his youth and a convinced Marxist, Bernstein became a close collaborator of Engels and one of his executors. However, partly under the influence of Fabianism, he began to be assailed by doubts as to the correctness of the theories. As he put it, "What is necessary is to become clear just where Marx is right and where he is wrong." [71] Bernstein argued that socialism should be a movement rather than a goal, not an apocalyptic vision but a march to freedom and equality by political process, cooperatives, education, and unionism. In his definition, socialism was a "movement towards, or the state of, an order of society based on, the principle of association." [72] In short, he wanted theory to correspond with what the party was actually doing.

Bernstein's articles caused a sensation in Social Democratic circles, and there were prolonged and impassioned debates over Revisionism at party congresses. It was difficult to gainsay the facts adduced by Bernstein, but there was one major fact he had overlooked: traditional Marxist doctrine was or seemed to be useful to the party and to the people wedded to the promotion of the proletarian cause.[73] The approach of the party majority was fairly well summarized by one leader's comment on Revisionism: "You don't talk about it, you just do it." [74] Radical language did not entail radical action. The party was "revolutionary" but not "revolution making."

In Russia, too, some hardships were mitigated. Legislation in 1897, although barely enforced, gave workers some slight protection. The country prospered, capitalism no longer seemed so disastrous, and the preoccupation of the intelligentsia with revolution waned. Reformism and liberalism grew. Lenin in 1901 lamented that "Russian Social Democracy is passing through a period of vacillation and doubt bordering on self-negation." [75]

The semirevolution of 1905 raised Marxist hopes briefly in Russia, and in Central Europe as well, but thereafter the tide ebbed. The semi-constitution which the tsar was compelled to grant gave a fair degree of freedom of speech and some civil rights; the legislative Duma, although unrepresentative and impotent, provided a forum for public opinion, including the parties of the extreme left. The older radicalism seemed outmoded, and revolution lost much of its mystique. Intellectuals tended to turn away from the Populist Chernyshevsky and the Marxist Plekhanov to idealists such as Dostoyevsky and Soloviev, and from revolutionary conspiracy to national traditions, the Orthodox Church, and religious philosophy.[76] Tolstoy became a more important intellectual force than Marx. The student movement lost intensity. In *Vekhi* (Signposts), in 1909, seven outstanding intellectuals, including such ex-Marxists as Peter Struve and Nicholas Berdyaev, made a root-and-branch attack on the old radical tradition as lawless, scornful of facts, and amoral.[77] The old Populism was revived in moderated form, mostly by Viktor Chernov, as the Socialist-Revolutionary Party; its aim was socialization of land and other socialistic policies to benefit the exploited peasant class without revolution. By 1914 the Socialist-Revolutionaries had far more adherents than Bolsheviks and Mensheviks combined.[78]

For the Marxists, the subsidence of the revolutionary fires of 1905 left ashes of disillusionment. The principal lesson for the Bolsheviks was their incapacity to take advantage of a revolutionary situation. The following years were discouraging. In 1906 the income of the Bolshevik Central Committee from its Russian membership was only 750 rubles.[79] Lenin several times expressed his gloom. Thus, in 1909: "A year of disintegration, a year of ideological and political disunity, a year of Party driftage lies behind us. The membership of all our party organizations has dropped. Some of them—namely, those whose membership was least proletarian—have fallen to pieces." [80] Inside Russia, at about the same time, Stalin wrote, "There was a time when our organization numbered thousands of members and could mobilize hundreds of thousands. . . . How different it is now. Instead of thousands, we count in our organization but tens, or at best hundreds of members. . . ." [81] Lenin found it almost impossible to maintain the ideological integrity of his group. Men nearest him began looking beyond Marxism for inspiration—for example, Bogdanov to Mach and Avenarius, and Lunacharsky to humanist religion. Lenin battled not only with the Mensheviks, but with sundry factions—"God-builders," "liquidators," and "recallers."

Lenin's policies and outlook changed also in the arid years of peace and calm. It was backsliding that he agreed in 1908 to discontinue the "expropriations" (i.e., robberies) by which the Bolsheviks had filled their coffers at the expense of the exploiters. With Bolshevik deputies in the Duma, Lenin found himself forced into the uncomfortable position of participating in parliamentary politics. In 1912, Lenin wrote about the electoral campaign much as any ordinary politician, calling Marxists "working class democrats" and urging his followers to exert themselves for a "democratic upswing." [82] The Bolshevik program as presented at the 1912 Prague Conference called for a democratic republic, an eight-hour workday, and land reform. Lenin was apparently well on the way to becoming a Social Democratic reformer like Kautsky, in practice if not in theory.

For the German Social Democrats the years preceding World War I were also a time of mellowing. The party became more and more an organization and less and less a movement. Together with the trade unions, it slowly built up an administrative apparatus, with its vested interests and union treasuries; accumulation of funds by the party was taken as progress toward socialism.[83] The party was a sort of workers' club, and the socialist bureaucracy came to see its task as competing with other parties for members and votes, not turning society upside down.[84] The party increasingly emphasized its ethical goals and deemphasized the Marxian analysis of capital and labor which was intended to support the revolution. Despite such caution, the electoral fortunes of the party leveled off after 1903, and it suffered its first setback in the election of 1907. As a result, it tended toward still more moderation.

In France the Marxists were only one of several socialist parties around the turn of the century. In 1905, Marxists, Blanquists, and reformist socialists united to form a single party, but this took on revisionist colors. The French government being much more democratic than the German, even the extremists in the French party were prepared to admit the possibility of socialism by the parliamentary path.[85] The leading socialist of the day, Jean Jaurès, was hardly a Marxist, and three nominal socialists entered the "bourgeois" government in 1910.

Like the national parties, international socialism was also being drained of most of what had earlier been understood as the essence of Marxism. The Second International, founded in 1889, never became more than a loose and feeble organization which tried bravely to reconcile Marxism and democracy, the flaming creed of the *Communist Manifesto* ("Let the ruling classes tremble at the thought of a communist revolution") with the mild tactics of its component parties. In 1907, for example, the "Red International" debated women's suffrage, rights of trade unions, colonialism, and militarism; the biggest theme of the International ordinarily was the prevention of war, although it was widely assumed that both capitalist interdependence and workers' solidarity made general war impossible.[86] Thus it was highly disillusioning when in 1914 the socialist parties of all the belligerent states (except Russia) rallied around their governments. The workers identified not with a class cause but with their national states; the minorities in the several parties who opposed the war effort were not workers but bourgeois intellectuals.

By the eve of World War I, the outlook for Marxism was dim. Marx himself was no awesome, semideified figure but primus inter pares among the publicists of socialism, along with such greats as Lassalle, Sidney Webb, G. B. Shaw, and Jaurès.[87] Neither Kautsky nor Rosa Luxemburg felt that Marx was above criticism or immune from error. There was no belief that people should be excluded from the International for being non-Marxist or anti-Marxist. Socialism, a word which was tending to lose favor, was little more than an expression of general discontent and equalitarian urges, hardly a belief in definite socialist principles.[88] As Sombart wrote in 1909, someone considering the socialist writers of the day might "perhaps still come across a revolutionary phrase here and there, but no one believes in it any longer. It is all ink; red ink if you like, but still ink and not life-blood." [89] It was no longer clear what socialism meant, whether it involved nationalization or class war; and it was an unquestionable disappointment that a half century of propaganda had achieved almost nothing.[90]

Marxist doctrine was subject to serious criticism among socialists for lack of ethical content [91] and for treating people as abstractions. Marxist economics was passé; "One hears less of surplus value now, as one hears less of Ricardo's theory of rent," wrote the young H. G. Wells, a socialist by conviction.[92] In the words of a less sympathetic critic,

. . . during the last twenty years, gradually at first, and of late with marked rapidity, the Socialistic theory of production has undergone a fundamental change. Nearly all its exponents who have any pretensions to be thinkers have by this time practically repudiated the doctrine of Marx altogether, and vie with each other in proclaiming their full recognition of the fact that the enhanced production of wealth in the modern world is not due to the labor of the average man alone, but to the co-operation with such labor of activities of a different kind, which are found to an efficient degree in exceptional men only. . . .[93]

It could be seriously asked whether Marxism was not moribund. Sombart saw its theoretical structure collapsing from age and criticism.[94] An Austrian student, Paul Weisengrün, maintained in 1911 that "all the really enlightened minds of Europe now recognize the fact that theoretical Marxism is nearing its end." He conceded that "the pious souls whose wishes take the form of social ideals for the future may still, of course, be counted by the hundred thousands. And in such souls the phrases 'exploiters,' 'increment of value,' 'inherent law of capitalistic development,' are still regarded as sacred formulas. But even in the army of believers the old dogmas are losing their magic; the doubters are multiplying daily." Marxism, moreover, "cannot adapt itself at all to a healthy capitalism . . . and it forgets the fact that there is in process a veritable rejuvenation of capitalism in general." [95]

In those relatively calm and prosperous years before 1914, Marxism was thus decadent. But the Götterdämmerung of the Great War put an end to "healthy capitalism" and gave new life to Marxism, albeit mostly in a radically altered form.

CHAPTER

III

Soviet Marxism

WAR AS A CATALYST

THE CALAMITY of 1914–1918 meant not only four years of grinding and purposeless slaughter but also the beginning of the end of European primacy in world affairs and the inception of a period of tensions and turmoil which has not yet fully subsided. World War I led to the triumph of a radical party in Russia and to the birth of Communism as a world political force, to the great economic depression of the 1930s, to the victory of fascism in several great powers, to a second world war, and ultimately to the rule of Marxist ideology over a third of the world's population.

The apparent progressiveness and stability of the prewar years were at an end. The unremitting carnage enthroned violence and unreason, mocked the prewar faith in progress through science and general goodwill, and spurred demands for fundamental change.

The war also undercut authority. To the vanquished, the government and the elite appeared responsible for human suffering and national humiliation; rulers in every defeated nation were overthrown. But even for the victorious, the gains, which were little more than glory, did not seem worth the cost. Someone had to be blamed for the catastrophe. Of the most likely scapegoats—the politicians, the militarists, and the capitalists—the last were the easiest target. Lenin's argument that finance capital was responsible for the mass murder was logically and factually weak, but it was as appealing as any at hand. The war contradicted Marxist theory by showing the overwhelming strength of nationalism over class solidarity, either of owners or workers. But it destroyed respect for inherited values and gave a new and powerful reason for radical change—namely, to make a peaceful world. In the suffering, utopia became more meaningful; in the atmosphere of violence, revolutionary violence no longer frightened. When insecurity gripped everyone, it was comforting to join a movement which promised total security.

Consequently, World War I gave a powerful boost to socialism in Europe. In Germany the Social Democrats, who had supported the Kaiser's government, were called upon to assume responsibility for the surrender. In France socialists shared in the government from the beginning of the war. In England the Labour Party, which had been declining in the last prewar years, joined the coalition government in 1915. After the war, having proclaimed its goal of socialization, Labour became one of the two leading parties. Everywhere socialists became acceptable as leading opposition or governing parties.

However, the moderate or establishment socialists, drawn into the sharing of power and responsibility, became less revolutionary, not more so; such socialists as Friedrich Ebert, the first president of the Weimar republic, and Gustav Noske, his assistant in military affairs, were prepared to repress efforts of Berlin workers in 1919 to carry out a revolution like that long promised by the Social Democrats. Nevertheless, beneath the often conservative leadership there was a ferment of radicalization. Unanimous or near-unanimous support for military budgets did not long outlast the first patriotic euphoria. A few, mostly young intellectuals, began expressing first reservations and then opposition, and their numbers grew as the war became more oppressive and futile. With Karl Liebknecht (son of Wilhelm, the collaborator of Marx and Engels) in the lead, a left wing split off from the German Social Democratic Party to form the Independent Social Democrats; most of the latter wound up in a few years in the German Communist Party. In other countries there similarly arose a set of new parties prepared to turn their backs on democratic procedures in order to reshape thoroughly the social order; and in the uncertainties and hardships of the first postwar years, they accepted the discipline, the vision,

and the promise of the successful revolutionary movement organized and headed by Lenin.

On the eve of the war, Lenin had made substantial progress
toward becoming a normal politician; his writings of the last peacetime months are uniformly trivial and nonideological. But with the
outbreak of war, revolution in Russia suddenly became, for the first
time since the Russo-Japanese War of 1904–1905, a practical possibility. Lenin could raise his sights from minor discomfiture of the
tsarist government to the achievement of power.[1] Lenin was at the
same time shocked by the decision of Marxist parties, especially
the German party, to support the war policies of their governments.
With little direct contact with the homeland, Lenin took seriously
the internationalist pretensions and slogans of the Second International and at first refused to believe the news. Feeling betrayed in
his faith, he broke emotionally and politically away from moderate
social democracy. Within days, Lenin was proclaiming that "the
Second International has died, overwhelmed by opportunism," and
calling for its replacement by a new Third International.[2] Communism was born.

Most of the slowly growing number of antiwar socialists were
for peace, but Lenin took the more truculent position that peace
would only restore imperialism. Instead, the imperialist war should
be converted into revolutionary civil war; the remedy, which he
demanded just a few days after war broke out, was not to patch up
an armistice between nations but to overthrow nations and capitalism, establishing a revolutionary United States of Europe.[3] He had
few followers at first, but the war gave him a platform and a hearing
such as he had never had before; and every month his position
became stronger.

Lenin's chief ideas of this period were set forth in his *Imperialism, the Highest Stage of Capitalism.* In writing it he had three
chief purposes: to fix on capitalism the blame for the catastrophe, to
explain the defection ("treason") of the Social Democratic parties,
and to justify immediate revolution in Russia. In Lenin's interpretation, the industrial capitalism of Marx's day had matured into the finance capital of the banks and monopolistic cartels. These needed
new markets and especially new fields of investment for their surpluses, which no longer could be profitably applied at home.
Hence came the scramble for colonies in the latter part of the nineteenth century. One result was that profits from colonial holdings
enabled the capitalists to improve the lot of their workers, or of a

labor aristocracy, sufficiently to buy them off and thus forestall revolution in the advanced industrial countries. Another result was that when the available territories of the globe had been partitioned, the captialists of different nations, ever greedy for more, had to come into conflict; hence the world war.

Lenin's small book was tedious, unoriginal, sloppily written, and logically weak. It espoused the claim of military-patriotic circles, which socialists had usually (and correctly) denied, that colonies enrich the nation. The idea of surplus capital piling up made nonsense of the Marxian rule of falling profits. The idea of the domination of finance capital deviated from Marx by separating capital from industry and the extraction of surplus value; in Lenin's interpretation, those directly in control of means of production were no longer the real capitalists. Lenin's history was faulty. After 1900, there was no more rush for colonies; the chief colonizer, England, came to amicable delimitation agreements with its chief rivals, Russia and France, to form a common political front, while colonial matters were not conspicuous in the rivalry of England and Germany. Lenin overlooked the fact that large areas, especially China, were still available for slicing up if the European powers had been really land hungry. His explanation for expansion was monumentally unsuited to his own country, Russia, one of the leading colonizers but an importer of capital. Lenin himself recognized in his work that French and German capital did not go to the respective colonies in any important degree,[4] while British capital did quite as well in Argentina as within the empire. Finally, the rivalries that directly caused the war were not between rich nations but between the relatively poor and underindustrialized Austria and Russia.

But Lenin's thesis was so useful that it has become something close to gospel for half the world. It explained why the predicted revolution had not come and why the workers of the West were so tame (their leaders had been bribed with part of the colonial plunder). It laid the blame for war squarely where most people wanted to see it, on the moneybags. It gave a basis for belief that capitalism was in its death throes, as Lenin's title indicated. Best of all, it in effect made the less industrialized countries a sort of proletariat exploited by the leading Western nations. Hence revolution was appropriate for the less developed but more exploited countries. Lenin counted Russia among the semicolonial exploited countries on the basis of the substantial amount of foreign capital invested there, so socialist revolution might appropriately begin in Russia;

this was the weak link in the chain of world capitalism, so the world revolution *should* begin there. Lenin gave a Marxist cast to the old Slavophile theory of the advantages of backwardness: Russian virtue, uncorrupted by the commercialism and bourgeois decadence of the West, would come forward to lead the world to redemption.

LENIN'S REVOLUTION

THUS Lenin went back to Russia in April 1917, armed with a theory and a mission to give a new direction, *his* direction, to the young Russian republic. The tsar had fallen a few weeks earlier, and the land was still giddy with new freedom. But already questions were arising as to the meaning of the war and the kind of government that should replace tsardom. Most people, or most of those who were vocal, were more or less convinced socialists of some variety, although the government patched together after the tsar's departure was ostensibly bourgeois. It was generally agreed that Russia, following the logic of Marx's historical pattern, had to pass through a capitalist stage on the way to socialism. The Mensheviks in particular adhered to this theory, according to which their party should not strive for power—indeed, should refuse it if thrust upon them, because, as Plekhanov contended, it could only lead to historical distortions and tyranny. They quoted Marx's and Engels's warning of the dangers of despotism through premature seizure of power.*

Lenin's party, too, shared the general hesitancy to seize power. Even Lenin did not claim that Russia could leap to socialism by itself. Like the others, Lenin assumed that the success of "proletarian" revolution in Russia depended on revolution in the West; in October his strongest plea was that the Bolsheviks must hurry because Germany was on the brink. As Brezhnev later put it, Lenin "had never regarded the revolution in Russia otherwise than as a component part and factor of the world revolution." [5] His was a position amply sanctioned by Marx and sometimes by Engels; even

* For example: "The worst thing that can befall a leader of an extreme party is to take over a government in an epoch when the movement is not yet ripe for the domination of the class which he represents. . . ." Engels, *The Peasant War in Germany* (Moscow: Foreign Languages Publishing House, 1956), p. 138.

Review Copy

TITLE: WHY MARXISM? The Continuing
        Success of a Failed Theory

AUTHOR: Robert G. Wesson

PRICE: $12.95

NO. OF PAGES 281

PUBLICATION
DATE: March 10, 1976

30-91881

For further information: Publicity Department

*We would appreciate receiving two copies of any review
or mention of this book.*

BASIC BOOKS, Publishers

East 53rd Street, New York, N. Y. 10022 • 593-7057

Kautsky at times looked hopefully to Russia for the start of a social-ist revolution in Europe.

While Lenin did not see Bolshevik victory as foreordained in the fall in 1917, he was desperately eager to seize a probably fleet-ing opportunity to fulfill a historic destiny. One Bolshevik leader, Piatakov, saw "the whole of Leninism" in the willingness to disre-gard "objective prerequisites" and invoke the creative will.[6] For Lenin there were no philosophic quibbles, no need to sit back and wait for history and economic change to do the work of the proletar-iat. It was not necessary to have popular backing. "It would be naive," he said, "to wait for a 'formal' majority for the Bolsheviks." [7]

Leninism rested on its founder's strong personality, domineer-ing will, and singleness of purpose. But his personality could domi-nate only because he could impress his faith on a group of men willing to dedicate themselves to his vision. Lenin's ideology gave the Bolshevik Party the coherence which could be translated in-to rulership at the opportune time; the faith made possible the discipline.

Lenin's substitution of the party for the proletariat implied a conviction of rightness and a consequent flexibility of tactics; to be a Bolshevik was more to be a follower of Lenin than to adhere to any particular doctrine.[8] It meant much more to be a Bolshevik than to be a Menshevik, Socialist-Revolutionary, or Anarchist, because the Bolsheviks had a leader, an ideological faith, and a purpose. The Bolsheviks could demand more of their men because they promised more; the makers of the new era should be heroes. Hav-ing faith in action, they attended to instruments of power and to the military aspects of revolution.[9] Lenin's was the only party with a military auxiliary, which was duly used to seize the government.

Marxism-Leninism, mixing the march of history with the mis-sion of guiding it (class-determinism plus voluntarism), served the Bolsheviks very well. Morality became class purpose, the goal of revolution, or in practice whatever the leadership saw as suitable for the higher goal. Lenin felt bound by no petty need for consis-tency. He could find the soviets, the workers' and soldiers' councils which had arisen almost spontaneously in 1905 and which were revived immediately after the tsar's abdication in 1917, to be the proper form of proletarian government, then turn his back on them in July when they seemed unhelpful, then exalt them again to seize power in the name of the Congress of Soviets, then send the congress home in a day to prevent interference with his new government. He could call a particular group the exponent of the march of history; as he wrote afterward, "during our revolution there were occasions when several thousand workers represented the masses." [10] He could promise (in *State and Revolution*) a practically anarchist revolutionary society of democratically chosen representatives, with everyone sharing equally in the management of official affairs, although he must have had some inkling of its impracticality, if not undesirability. Similarly, Lenin could proclaim the much applauded Marxist goal of workers' control of industry with no idea of putting it into effect until some distant day when the proletariat should have sufficiently ripened. He could accept German funds, which were perhaps crucial in sustaining the Bolshevik press and party apparatus prior to November 1917, just as he had earlier been willing to fill Bolshevik coffers by "expropriations" and gifts from capitalist class enemies.*

Lenin's flexibility enabled him to handle the peasant problem, which would have been insoluble within the strict framework of Marxism. The peasants wanted neither to be turned into workers on state farms (Lenin's preference) nor to be required to join communal farms; they wanted more land for themselves. Lenin's answer was simply to take over the Socialist-Revolutionary program of land for those who worked it, making nationalization only a formality. Consequently, when the Provisional Government failed to act and jacqueries rose in the summer of 1917, Lenin could present his party as a friend of the peasant masses. Here again, however, Lenin must be credited with being a better follower of Marx than most Marxists realized. In 1847, Marx proposed the same strategy of promising land to the peasants with the ultimate design of taking it away.[11]

Lenin was also free to oppose the war. In April 1917 nearly everyone felt that newly free Russia had to be defended; but it became more and more acceptable to oppose the war as it deteriorated in succeeding months, until peace became by the fall the biggest single issue raising the Leninists to power. The peasants in uniform who did not want to be sent to the front but did want to share in the land grabbing gave victory to Lenin if only by refusing to fight for Kerensky. Lenin blamed the capitalists for the war, and so took advantage of the growing anti-Western sentiments and the common

* That the Bolsheviks received German financing to assist their antiwar activities is generally accepted on the basis of documentary evidence. See Adam B. Ulam, *The Bolsheviks* (New York: Macmillan, 1965), p. 327.

belief that Britain and France were spending Russian blood. The war, Lenin proclaimed, was a product of bourgeois society and of no interest to the people; their interest was the overthrow of the old order of exploitation and militarism. Hence Lenin could raise a strong cry for peace without indicating surrender.

For these reasons, as the Kerensky government began falling apart in the late summer of 1917, many turned to Lenin as a possible savior in an apparently almost hopeless situation; supporters of the Provisional Government increasingly withdrew to the political sidelines. The Leninists needed only the boldness to call out a few thousand half-trained Red Guards and step into the gap. In all probability, Lenin could have carried out his coup peacefully, but he preferred the drama of an armed uprising to mark the inauguration of proletarian power.

However, the storming of the Winter Palace, where Bolshevik sailors burst in on the ministers sitting around a table, did not complete the revolution. It was necessary first to vanquish in civil war the opposing forces which began to gather strength and go into action as they became aware of the reality of Bolshevik power. Again, ideology helped the Leninists to victory in often nearly impossible situations. Only the Bolsheviks had a real program and purpose; the anti-Bolsheviks were fragmented into a dozen different groups which could never cooperate effectively and which the Bolsheviks could destroy seriatim.

Marxism-Leninism also gave the little group around Lenin the confidence to govern ruthlessly. Debate within the party was gradually repressed; others might talk, the Bolsheviks acted. With his confidence in ultimate rightness, Lenin could insist on a one-party government instead of a probably less effective coalition. He could immediately begin destroying the freedoms Russian revolutionaries had clamored for during previous decades. He repressed other parties, restored censorship of the press, brought back the political police, and set aside the freely elected Constituent Assembly, which had long been the aspiration of all popular forces. Trotsky, who had helped break down discipline in the old army, could in apparently good conscience and with the assent of fellow commissars impose a new hierarchic discipline, not just restoring the death penalty but applying it as freely as any tsar. Any means could be used to defeat the class enemy—and any opponent was a class enemy.

The Leninists were sustained by confidence not only in the

rightness but also in the inevitability of their victory. It was inconceivable that the proletariat should yield to regressive forces. If things seemed momentarily to be going badly, salvation could always come from the class-comrades abroad. Soviet-style governments in Hungary and Bavaria furnished a badly needed lift for the hard-pressed Bolsheviks in 1919; Soviet leaders were perpetually scanning news reports and seeing in every riot, strike, and leftist proclamation a revolutionary spark. Marxism-Leninism also made Russia the champion of socialist justice against the combined forces of world capitalism, and the desultory interventionist efforts of the Allied powers were depicted as a grand reactionary crusade to crush the workers' state.

Marxism was further indispensable as a principle of supranational unity. Lenin had to turn away from Russian nationalism (in the direct and obvious sense), a weapon which could in any case be more effectively wielded by his opponents. Nationalism had been problematic for the old empire, whose population was less than half Russian. Anti-Russian sentiments had been a major cause of dissatisfaction, and many of the best recruits for the revolutionary movement had been non-Russians. Lenin himself was of mixed Tatar, German, and Scandinavian blood; and a large part of the Bolshevik revolutionary leadership belonged to the Jewish minority, the most maltreated of all. It was Lenin's problem to mobilize these people against the Russian regime without at the same time destroying the unity of many peoples that Russia had hammered together in the course of five centuries.

Marxism gave the formula. Lenin's approach was to say that the peoples should be set free from their prison house and liberated beyond all previous notions of freedom by being released from class as well as national oppression; but, having been thus liberated, they should be joined through the international class solidarity of all working people. In practice, this amounted to saying that the nationalities should be given the promise and some appearance of freedom but should in fact be united under the leadership of the centralized vanguard party. The deception was not so obvious as to be ineffective. The most reliable military force on the Bolsehvik side in the disorders of the revolution and civil war was a detachment of Latvian sharpshooters; and the Cheka, the sharp sword of the revolution, was dominated by Poles and Latvians.

Lenin's politic approach to the nationality problem practically won the civil war. The forces of Russian conservatism felt that they had to advocate the restoration of the united empire; this made the Bolsheviks seem the lesser evil to nationalists who wanted, above all, an end to Russian domination. Hence the two greatest potential forces in opposition to the Moscow-centered Bolshevik regime were completely at loggerheads. It was the misfortune of the Whites, moreover, that they were operating for the most part from minority areas (the Caucasus, the Ukraine, and the eastern territories) where they encountered little sympathy. The basis of Soviet strength was in the center, but the Bolsheviks had enough genuine internationalism to carry an air of liberation wherever they went. Everywhere but in Poland, which they had to surrender, they could count on a friendly party willing to help them against the native "bourgeois" or "capitalist" nationalist regimes, to open the gates and help set up a collaborative government.

Thus Lenin, convinced of the basic approach of Marxism but most of all impelled by a drive to overthrow the tsarist state, adapted the teachings of Marx to the special conditions of Russia, then to the political needs of the hour. As refashioned by Lenin, Marxism served to integrate, stiffen, and inspire the movement of discontent in troubled times. It helped a group of middle-class intelligentsia and *déclassés* to set themselves up as leaders of the proletariat in particular and the "masses" in general, and so to assume the government of the world's largest country. It made the desire to establish a perfect society into a powerful means for the conquest of power. Finally, it fit the spiritual and political needs of a country weary of traditional autocracy but unready for democracy. Lenin would seem to have been appointed by destiny to remake the Russian empire in a more modern image.

Yet only in retrospect does Lenin's victory take on the appearance of inevitability. In the chaotic times of 1917, the intransigence, determination, and discipline of Lenin's party and the unifying power of its doctrines enabled it to push itself into the center of power. But some of the characteristics which helped the Bolsheviks in the difficult and uncertain days of military defeat and leaderlessness would have remained a liability in more tranquil times. The Bolsheviks' narrowness and intolerance would have tended rather to repel, and the utopianism of Leninism would have seemed absurd. Its harshness, authoritarian manners, and penchant for dictatorship would, in a Russia increasingly influenced by Western individualism and democracy, have condemned the Bolsheviks to remain nothing more than a sect of doctrinaire malcontents.

FROM LENINISM TO STALINISM

AT THE BEGINNING of the nineteenth century, Philippe Buonarroti, a follower of Babeuf, thought about the problem of building a just society and foresaw a class

> which would find in the superiority of its own spirit, and above all, in the ignorance of its compatriots, the source for creating distinctions and privileges. Exaggerating the importance of its services, it would easily come to think of itself as the protector of the nation. And clothing its own audacious enterprises in the public good, it would still speak of liberty and equality to its unperceptive fellow citizens, who would be subjected to a servitude all the more harsh because it seemed legal and voluntary.[12]

The revolutionaries turned governors would still need an ideological justification to persuade the masses that obedience was the freedom for which they had chased out the erstwhile parasitic rulers.

However, the ideology of revolution cannot be that of government. Revolutionaries stand for disorder and demand equality and freedom, while rulers want order and security. This antithesis appeared especially sharp when the revolutionary Leninists, who had endeavored to undermine the state and had promised total equalization and utopian freedom, suddenly becoming masters of a new Soviet state required far more obedience than had the tsars and held the entire country virtually as their property. Thus, once the Bolsheviks took power, the Marxism of the old Bolshevik movement had to become something essentially new. From a commitment to change, Marxism was transformed into a means of assuring stability; the ideal became the backdrop to careers and to the realities of power, ambition, and status. The transformation was like that of Christianity from the creed of the Roman catacombs to the state church of the empire. Indeed, it was even sharper, for Christianity never made rebellion its principal tenet and was never reduced entirely to being an apology for the imperial regime.

It was never admitted, of course, that anything was changed; and Lenin's works are still canonical, although Marx's have been largely retired from sight. For two decades and more, the world was inclined to agree that the Soviet Union was on the ideological course plotted by Lenin in exile. Even today the feeling is widespread that the Soviet Union aims (although more calmly than in the original vision) at the Leninist goals of equality and freedom.

Soviet Marxism

A major reason for the persistence of this belief in the essential continuity of Marxism-Leninism is propaganda. The Soviet state has made every effort to convince its people and the world that all its measures have been undertaken in fulfillment of Lenin's lofty dreams. Every deviation from Leninism has been made in the name of Lenin, almost always supported by citations from his works. This was not difficult, because the Marxist-Leninist vocabulary was retained, the users of the words being the masters of their meanings. Moreover, flexibility in the pursuit of vague but noble goals was central to Leninism from the beginning, and rationalizations could be piled on reinterpretations without doing violence to the spirit of the founder. It was the more feasible because, whatever the shimmering promises of Lenin's Marxism, the urge to undivided power was a large part of its substance; power in the state became an extension of power in the leadership of the party. It was highly desirable, in any case, to maintain as much continuity as possible from revolutionary movement to ruling party, because the latter based and to a large extent still bases its legitimacy on the grand revolution.

But neither propaganda and indoctrination nor the desire of Soviet leaders to see themselves carrying on the heroic revolution would have carried Marxism-Leninism very far into bleak Soviet reality if revolutionary themes had not continued to be useful; to some extent, they are still useful today. It was very fitting to see the civil war as a campaign for social renewal and proletarian revolution. After Lenin put an end to the purely revolutionary phase by making peace with imperial Germany at Brest-Litovsk (March 1918), there might have begun a strong turnaround toward the normalization, in the Western sense, of Soviet Russia; but the renewal of fighting a few weeks later restored much of the intensity of the ideological commitment. The Bolsheviks regarded their opponents not as domestic counterrevolutionaries but as exponents of the general evil of world capitalism. The Leninists could see themselves not as mere seekers after power but as the supreme idealists in the greatest of causes, scientifically supported by the Marxist analysis of society; and they were spiritually nourished by hopes that the workers elsewhere would do their duty and that the proletarians were bound to vanquish historically backward forces. The internationalism of the class struggle, moreover, squared the Bolshevik conscience with the restoration of the rule of Russia over the minority peoples, even as their independence was being proclaimed.

The claim to represent the revolutionary cause also sanctioned the demand that the people in general and party members in particular sacrifice personal welfare for the higher aim: the victory of truth, virtue, justice, and the working class. The Russians passively endured privations incomparably greater than the hardships which toppled the tsarist regime.

The Bolsheviks entered the struggle without skills, trained personnel, or any idea of how to run a government. On the other hand, the elite could demand more of the people because it was itself inspired by revolutionary ideology. Party members were expected to occupy the most dangerous positions in battle, to work the longest hours and most diligently in factories or offices, and to earn, even in the highest ranks, no more than an ordinary worker. People took pride in poverty and humble origins; the only merit was service. It was possible to organize poor peasants to cooperate in the requisition of grain for which the Soviet state could give little or nothing in return. It was possible also to establish a controlled economy, partly as a war measure, partly as the realization of the utopia of communism. Money went nearly out of use; all goods were theoretically disposed by the community (that is, by the state) and distributed according to need (the need of the state more than that of the recipient)—in other words, rationing.

This required stern dictatorship, and Marxism-Leninism paved the way by admitting the "dictatorship of the proletariat" for an indefinite transitional period to the society of absolute freedom. Lenin had long seen "spontaneity" as the enemy of his cause; the organization and the unity of the organization was practically the summum bonum. Despite this, there was initially some freedom within the top level of the party to criticize and oppose policies. This came to an end a few months after the seizure of power; the debate over the Peace of Brest-Litovsk was the last in which the outcome was in doubt. At this time, too, Lenin celebrated the departure from Social Democratic tradition by changing the name of the party to "Communist." Truth became ever more closely defined by the leadership. As Lenin saw it, there were only "socialist" (Leninist) ideology and "bourgeois" ideology, with no unsettled territories; "truth" was what served class (i.e., party) interests. At times, Lenin was rather candid about dictatorship; thus, soon after Brest-Litovsk he said, "The irrefutable experience of history has shown that in the history of revolutionary movements the dictatorship of individual persons was very often the vehicle, the channel of the dictatorship of the revolutionary classes. . . . But how can strict unity be ensured? By thousands subordinating their will to the will of one." [13]

During the war, it could be hoped that victory would bring utopia. But as the war petered out in 1920 and 1921 and the hoped-for revolutions elsewhere failed to materialize, War Communism had to be abandoned. Military mobilization of the economy was no longer possible. Trotsky's idea of reconstruction by labor armies was politically attractive but humanly impractical. The Kronstadt sailors, successors of those who had been most ardently pro-Bolshevik in 1917, saw no reason for continuing dictatorship after the war and mutinied in the name of democratic communism. The peasants began to resist requisitions of their crops when they were no longer frightened by the prospect of returning landlords and tsarist tax gatherers.

Lenin's realistic response in the spring of 1921 was his New Economic Policy, a retreat on many fronts. No longer expected to deliver all their surplus, Communist-style, peasants could treat the land they farmed practically as private property and even hire labor. Private trade was legalized. Small-scale private manufacturing was permitted, although basic industry was kept in state hands. But concurrently, the party tightened its internal discipline and political monopoly. The non-Bolshevik socialist parties, which had been permitted a shadowy existence in return for supporting the Soviet side in the civil war, were now proscribed, and censorship became more stringent. Within the party, decision making became concentrated in the narrower circle of the Politburo; the larger Central Committee fell into the background. And Lenin himself became more of an autocrat. The effort of the Workers' Opposition at the Tenth Party Congress (March 1921) to claim political rights for the trade unions as representatives of the proletariat was sharply rebuffed; a rule was adopted prohibiting factions—prohibiting, in effect, any efforts to promote any policy not approved by the party leadership. The ideology which had served to stiffen a popular dictatorship became the crutch of an unpopular one.

It was also necessary to take into account the situation of Russia in the world. After the civil war it was still hoped that revolution in the West would come to the rescue. In the early 1920s world revolution was taken seriously enough for Lenin, Trotsky, Zinoviev, and others to express the belief or hope that other countries (Germany in particular) would take over the lead in the world movement. As late as August 1923, Trotsky offered to resign as war commissar to dedicate himself to helping the fantasy of a German Communist insurgency.[14]

Yet this was mostly an expression of the schizophrenia of the Leninist revolution, which still wanted to think of itself as something universal while acting more and more like something national. As soon as the civil war wound down and the Allied blockade was lifted (January 1920), the Soviet state began promoting profitable peaceful relations ("Peaceful Coexistence") with the capitalist states it was trying to subvert. Trade gradually started up again; Bolsheviks bargained with capitalists over prices and even tried to peddle concessions for the exploitation of Russian resources while arming and prodding Communist parties. By the end of 1924 the Soviet Union was a recognized member of the international community, having diplomatic relations with most important powers.

Ideological accommodation was required. It was regretfully recognized that capitalism had achieved "stabilization," but this was accounted only temporary. Lenin insisted that the renewal of violent conflict, a new anti-Soviet onslaught by the "bourgeois" powers, was sure to come someday; he was not officially contradicted until Khrushchev refurbished Peaceful Coexistence in 1956. But since the world revolution, in terms of which a Russian revolution could have Marxist meaning, failed dismally to appear, the question was: What was the Soviet Union doing? Stalin, who had become the strongest individual in the Soviet government, gave the only possible answer in his theory of "Socialism in One Country" (1924): the Soviet Union was building socialism on its own. This was a major innovation, although Stalin argued that it was just what Lenin had intended all along. It was shocking to the more consistent Marxists, led by Trotsky, those who had grown up with faith in the world movement and whose political fortunes were tied to the Comintern. It meant shrinking Leninism from a theory of world revolution to a theory of Russian revolution.[15] And it meant standing Marx on his head by claiming that the party was to make socialism in a feebly industrialized country, instead of acting merely as the midwife of a socialism that had gestated in the womb of advanced capitalism (to use Marx's obstetrical metaphors). Only political, not economic, factors counted.

Stalin's thesis was popular, however, with Russians who liked to be told that they did not have to wait for the slothful or cowardly German or British workers but could go forward on their own to build the ideal society—always with the qualification that the Soviet state could not enter the "higher stage" of communism so long as it was surrounded by class-hostile powers. It was an example of "creative Marxism," whereby Marxism is always to be remodeled for the needs of the day, without change of general spirit or direction. It was an expression of de facto policy, and almost anyone in power would have been constrained to act in terms of "Socialism in One Country" even if he might have shrunk from saying so. Marx might well have done the same. He certainly did not contemplate socialism remaining confined to a single country, much less an industrially backward one; but there is no reason to suppose that, if he or his followers had come to power anywhere, he would have favored renouncing power for theoretical reasons.

The explicit disavowal of world revolution as an immediate necessity (although it remained a long-term theoretical goal) was an important step in the emergence of Stalinism. It meant turning away from the revolutionary intellectuals of Lenin's day. Stalin brought forward the home-bred boys of suitably lower-class origin who, while less adept in Marxist subtleties, were also less scrupulous and more willing to act harshly, as required by the needs of the party.

Stalin's notorious achievement was to make the most of the potentialities of Marxism-Leninism to build up one of the most spectacular despotisms in history. It was not easy; Stalin took six or seven years from the time he became General Secretary of the party (April 1922) to exalt himself above Lenin, and another nine years to crush the last remnant of opposition to his will. But his progress was so steady as to seem historically decreed. One means was to make himself the exponent of Leninism, somewhat as Engels made himself the exponent of Marxism. In both cases, the new "ism" took shape upon the departure of the older master; the birth of the cult of Lenin may be marked with Stalin's semiliturgical postfuneral eulogy,[16] much as the cult of Marx received its impetus from Engels's graveside speech. Stalin, like Engels, made himself interpreter of his senior's ideas, formulating them more simply and reshaping them to the needs of the age, while acting as the most faithful of disciples. Engels adapted Marxism to social democracy; Stalin made a new support for arbitrary rule out of the cult of Lenin, whose works were made canonical. Marxism-Leninism, due to become Marxism-

75

Leninism-Stalinism in the 1930s, was made the rationale not for proletarian revolution but for "revolution from above," the total imposition of the will of the ruler in remaking the country.

To achieve this, Stalin had to gather the reins of power in his own hands, isolating and eliminating first the internationalists, who took world revolution seriously, next the "leftists," who wanted to press forward by squeezing the peasants and pushing industrialization, and then the "rightists," who wanted to take a cautious approach and encourage growth by market mechanisms. Once opposition in the party was essentially liquidated, Stalin undertook the social transformation of the peasants, whose way of life had thus far been little changed by the revolution. Marxism could be squared with almost any form of agricultural production—small owners, peasant cooperatives, municipal or state farms (anything except big capitalistic farms, which did not exist in Russia)—but "Socialism in One Country" implied that the peasants were to be socialized. They would otherwise represent a perennial danger to the Soviet way, a population (then about four-fifths of the total) virtually outside the system and always a potential source of opposition. Moreover, Stalin also wanted to achieve control of agriculture, particularly grain production.

The rationale for the collectivization of agriculture was partly modernization; fields were to be joined to permit the use of modern machinery, which Russia did not have. It was also Marxist, the necessity for socializing means of production. The peasants had to be made workers in the workers' state, co-builders of "socialism." However little Marx's arguments against capitalist exploitation applied to peasants who owned two cows or could afford to hire a hand at harvest, it would nevertheless have been impossible to push through this brutal and costly program without a conviction of historic right. Stalin sent out thousands of ex-peasants and sons of peasants to push peasants into collectives by every means from suasion and promises to crude violence, force being necessary because the state farms and party-sponsored cooperatives were too inefficient to attract more than a tiny minority. When resistance arose, this could only be viewed as class war, an attack of the village "capitalists" (kulaks) on the Soviet state. Hence the kulaks had to be "destroyed as a class." They were the supposedly cunning class enemy, and in the Marxist-Leninist outlook the troubles of Russia, the failure of socialism to bring any fair facsimile of abundance and bliss, could only be ascribed to the class enemy.

Driven by ideology, ignorance, and the urge to total power, collectivization marched on to disaster—the loss of about half of Soviet livestock, massive suffering, and the deaths of millions who could be classified as "capitalist" only by the most tortured political reasoning. Soviet agriculture was set back for a generation, and the majority of the population remained alienated until reunited by World War II. But doctrinal fixation enabled Stalin and his loyal followers to carry through. If millions of peasants starved in the early 1930s because the grain collectors did not leave them enough to survive the winter, it did not matter, because they were a backward social class. Stalin won, in the name of Marxist history and socialism; the peasants became bound to service to the state, much as the serfs had been bound in the eighteenth century.* They had the consolation of being told that they were toiling for themselves, for their own proletarian state, and for the class victory of the workers, of whom the party was representative.

Eager to press forward in the appointed way, Stalin undertook the industrial transformation of Russia at the same time he was harnessing the peasantry. State control and planning of industry, like collective farms and party purges, antedated Stalin, but he made so much more of them than his predecessors that one might speak, in the language of dialectical materialism, of a quantitative difference becoming qualitative. Lenin had refreshed his spirits in the depressing days of the civil war with schemes for the electrification of Russia; throughout the 1920s a planning agency tried to project economic development as a guide to policy. Stalin's contribution was to apply the Marxist vision of the collectivist economy to justify the non-Marxist program of imposing industrialization by state fiat, extracting surplus value from the workers and depriving the peasants of all their output above the barest subsistence level. Forced industrialization, emphasizing large plants and heavy industry, was necessary to provide Russia with a defense industry, with the economic basis for "socialism," and with a proletariat for the party to represent. It was also a surrogate revolution in the spirit of "Socialism in One Country." The political revolution had failed to bring the millennium; now Russia, advancing by its own efforts in the vanguard of history, would bring socialism by an economic revolution.

---

* There are obvious parallels with Marx's "Asiatic mode of production," the prime characteristic of which was state ownership of land. This element of the Marxian scheme had to be omitted from Soviet ideology.

The first years were fearfully hard. Poor planning and lack of managerial and engineering skills wasted much of the resources painfully poured into industrialization. As fast as heavy industry was built, craft production and consumer industries were destroyed or depressed. The standard of living, which had barely returned to the prewar level, sank precipitously. But many believed in and cooperated with the program zealously, working selflessly despite cruel hardship (and frustration by party and bureaucratic stupidities), in a rebirth of revolutionary spirit.[17] Thanks to this spirit, Stalin again succeeded, despite miscalculations, creating a mighty industrial plant totally under state and party control and capable of arming a potent military machine.

Having subdued agriculture and industry, Stalin turned between 1934 and 1938 to his most celebrated achievement, the total subjugation of the party and the Russian people. Sense cannot be made of madness, but whatever the reasons for the purges, which killed approximately 13 million people directly or through the hardships of the labor camps, the devastation of human resources would, like collectivization and forced industrialization, have been impossible without the creed which dictated that the party, representative of the workers, could not be wrong. The entire lives of the leading purge victims, from Trotsky, Kamenev, Zinoviev, and Bukharin on down, were bound up with the party, and they were defenseless against it. If the party was wrong, there was no truth. By extension, Stalin, always backed by his party majorities, could not be wrong either. In the name of defense of the revolution, Stalin got men to pursue thousands of their own kind, sometimes even to destroy their own families. Foreign Minister Litvinov knew that his colleagues were being picked off and shot one by one; only by a miracle could he expect to survive. He slept with a loaded pistol by his side, awaiting the GPU's visit; yet he remained caught up in the great cause, a faithful and effective servant of the great destroyer. As Solzhenitsyn said, "We submitted *with pleasure*." [18]

Stalin could smash resistance because he was the center, the unifier; others felt that if he went, the party might be unable to hold together and sustain its supremacy. From 1925 onward the cult of Stalin's personality became an integral part of Marxism-Leninism-Stalinism. The leader was not explicitly equated with the working class, but he was the exponent of its victorious march. This implied several ideological adjustments. Marxism came to represent less a theory of class struggle and historical materialism than an example furnished by the party and its leaders, Lenin and Stalin, in past and present. Since Stalin rested his power to a large extent on the state and state organs, particularly the police, the idea of the state withering away in socialism became taboo, and those who were unfortunate enough to have espoused it were purged. On the contrary, it was discovered that the state under socialism had to become more coercive instead of less, because a class enemy nearing total defeat supposedly becomes more dangerous and vicious. Along with the end of the state, other utopian goals were also set aside. Equality was denigrated as "petty-bourgeois." Marx's practical comments in the *Critique of the Gotha Program* on the need for payment according to work done were cited against the fundamental equalitarianism of Marxism. Men in Stalin's new elite of bureaucrats and technicians might earn forty or more times as much as an ordinary worker, a disparity comparable to that in tsarist society. When the major transformations were accomplished and Stalin sought no longer to change but to maintain, his state became conservative. The old Russia was returned to respectability; history was rewritten to make tsarist imperialism "progressive."

The exaltation of the individual and the state was antithetical to traditional Marxist theory, but there was little effort to reconcile the opposites by rethinking doctrine. Creativity was extinguished by terrorism; symbols and words took the place of theory. As the Marxologist David Riazanov remarked in 1929, "They don't need any Marxists in the Politburo." [19]

About the end of 1938, as the slaughter of the great purge years wound down to mere chronic terrorism, Stalin had nothing more politically to achieve at home. Fortuitously, the world outside was becoming at this time both more dangerous and more promising, as the Axis powers, Germany and Italy, aligned with Japan, began hammering at the shaky international order set up in 1919. Stalin had long ago turned his back on world revolution, and he had made the Comintern and foreign Communist parties instruments not only of Soviet policies but also of his personal needs. In 1935 he turned to something like a collective security policy, entering a defense pact with France and promoting Popular Fronts against fascism. In 1939 he embarked on a policy of almost pure realpolitik, bargaining with both Hitler and the Western democracies for recovery of lands lost from the Russian empire in 1918–1920 along the western marches. The result of the pact with Hitler was the outbreak of war, which Stalin probably intended and from which he rightly expected great gains.

By the time of the German attack, there was hardly a shred of

79

Marxism in Soviet foreign policy. Internally, Marxist themes nearly disappeared when the Russian people found themselves fighting for survival. Stalin appealed to native patriotism and hatred for the brutal invader much more than to loyalty to the cause of the workers or even socialism. Communism was buried in nationalism, and Stalin even came to an amicable modus vivendi with the Orthodox Church. It was possible in 1943 for a deputy foreign minister to prefer "the tradition of the Russian and Ukrainian people" to the "old ideology of leftist trends." [20]

But ideas of proletarianism, class struggle, and international vocation became useful and relevant again after the war, when the Soviets found themselves both masters of a new empire and cold war antagonists of the United States. When Russian armies surged over minority-inhabited areas of the Soviet Union and even more when they staked out a Soviet sphere of influence in Eastern and Central Europe, it became again suitable, perhaps indispensable, to justify the rule of the party in supranational terms of proletarian class interests and international socialism, the universalist movement headed by the Soviet Fatherland of the Workers and its genius leader, Stalin. Concurrently, the former valued allies, Britain and the United States, became subversive influences working against Soviet dominion; they were now near-enemies, driven by capitalist-reactionary hatred for socialism and the workers' cause.

Postwar Stalinism thus settled down to a crude semi-Marxist view of the world, mixing claims of superior socialist justice with the apotheosis of Stalin and with Russianism, a despotism with ideological varnish. "Socialism in One Country" became "Socialism in One Bloc," a capitalist-encircled fortress. The Soviet-dominated countries of Eastern Europe were made "socialist" by coercion. Russian artists and scientists were castigated for bowing to the decadent West. The outside world was viewed as filled with reactionaries, capitalists, and their dupes and flunkies; only faithful Stalinists were friends. At home, it was necessary not just to refrain from criticism but to be loud in praise of Stalin and his works. The autocrat shut himself up in his palace, and his bureaucracy ran the country, confirming Trotsky's contention that a would-be socialist revolution in a less advanced country was condemned to bureaucratic degradation. But the Soviet state still claimed to be carrying out the ideals of Marx as developed by Lenin. Stalin even showed a flash of the old dreams when, in his last work, *Problems of Socialist Economy*, he called for barter of commodities between city and countryside.[21]

POST-STALINISM

THE HEIRS of Stalin were disturbed and fearful at the loss of the man who had stood at the center of the Soviet system and held it together for thirty years. When they warned the people against "disorder and panic," the only sign of panic was in themselves, as they put Moscow under tight guard. They had, on the other hand, reasons to be relieved. Stalin in his last months was apparently planning a purge of his close associates, to bring back the heady days of the 1930s. And the iron grip, no longer capable of innovation but only of repression, was choking the country. It was necessary to modify his negative approach to foreign affairs, to slacken controls on the economy, to release artistic creativity, to allow the inflow of modern ideas and technology. In short, it was time to permit the country to start growing again.

For nearly three years nothing major was done overtly, as the new oligarchy took many little steps toward more sensible policies at home and abroad while settling relations among themselves, with the resultant ascendancy of Nikita Khruschev. Khrushchev, who like Stalin had used the senior secretaryship of the party to push himself to dominance, felt strong enough by 1956 to attempt (chiefly at the Twentieth Congress of the Party, in February 1956) to bring Marxism-Leninism into better harmony with modern conditions. In his public statement, Khrushchev dealt mostly with foreign affairs, propounding the idea of Peaceful Coexistence and its consequences. This was an old topic of Lenin's, but Stalin had turned away from it; Khrushchev stressed it with a new argument: the inadmissibility of nuclear war. No longer was an Armageddon between rising socialism and desperate capitalism unavoidable. The final victory of socialism could and would hence come by peaceful process, with the gathering of strength of the Soviet Union and its allies and their example of progress and prosperity. This implied that although "wars of liberation" were welcome, violent revolution was not necessary; Khrushchev accepted a revision of Marxism made by the older Marx (at least for a few democratic countries) but strongly rejected by Lenin. It further followed that there were different ways to socialism; it was not necessary for other countries to tread in Soviet footsteps. This again was backsliding from Lenin's approach, but it was most advantageous for Soviet foreign policy. If it was no longer necessary to classify states as either members of the "socialist camp" or as enemies, the Soviet

Union was free to look for friends around the world, particularly among those many nations which, while not Communist governed, were not industrialized capitalist powers. The Soviet Union, Khrushchev hoped, could become leader of the whole anti-imperialist world.

This represented the most substantial overt revision of Marxism-Leninism in its history. But it was put in the shadows by Khrushchev's secret speech to the delegates of the Congress, in which he undertook to erase Stalinism from Marxism-Leninism-Stalinism. Khrushchev shocked the party, though not yet the public, with an account of a small fraction of Stalin's crimes and even exaggerated his incompetence. The leadership cult was shattered for many years to come. Khrushchev's purposes were doubtless mostly political—to help himself (he had been outside the innermost circle) against others more closely associated with Stalin—but he also seems to have wanted to restore some of the revolutionary idealism of Leninism.

As a result of anti-Soviet movements in Poland and Hungary in the latter months of 1956, Khrushchev felt compelled to retreat to a harsher line and restore some grace to Stalin's memory. Still, he continued a modest effort to revitalize Soviet life. This included some slackening of controls over the creative arts, a partial decentralization of economic administration, and a revival of the life and authority of the party. Khrushchev reduced emphasis on nationalism and Russia, encouraged more talk of classes and class conflict, and stepped up antireligious propaganda. Also in the Leninist spirit, he mildly favored an equalitarianism out of harmony with the increasingly stratified Soviet society.

Khrushchev also made some moves toward a utopian society—reducing pay differentials, educating children to communism in boarding schools, and mixing manual with academic training, as Marx had proposed—and tried to blueprint his vision of the way to the communist society, the theoretical goal of all Soviet strivings since the revolution. His revision of the official program of the CPSU in 1961 promised a partially communistic (i.e., moneyless) society by 1980, to be achieved through a mighty upsurge of production which would make it possible to furnish many more services without pay. Meals would be communally prepared to relieve women of housework; along with the boarding schools, this would begin to dissolve the family into the great socialist collective. Bowing to the ageless dream (popularized by Marx and Engels) of the disappearance of the state, Khrushchev also foresaw volunteer citizens' organizations taking over public functions, particularly that of keeping order. But these developments, along with economic administration, were to be guided by the party; it was never suggested that the party, too, should fade out. In 1961 the party felt able to promise much less than in 1919, when it had looked sanguinely to the early dawning of utopia.

By the time Khrushchev could get his vision into print, his fortunes were already waning because of his economic and foreign-policy failures; three years later he was ousted. But if his successors proved in many ways better managers, they were ideologically less productive. They added nothing specifically and amended only by omission. Khrushchev's egalitarian initiatives were allowed to lapse; his utopianism was forgotten; Stalin's contributions were again emphasized, particularly collectivization and planned industrialization. As a result, Soviet ideology became more than ever a diffuse mélange of ideas and slogans drawn from the works of Marx, Engels, and Lenin (plus occasional trite utterances by General Secretary Brezhnev), along with the cult of Lenin's personality, glorification of the party and its history and of the Soviet Union, land of socialism. All this was mixed with logically disparate themes of Russianism, patriotism, and militarism. Soviet ideology remains essentially as it was put together by Stalin, just as the present Soviet government is like Stalin's with the rough spots smoothed out, a fabric woven of revolutionary and conservative motifs to make a suitable garb for a basically conservative state whose ruling elite feels the need to legitimize its political privilege in modern terms.

Of Marx's writings, only selected works are made available to the Soviet citizenry. His calls for freedom of the press and his few utterances in favor of democracy are neglected. The idea of doing away with the slavery of speculation of labor is wholly unsuited to Soviet society, which demands even more specialization than other industrial nations. There has been little attempt ever to apply Marx specifically to the Soviet economy—he had nothing to say about the organization of production under socialism—and the labor theory of value has been counterproductive. It accorded no value to natural resources, so the Soviets still find it difficult to reach rational assessments of the value of land and minerals. At one time they did not even count the cost of prospecting, and energy is still counted as free in Soviet industry. Since capital, in the Marxian view, could not produce value, no interest was charged on loans to enterprises, which had no incentive to economize but only to grab as much as possible. The planners were compelled belatedly to introduce a charge on capital, which could not be called "interest."

The Marxian fundamental of class struggle remains alive in Marxism-Leninism; but this, too, raises problems. Although no conflict of classes can be admitted in the socialist states, differences in economic status are obvious. The Soviets get around this by insisting that, as co-owners of the socialist economy, all have the same relation to the means of production: managers as well as janitors are workers. Marx's manual laborers are joined by the intelligentsia, bureaucrats, and political manipulators to form the Soviet working class. The members of the elite, with their chauffeured limousines, private lodges, special stores, and so forth, are merely being compensated as befits the best workers. Class thus becomes more a political than an economic category. As a Soviet writer put it, "Our concept [of the working class] is linked primarily with its class essence, its morality and monolithic ideological and political character." [22] Party secretaries can speak to the masses as fellow workers, and managers and technical personnel belong to and exert leadership in Soviet trade unions.

If the idea of class struggle is axiomatically excluded within the Soviet Union, it is projected abroad as the prime reality of Western industrialized countries. For many decades, the Soviet press has gloated over strikes, riots, and persecutions of workers in the West, seemingly always looking, as in civil war days, for the proletarians to come to the aid of their Russian comrades or at least to tear down Western societies. The Marxian view of the state as simply an agency of the capitalists is accepted without qualification; indeed, according to Soviet scholars, the state stands for the interests of the capitalist class as a whole even when individual capitalists don't know it.[23]

The idea of revolution, the ultimate expression of class struggle, is likewise excluded from the Soviet scene but upheld abroad. This has worn thin after so many years, and it is no longer clear that the staid Soviet leadership wants revolutionary disturbances in any important area lest there be uncertainties and complications for Soviet foreign policy. But Khrushchev rather eagerly espoused "wars of liberation" as a means of hastening the general victory of "socialism" over "imperialism," and his successors have willingly cheered anticapitalist movements of various hues, backed demands by less developed countries against the West, and welcomed every economic or political setback to their rivals on the world stage. Even as détente was getting under way, it was authoritatively stated that the Soviet Union "wages a relentless economic, political, and ideological struggle against world capitalism. True to its internationalist duty, it gives comprehensive assistance and support to the working class and to all the revolutionary forces of our time." [24]

Yet the Soviet Union lays no great stakes on Communist parties in the countries where they might seem to have best chances of coming to power—namely, in the Third World. It has preferred to deal with existing governments, sometimes even cultivating close relations with leaders who may, as in Egypt and Algeria, firmly repress the adherents of Moscow. The Soviet Union has not been inhibited by Marxism from welcoming "progressive" military regimes, whose progressiveness consists chiefly in friendliness for the Soviet Union and hostility to Western interests, perhaps fortified with some use of Marxist language. For ideological purposes, it is considered in such cases that the state is independent of any particular class.[25]

The general Marxist-Leninist view of history is also canonical but not very consistently applied. The periodization of primitive communism, gentile society, slave society, feudalism, capitalism, and socialism-communism is accepted despite the difficulty of fitting facts to it. Soviet historians strain to find slavery dominant in ancient societies where there was little of it, and feudalism becomes a catchall for almost any precapitalist system. An intermediate category of "people's democracies" had to be invented for states which the Soviet Union approves but which cannot be embraced as socialist. The important essence of the historical scheme is that the pattern unfolds ineluctably to the victory of the proletariat, socialism, the party, and, practically speaking, the Russian system, if not Russia itself, over the whole earth. Little is said about the shape of the communist society which is abuilding in the Soviet Union, the land of "developed socialism," or how long it may take to arrive in Russia and around the globe; but it is on the way. The Soviet workers are "builders of communism," and it is their glory to "pave the way to a communist future for all mankind." [26] The troubles of the West, meanwhile, are again and again described in terms which suggest that the death throes may be at hand.*

* For example, V. Ponomarev wrote of the "sharpening of the general crisis of capitalism" and claimed that efforts of the capitalist countries to adapt to the technological revolution could only deepen their troubles. See *Kommunist*, no. 15 (October, 1971):37, 39.

The generalized logical foundation for the historical sequence is dialectical materialism. Soviet philosophers have to follow Engels and Lenin, and Soviet scientists are supposed to use the dialectic of nature as a guide in their researches, but very little evidence has been adduced that they have found it useful. On the other hand, the requirements of dialectical materialism caused serious difficulties for Soviet science under Stalin. For example, belief in the fixity of matter and the knowability of all phenomena seemed to conflict with some aspects of relativity and quantum mechanics. Cybernetics was likewise outlawed as a bourgeois perversion. Under the recent rulership, however, cybernetics came into vogue as an aid to party management; and physics and chemistry suffer little more than the requirement of an occasional formal bow to the "masters of scientific socialism." But dialectical materialism is still cherished as a basis for claiming that socialism is scientific and that Marxism forms a total and coherent world view.

For most purposes, the Soviet citizen gets his Marx and Engels through Lenin and the party, much as Catholics were to understand the Bible through the priest. In the ordinary Soviet press, citations from Lenin (or his latter-day interpreter, Brezhnev) are common enough; those from Engels are scarce; those from Marx, rare. The birthday of Lenin fills the press every April, yet Marx's goes unnoticed. In the higher ranges of ideological study, Marx receives more attention; but students are discouraged from going into Marx until they have had sufficient training to internalize the correct approach. Marx, always useful to those who oppose the system, is potentially subversive.

Mixed with reverence for Lenin is study of the glorious history of the party, "the greatest legacy that Lenin has bequeathed to the world revolutionary movement." [27] It is an epic story, retold in minute detail, from Lenin's struggles in exile for the true doctrines through the glamour of the revolution and the trials of the civil war, collectivization and industrialization, the ordeal of the Great Patriotic War and reconstruction, down to the latest feats of constructive labor in the decisive year of the Five-Year Plan. Whatever the mistakes of its leaders—and most high leaders except Lenin have been retrospectively denigrated—the errors have only been of individuals; the party itself has always been correct. The strength of the party is equated with the prosperity of socialism, even democracy: "The guidance of the party is the decisive condition of the further strengthening and development of socialist democracy." [28]

Although the primacy of the party was the main contribution of Lenin to Marxism, and although the party is the effective governing body, the great Soviet state shares in the exaltation. More than a mere country, it is the exponent of the new order, "the first country of socialism" and its defender. The Soviet state stands for the historic mission of the Soviet people. It cannot be merely a superstructure of the economic base, like non-Communist states; or, if a part of the superstructure, it possesses an autonomy which belies the original understanding of that term: "The superstructure does not passively follow its base. . . . Finally, the development of socialism does not take place spontaneously but in a planned way. . . ." [29]

Pride in the Soviet state means pride in eternal Russia, at least for the Russians who are the dominant half of the population. Moscow is not just the capital of the Soviet Union and the center of the world socialist movement but the focus of post-Mongol Russian history. The working class, the party, the state, and the Russians are all part of the ideological mixture, along with such non-Marxist elements as visions of incalculable riches in Siberia. *Pravda* headlines patriotically, "I Love My Native Land." [30]

The growth of Russianism out of Marxism-Leninism reflects not only increasing conservatism and decline of interest in the universalist cause but also the changing composition of leadership. The Bolshevik Revolution represented to a larger extent than commonly realized a movement of minority peoples against the oppressive, Russian-dominated empire. A very large part of Lenin's coterie was Jewish, including Trotsky, Kamenev, Zinoviev, Radek, and many others; Dzerzhinsky, head of Lenin's political police, was Polish; Stalin was Georgian. Such men were far readier than most Russians to embrace an international cause and to destroy the tsarist regime root and branch. But after the revolution, the non-Russians lost ground. In the administration of the new state, leaders of the exile party were swamped by the holdovers of the older bureaucracy and by new recruits; eventually, Stalin removed nearly all of the old Bolsheviks, especially those of Jewish background. After Stalin's death, the last strong non-Russian group at the center, Stalin's Georgian clique, was eliminated. Today the core of the party is almost purely Russian, with some admixture of the closely related Ukrainians. In the first years of the Soviet Union, there reigned a truly internationalist spirit, and a genuine effort was made to combat "Great Russian chauvinism"; now only the "bourgeois nationalism" of minorities is castigated. Russification is pressed in many forms, and Russianism is implicit in official ideology.

Hardly any state in modern times, except prewar Germany, Italy, and Japan, has made so much of war and heroism as the Soviet Union. Thousands of impressive and costly war monuments have been erected, and the armed forces are daily and intensely publicized and glorified. Military-patriotic lore is supposed to be taught in every school, and motifs of battle are recurrent in semiliterary writing. For example, a poet noted the appearance of the sea behind the mountains in Crimea: "My comrade said, 'It was like when the marine fighter was pushing his way south in battle, under his jacket, faded from sweat, a sailor's jersey suddenly appeared.' There was a white scar on his skin; and in the distance one saw ships, and nothing was fairer than this land steeped in hot blood." [31] Perhaps it is simpler and more effective to teach men to revere the heroes of the past, and to be brave, loyal, and self-sacrificing for the fatherland, than to convince them of the need to fight for a proletariat which does not exist at home or for a world cause that few take seriously.

Yet Soviet militarism and the call to duty are still entwined with ideas that may be called Marxist. As the army paper tells us, "Soviet man, growing up under socialism, is the builder of communism; patriot and internationalist, armed with a scientific philosophy, he is distinguished by high moral qualities and enjoys the esteem of all progressive people of the earth." [32] The Soviet leadership wants the best of both worlds: loyalty to the state as it is, and loyalty to the general cause of "proletarian internationalism," the broad movement led and defined by Soviet ideology. This is characteristic of the age-old ambivalence of Russia, at once national and universalist.

LENINISM ABROAD

THE YEAR 1917 was the second great watershed in the life of Marxism. With the Russian Revolution, the meaning of Marxism underwent a radical transformation. Previously, Marxism was a somewhat offbeat, semiradical philosophy which did not seem likely ever to amount to anything of importance; to be Marxist after the revolution, meant being a citizen and supporter of a powerful government, or, for many outside the Soviet Union, being a supporter of the great alternative to the traditional patterns of society. The rather loose and hardly obligatory philosophy of some opposition parties, mostly in Germany and Austria, yielded place to the compulsory ideology of a great state. Marxism, a designation not much used before 1917, became a leading term in the political vocabulary.

Karl Marx was elevated by the triumph of his Russian disciples from a radical economist and political agitator of the days of early industrialization, a man hardly taken seriously in proper circles, to intellectual godhood. For such loyal Marxists as Karl Kautsky and Rosa Luxemburg, Marx was simply a thinker, outstanding but fallible. As a result of the Russian Revolution, Marx was deified as the official prophet of a great power, an authority to whom millions bowed, whose importance lay not merely in truths he may have expressed or even in the inspirational qualities of his works but in his political standing. For nonbelievers as well as believers, Marx assumed a singular and unparalleled stature in intellectual history, the philosopher who visibly and emphatically changed the world, a figure comparable only to such hallowed greats as Aristotle.

This transmogrification took hold as the Soviet state became a reality, and Marxism has advanced in step with the enormous expansion of Soviet power in the decades since. Logically or not, the world came largely to equate Marxism with Marxism-Leninism, the variant propagated by the Soviet Union. The Russian Revolution and the Soviet experiment became central to Marxist thinking, even for persons opposed to Soviet policies. Everything written about Marx and Marxism for the past half century is informed by the immanent reality of the Soviet Union, its claims, its victories, its shortcomings. Only since World War II, as the split of some Marxist-Leninist states, especially Yugoslavia and China, from the Soviet bloc has facilitated the development of independent Marxist or semi-Marxist movements elsewhere (and as ideological zeal has decayed in the Soviet Union itself), has the world reverted more to the earlier view of Marxism as a broad tendency, the Soviet "scientific socialism" being only the most potent variant.

Not only Soviet power, of course, but also the trials and disturbances of the world since 1914 gave life and strength to Marxism—the great wars, economic disorders, and the menace of fascism.

89

Even without Lenin's somewhat fortuitous triumph, World War I would certainly have put revolutionary change back on the agenda. But the successful revolution in Russia channeled and shaped the radicalism inherent in the war and early postwar situation, giving it great impetus on the one hand, dividing and confusing it on the other.

Socialists and Marxists were thrilled by the unexampled achievement of their fellows in Russia and were eager to believe that Lenin's revolution was indeed Marxist. The Bolshevik success showed that the dream could become reality; and to be a true revolutionary one went along with the revolutionary state. Others had talked endlessly, while Lenin's party had clutched the opportunity to put socialism into practice. Lenin did what Western socialists had come to think impossible, and their impotence had been shown up in the war. It was immensely promising, this first socialist revolution in the name of Marxist teachings, all the more exciting because the West saw the Bolsheviks not as inaugurators of a new order in Russia but as they presented themselves—as part of an antinational universal movement relevant for all peoples, the cracking if not the cracking up of the capitalist world order, the new socialist dawning.

Lenin attracted a large international following for several reasons. Awe of power and respect for what worked led a large majority of Western Marxists at least at first to overlook doctrinal differences and inconsistencies of Leninism with Marxism as they understood it. The prestige of actually having made a revolution enabled the Russian comrades to speak with an authority above mere logic. The fact that Lenin was the most consistent opponent of the war and that his party rode to power on a platform of peace added to their appeal as soon as the nations began counting their losses. In France, for example, the antiwar movement gave the impulse for the formation of a Leninist Communist Party in 1920. The postwar recession made labor and many others more hospitable to the Bolshevik message, although it alarmed conservatives. Democrats disappointed in the harvest of Western democracy were willing to look to the soviets as a new form of popular government. Many anarchists and general revolutionaries with little interest in Marx joined extremer Social Democrats in trooping to the side of Lenin in the first years. Until the summer of 1920, when the Soviet invasion of Poland was repelled, no one could be sure but that Communism might indeed sweep over Europe.

90

But the first influence of the Russian Revolution was much reduced by the fact that it came in the middle of the war which occupied all attention. For the Germans, the Leninists were enemy nationals not easily to be accepted as models or saviors, the less welcome because of traditional German feelings of superiority over the Slavs. For the Allied powers, the Bolsheviks were traitors, effectively if not literally servants of the enemy. Moreover, communications and travel were practically shut down by the war and by the Russian civil war; there was little real information as to what was going on in Russia, only a multitude of rumors, ranging from the nationalization of women and the alleged destruction of morality and religion to workers' management of factories.[33] It was not until 1920 that the Bolsheviks could establish extensive personal contact with the Western socialist movement.

By then, however, a reaction had set in. It became apparent that Lenin was not the libertarian many had hoped and that he was repressing not only reactionaries but socialists whose ideas were different from his and usually more like those current in the West. The workers were not taking charge in Russia, there was not much pretense of democracy, and the practical results of the revolution bore little resemblance to the Marxist dream. The Soviet takeover (in defiance of treaties and promises) of briefly independent Georgia, a Menshevik-run state with perhaps a better claim to the title of "socialist" than any other, shocked socialists in 1920–1921 much as did the invasion of Czechoslavakia in 1968. The Bolsheviks showed themselves aggressive, powerminded, and domineering beyond anything Western Social Democrats had known. Consequently, while the majority of members usually preferred to side with Lenin, the majority of Marxist or socialist leaders in non-Russian Europe refused the stiff conditions imposed by Lenin for affiliation with the new International he organized, and Western socialism became split between anti-Soviet and pro-Soviet forces. The split became permanent and deep, with many issues dividing the two sides: the possibility of reform versus the necessity of violent revolution, legal versus illegal tactics, loose versus tight party organization, tolerance versus intolerance of religion, patriotism versus internationalism (or pro-Sovietism, as it came to amount to). The key division, however, was over the rejection or acceptance of the right of the Soviet Communist leadership to speak in the name of the proletariat.

Those socialists who rejected Lenin (and subsequently Stalin)

mostly clung to the name of Marx; they did not see Marx as misleading but Lenin as misled, mostly because of the un-Marxist conditions of the Russian Revolution. But the rise of Leninism pushed
the moderates farther to the right. The Soviet-sponsored Communist movement drained off the extremists, especially young activists who preferred movement to theory and who were weary of
the staid and aging Social Democratic directorates. The moderate
socialists had also become much more involved with the governing
apparatus during and after the war; as members of governments
they found themselves repressing riots, persuading workers not to
strike, and using the coercive arm of the state to maintain order. As
such, they were increasingly the target of Communist abuse.

Yet the parties which followed the traditions of the Second
International were always confused in their attitude toward the Soviet state, uncertain whether to defend it as socialist or condemn it
as totalitarian. While moving farther from intransigent positions
toward attitudes more humanitarian than revolutionary, they continued to long for proletarian unity. They never quite gave up the
faith that communal ownership of means of production made the
Soviet Union something different and more promising, a state
whose misdeeds were more aberration than essence. At any time,
most of them would probably have welcomed a reconciliation if the
Leninists (or Stalinists) had been willing to submerge differences.

But instead of submerging differences, Lenin raised them.
Disgust with what he regarded as treason to internationalist duty in
1914 enabled him to think in terms of a split with the Western
Social Democratic movement; very soon after the war began, he
was proclaiming "Long live the Third International." As soon as he
got back to Russia in April 1917, Lenin proposed establishing his
new International to replace the collapsed Second International.
He had so much else to do that the First Congress of the
Communist International was not held until March 1919. But conditions were still so bad that only a handful of foreign "delegates"
could be assembled; the real founding congress was held in Moscow (as were all Comintern congresses) in July and August 1920. It
set in motion the Moscow-directed international Communist movement, which has endured essentially unchanged to this day. Its secondary achievement was to draw a hard, sharp line between those
who would and those who would not follow the Russian example.

This was achieved by Lenin's rigorous Twenty-one Conditions
for affiliation. To be accepted in the new movement, parties had to

bind themselves to purge reformers and waverers, to carry on illegal as well as legal activities, to subvert the armed forces of their countries, and to help so far as possible the Soviet state. As though these and other similar conditions were not enough, parties had to pledge to obey decisions of the Central Committee, which under the circumstances could be nothing but an arm of the Soviet state. For Lenin, revolution was to be made in the way he had proved successful in Russia; any people or groups who stood for a different approach were hindrances to be cast aside. Lenin also pointed to the failure of the Second International and demanded that the Third be different. This meant having a central organization to run the show, coordinating the political action of the various sections of the world proletariat. If this entailed placing the whole under Russian leadership, so much the better, although in the first years most Bolshevik leaders seem sincerely to have desired the prompt transferral of headquarters to the more industrialized West.[34]

The prestige of the Russian revolutionary center was such that a large part of the socialist movement voluntarily subordinated itself, although many joined with little awareness of how far the ideals of the Comintern differed from their own. For example, the moderate and enlightened Norwegian Labor Party went along for a few years.[35] Leninist organizational practice was fairly effective not in making revolution but in keeping a coherent army of believers mobilized to propagandize, subvert, and recruit. The Leninists erected and used many correlated and front organizations, in imitation of the domestic Soviet practice whereby the party spread its influence through control of nonparty organizations. There were the Red Trade Unions, the Sports International, the Peasant International, relief and charitable organizations, youth leagues, and the like. It was also the good fortune of the Bolshevik leaders, who were mostly quite young, to attract the socialist youth of the West to their fold. Around 1920 the overwhelming majority of Communist leaders were under 30, and many of them were under 25.[36]

The Comintern made no progress in its avowed aim of establishing the "dictatorship of the proletariat and the International Soviet Republic," despite the best subversive and revolutionary efforts of its agents, especially in Germany. But Lenin and his successors could never admit defeat in principle, only a "temporary stabilization of capitalism." And failure could not be due to the application of Russian and Leninist methods where they were inappropriate, nor to the plain fact that a Leninist-type revolution was possible only in a socially disintegrating situation not likely to occur in peacetime. To the contrary, failure must be due to insufficient vigilance against treasonous reformist elements and to the indiscipline or cowardice of the leaders. This could only imply closer direction from the Russian center, which was imposed the more easily because each failure discredited and weakened the non-Russian party involved.

In the postwar recovery of the 1920s, many revolutionaries lost heart. The vibrant movement decayed into a bureaucratized organization like its parent, the Soviet state. In the logic of "Socialism in One Country," the movement became the instrument of Soviet state policy; if it could not bring other countries to the side of the Soviet Union by overthrowing their governments, it should promote the cause of socialism by serving the Fatherland of the Workers. Lenin's idea that the Russian Revolution would liberate the world proletariat was reversed into Stalin's belief that it was the world proletariat's duty to help the Soviet Union. Stalin, who never took any great interest in the Comintern and foreign revolution in any case, made it his agent; foreign Communists, so long as they were obedient, were a material asset, although rather less valuable than imported machine tools.

The result was to kill whatever revolutionary spirit survived the relative prosperity of the middle and latter 1920s. The Comintern and its component parties became narrow and authoritarian, little despotisms within their limited spheres of power. The intellectuals, sometimes useful but always unreliable, were pushed out and replaced by unimaginative hacks of more proletarian background. Total conformism became the rule. In 1924, E. Varga asked Zinoviev, then president of the Comintern, whether he should report to the upcoming congress on the momentary stabilization of capitalism or its imminent collapse; [37] and in subsequent Stalinist times, independence of mind was even less conspicuous.

In 1928, Stalin took a sharp left turn in domestic policies, so his international claque had to go along; and the Comintern rose to a pinnacle of empty phrasemongering. The Comintern had also to reflect Stalin's expulsion of his rivals from the Soviet party and his distrust and hatred for any who might be faintly suspected of liberal weaknesses. While talking grandly of overthrowing capitalism, the Comintern dedicated itself between 1928 and 1934 principally to attacking "Social Fascists," as Social Democrats were called, with an enmity much fiercer than that turned against capitalists or genuine fascists. The prime task was to eliminate the rivals for the loyalty of the workers. But in the process, the Communists themselves suffered; most Communist parties shrank to a small fraction of their early postwar membership.

The sagging Communist movement was revived by the economic depression which began at the end of the 1920s and sent the economy of the non-Communist world plunging downward until 1932–1933. Unemployment, an unexampled commercial crisis, and underconsumption rekindled Communist hopes and brought the parties a flood of converts. The rise of fascism and the Nazi threat were even more helpful. Stalin was slow to recognize that Hitler could destroy Communists as well as Social Democrats, but by 1935 he was prepared to turn to a defensive, antifascist policy. The Soviet Union bent ideology by signing an alliance with France, and the Comintern congress decreed the Popular Front policy: Communists, in the defense of democracy and collective security, should join with socialist or even "bourgeois" parties as far as possible. This sensible redirection brought a great accretion of strength. The movement's effectiveness was still limited by Stalinist narrowness; the Stalinists in the Spanish civil war were as much exercised to annihilate Trotskyites on the republican side as Franco's fascists. But the Communists, with their organizational and propagandistic talents, became the most visible and emphatic opponents of fascism and gained corresponding credit. Their authority and electoral appeal shot up; in France, for example, Communist representation in parliament increased sevenfold.

All that was gained thereby was cast away, however, by Stalin's deal with Hitler in August 1939. The Communist parties obediently swallowed their principled antifascism and showed themselves mindless and antinational tools of Stalin and his foreign policy ambitions. During the nearly two years up to Hitler's assault on the Socialist Fatherland, which began on June 22, 1941, the Comintern's member parties assiduously denounced the "imperialist" war carried on by plutocratic Britain and France against the inoffensive Nazi friend of their Russian master. But with Russia in the fray, the parties leaped into action on behalf of the antifascist cause. Again, thanks to their discipline, organization, and ability to call upon the moral and material devotion of their members, the Communist parties were more effective in a situation of stress and disorder than their competitors. Their unseemly behavior during the first part of the war was forgotten in the ongoing struggle and buried under appreciation for their subsequent valiant service. The Communists naturally became leaders of resistance movements across Nazi-occupied Europe.

The Soviet state also achieved a new status. During the interwar period, it had never fully recovered the international standing once held by tsarist Russia. Through all negotiations about collective security there was an undercurrent of distrust (not without justification) for Stalinist Russia. There was hardly a thought of bringing the Soviet Union into the 1938 Munich settlement. But in the war the Soviet Union became the valued and respected ally of Britain and the United States; and the Russians, who bore the heaviest burden of fighting, by the end of the war rose to a pinnacle of prestige unknown since Alexander I rode into Paris. Stalin, his crimes forgotten insofar as they had become known, became a great war leader on a par with Roosevelt and Churchill. As a Yugoslav partisan officer saw him, "Stalin was not only the undisputed leader of genius, he was the incarnation of the very idea and dream of the new society." The admiring Djilas bowed to the "crystal clarity of his style, the penetration of his logic, and the harmony of his commentaries, as though they were expressions of the most exalted wisdom." In short, "he was the incarnation of an idea, transfigured in Communist minds into pure idea, and thereby into something infallible and sinless. Stalin was the victorious battle of today and the brotherhood of man of tomorrow. . . ." [38] Marxism and Communism were likewise uplifted; the guiding philosophy of a country that fought so well against the Hitlerites could not be all bad (it was not suggested that the philosophy which had helped the Nazis to fight with exemplary effectiveness was correspondingly praiseworthy). Russian military success made Marxism again a subject of intense interest in Europe.

Like its predecessor, World War II left a highly revolutionary situation in Europe. Again, as during and after World War I, the prestige and presence of the United States reduced the gains which Marxism harvested, partly by shoring up and protecting non-Communist governments, partly by sponsoring the economic reconstruction which made Communism seem less desirable and relevant. Despite the atmosphere of violence, desperation even deeper than in 1918–1919, and the discrediting of the old order, Communists were able to achieve power in Europe only where they came in directly on the tides of war (as in Yugoslavia and Al-

bania) or were placed in power by Soviet armies. The popular revolutionism of 1945–1947 was too much influenced, channeled, and
harnessed by the Russians to have much dynamic force, and most
Communist parties receded as rapidly as prosperity returned. Only
in France and Italy did large Communist parties become a prominent and seemingly permanent part of the political landscape.

Despite the failure of postwar revolutionism, World War II
meant another great leap forward for Marxism, because Marxist-
Leninist parties attained power in a dozen additional countries:
China and the northern parts of Korea and Vietnam, the countries of
the Soviet sphere in Eastern Europe, and Yugoslavia and Albania.
Marxist-Leninist Communism came to rule a third of the world's
population. It seemed a tremendous, perhaps irresistible ava-
lanche, which had only to go forward a little more, as it had gone
forward ever since 1917 with only brief setbacks, to become the
dominant force on earth. But success carries germs of trouble, and
the movement which the Russians found manageable as long as
they were the only possessors of political power could no longer be
held together. Bitter enmity arose between the two chief
Communist powers, and hostility or dissidence developed to varying degrees between the Soviet Union and those Communist states
that were in a position to take an independent stance.

The Soviet Union nonetheless has to keep up a universalist
movement of some sort for the ideological reasons stated earlier,
even though the Soviets may not greatly desire revolution anywhere. After the formal dissolution of the Comintern in 1943, the
Soviet Union nevertheless managed to maintain a remarkable degree of control over the nonruling parties despite the Chinese challenge and the invitation to self-will in a world of competing
Communisms. This has been ascribable to inertia, old habits of
generally aging party leaderships, the prestige of the Soviet Union,
and political and economic dependence on Moscow. The Soviets
continue to put much money and effort into the movement, hold
congresses, consult with leaders, furnish publications, and maintain a multitude of organizational linkages. Their reward has been a
fairly obedient movement with branches in almost every country.
Charisma and idealism have largely vanished and organizations
have become calcified, with no room for new ways, ideas, or emotions. But the parties abroad still serve as channels through which
Marxist-Leninist vocabulary, modes of thought, and philosophy are
continually poured into the political and intellectual world.

CHAPTER

IV

―――

Marxism
for Precapitalists

STEPS AWAY FROM THE CENTER

"COMMUNISM," John Kautsky wrote, "is a phenomenon of underdevelopment." [1] Russia was and felt itself relatively backward at the time of the Leninist Revolution; and Albania and Yugoslavia, the other European countries where Communist parties fought their way to power, were among the poorest and least industrialized on the continent. China was a very backward country in terms of Western technological culture when a Marxist-Leninist party took power. Several countries of Africa, such as Guinea and the People's Republic of the Congo, have had semi-Communist governments; and Cuba, suffering especially from backwardness by comparison with its great neighbor, upgraded a bourgeois-democratic revolution under Castro to Marxist-Leninist socialism. Yet nowhere in the advanced industrial world has a Communist revolution come near success except briefly in times of exceptional disorder.

It is also in the less developed countries that Marxism is most fervently and uncritically maintained by people under no physical compulsion in their choice of ideology. Very many intellectuals in non-Soviet Europe have been much influenced by Marxism in recent years, but they are apt to be more critical; Marxism or Marxist-influenced ideas in Germany, France, or Italy encounter competition and opposition.

This anomaly has attracted much comment. Marxism, the doctrine of the industrial proletariat, preaching the doom of overripe capitalism, has proven most useful and attractive in countries which have an insignificant proletariat in the Marxian sense and which have barely set out on the road of capitalist construction. From a doctrine based on the results of industrialization, Marxism has become an ideology for industrialization and modernization under political guidance; a study of the outcome of change has become a motivation for change.

Marx had little sympathy for the victims of colonialism and approved the modernization brought by British imperialism, particularly in India, the only colonial territory to which he paid any considerable attention. There, he wrote, "English interference . . . produced the greatest, and, to speak the truth, the only social revolution ever heard of in Asia," with the building of railroads, the beginnings of factory industry, and the establishment of regular means of communication.[2] He saw the communism of Indian villages as entirely negative; British rule was to break the age-old fetters on Indian society. Engels was equally scornful of the virtues of primitivism. As he wrote in 1848:

> All these nations of free barbarians look very proud, noble, and glorious at a distance, but only come near them and you will find that they, as well as the more civilized nations, are ruled by lust of gain, and only employ ruder and more cruel means. And after all, the modern *bourgeois*, with civilization, industry, order, and at least relative enlightenment following him, is preferable to the feudal lord or to the marauding robber, with the barbarian state of society to which they belong.[3]

Marx and Engels at one time evinced a weakness for the virtuous Russian peasant commune, presumably in order to please the Russian revolutionaries, but Engels later recanted. Writing of state control of the economy in the Netherlands Indies, he held that this "is proof of how today primitive communism furnishes there as well as in India and Russia the finest and broadest basis for exploitation and despotism. . . ."[4]

Before the Russian Revolution, Marxist parties generally disapproved of colonialism and colonial wars but held no expectations for the exploited peoples of the non-European world. This accorded with the logic of Marxism and with the facts. Native peoples from Indochina to the Niger offered only slight or occasional resistance to European conquest and seemed to accept the rule of the superior European powers with Oriental fatalism. European socialists assumed for themselves the leadership assigned them by the Marxist historical sequence; one day they would assist the less fortunate lands toward socialism.

But if Lenin's conversion of Marxism into the battle cry of the less developed countries was a perversion of Marxian teachings, Marxist dialectics teaches us to look beneath appearances to find the essence. Antithetical to systematic, "scientific," economic-determinist, evolutionary Social Democratic Marxism there is romantic, voluntaristic, revolutionary, Communist Marxism. Both are present, sometimes side by side, in the works of Marx and Engels. The two sides are antithetical but never entirely separated, and one can brew his own variety of Marxism by bringing in elements of both in varying proportions, as all true Marxists have done. Voluntaristic revolutionism, which uses economic determinism as little more than a cover of scientism, follows quite as much in the way of Marx and Marxism as Kautsky's social democracy, which used revolutionism as a cover of activism for a reformist approach. Without determinism, Marxism becomes anarchism; without revolutionism, it becomes democratic reformism.

Marxism and the socialist movement have arisen from the clash of capitalism with the precapitalist disposition,[5] which is an anticapitalist disposition. In 1848 revolutions were briefly successful in Hungary and Italy, where there was not a trace of modern industry, and old governments toppled across the continent. But England hardly stirred. Marx thus looked away from the leading capitalist state toward continental Europe, regardless of theory. Industrialization in France was far behind Britain, French capitalism was less "bourgeois" in mentality, and French institutions were more authoritarian. Not despite but because of these factors, socialism was much stronger in France and more revolutionary. In Germany there was much less democracy than in England, and a weaker bourgeoisie; German industrialization really began only in Marx's later years, yet Marxism was far stronger there than in Britain. The same was true to an even greater degree of Russia prior to World War I.

Marx was ready to welcome revolution almost anywhere—in

100

Ireland, Italy, or the Russia of the 1880s, which was much less industrialized even than the Russia of 1917. He was excited by the Taiping Rebellion which wracked China between 1850 and 1864, seeing it as an admirable agrarian-proletarian, anti-Western capitalist outburst. Engels, although he stressed economic determinism, did not overlook the possibilities of revolutionary action where conditions were propitious. He also prepared the way for Lenin's analysis of imperialism by blaming the otherwise unaccountable quiescence of the British proletariat on colonial exploitation. In England, he wrote, "the workers gaily share the feast of England's monopoly of the world market and the colonies." [6] He also recognized that Marxism appealed to countries in transition from an agricultural to an industrial society and pointed in passing to the army (in Germany) as a possible starting place for revolution.[7]

Late in life, Engels was much interested in the progress of socialism in such primitive parts of Europe as Romania and Bulgaria.[8] In 1894 he opined that less developed countries could proceed quickly to socialism if guided by the advanced countries; they would not have to undergo the travails of capitalism. It was only a short step to the conclusion that the less developed might achieve socialism concurrently with the leaders. Engels prepared for this by assuming that revolutionary leaders in a country like Russia could be more advanced than their society (as Lenin was to claim) because they had the benefit of socialist theory developed under capitalism.[9] If Marx and Engels were prepared to say that native institutions might serve as a basis of socialist development in Russia and that revolution there might be part of a general wave, such thinking was perfectly applicable to still less industrialized countries.

Such occasions seemed to be arising in the first few years of this century. The Russian revolution of 1905 had echoes across Asia, especially in Turkey and Iran, where anti-Western Westernizers hoped to strengthen their countries by constitutional reform. Lenin, seeing Russian and Western European radicalism in disarray, looked expectantly to these stirrings in Asia. In 1911 he greeted the overthrow of the Manchu empire in China, hoping that a nonexistent Marxist party might come to power.[10] Disorders in the Netherlands Indies similarly cheered him. He wrote in 1913: "The awakening of Asia and the beginning of the struggle for power by the advanced proletariat of Europe are a symbol of the new phase in world history that began early this century." [11]

Lenin's theory of imperialism, wherein he stressed more strongly than previous writers the dependence of Western capitalism on colonialism, sanctioned revolution not just in Russia but almost anywhere. Socialist activism was thereby legitimized regardless of economic development; this implied that the peasantry was to be accepted almost as a substitute proletariat. The chains of world capitalism were to be broken wherever their breaking might prove them weak. It was up to the poor countries to take the lead.

During World War I, Lenin tied his hopes for Russia to prospects for overthrow of the ruling classes in the leading belligerent states; as a proper Marxist, he did not pretend that his movement could succeed without the greater one, which the logic of historical materialism made more appropriate. Nonetheless, he posited an alliance of Russian Bolshevism with Asian nationalistic revolution, proletarian or not.[12] The success of October 1917 radically changed the situation, and for the next few years the eyes of Lenin and his fellows were hopefully scanning the western horizon for signs of rescue through the breakdown of the European order. But the flare-ups of Communism in Central Europe (especially Hungary and Bavaria) died down; and the duller prospects in the West became, the more Bolshevik attention turned eastward. At the Comintern congress in the summer of 1920 much attention was paid to Asia, especially India, where Lenin hoped to find support for the young and very weak Soviet state by an indirect attack on world capitalism—that is, practically speaking, on Great Britain. The road to London and Paris, as Lenin saw it, passed through Peking and Delhi. Lenin, in effect, equated exploited nations with the exploited class; but he was unwilling to go so far as the Indian Communist M. N. Roy, who held world revolution to depend entirely on Asia.[13]

Since Marxism is theory as well as practice, discussions inevitably arose as to whether the Comintern should work for nationalistic, anti-Western but "bourgeois" movements, or for Communist, party-led, and lower-class (if not proletarian) revolution. The answer was to propose both, hoping the "workers' " party could seize control. Lenin favored any activity which would harm the antagonists of the Soviet state, and in practice this meant non-Communist nationalistic rebellions. Yet he encouraged the poorer countries to follow the Soviet example as closely as possible. They, like Russia, could skip the capitalist stage of history with the aid of more advanced proletariats; soon it would be said that they need only count on the support of the Soviet fortress of socialism. He recognized that the colonial or semicolonial countries had no proletariat, but he argued that "the idea of Soviet organization is a simple one, and is applicable, not only to proletarian, but also to peasant feudal and semi-feudal relations." Hence these countries should form peasant soviets, so that "with the aid of the proletariat of the advanced countries" they could "go over to the Soviet system and, through certain stages of development, to communism, without having to pass through the capitalist stage." [14]

The Comintern congress was quickly followed by the First Congress of the Peoples of the East, held at Baku, in Soviet Azerbaijan, in September 1920. Here radicals and nationalists of Asia assembled to cheer holy war against British imperialism. Soviet leaders spoke of the destinies of the oppressed masses everywhere, of whom the Communists were the vanguard. Stalin spoke for Russia at about the same time: "Here I . . . draw together the strength of the proletariat of the West and the peasantry of the East to smash the old world." [15] Not much more came of hopes for the East than those for the West, but the promise of the former remained the brighter. As Lenin saw the world at the end of his active life, "the East has been definitely drawn into the revolutionary movement," a development which he found promising: "In the last analysis, the outcome of the struggle will be determined by the fact that Russia, India, China, etc., account for the overwhelming majority of the population of the globe." [16] Russia would lead Asia against the West.[17] And in the Comintern the Leninists had a staff and organization to mobilize the uncountable Asian masses in the cause.

MAOISM

THE EMISSARIES of the Comintern found a warm welcome where people long treated as inferiors were rising to a new anger at the European intruders. The missionaries of Lenin's new dispensation went out with little backing of political or economic power, but with the word that the poor would be uplifted and the powerful cast down, as proved by the famous philosopher Karl Marx and as demonstrated by a great friend of the people, Lenin, and, after 1924, by his peerless successor, Stalin.

Nowhere was the soil more fertile for the message than in China. The breakdown of Chinese society, torn by warlordism and civil conflict since the fall of the decadent dynasty in 1911, was much more extreme than that of Russian society in 1917; efforts to establish a Western-style republic had brought only disorder and frustration. Relations with the West had for a century been disagreeable, and their impact was peculiarly painful and humiliating because the Chinese had been perhaps the proudest of all peoples. The Russians gloried in their great empire but had never felt quite safe in the world; for centuries they had been busily borrowing from and adjusting to the technological civilization of their neighbors. The Chinese felt wholly satisfied with their own civilization, in comparison with which they held all others to be barbarian, acceptable only so far as they were deferential. Yet the Westerners came in the nineteenth century with superior military power, and the Chinese found themselves treated as weak, backward, and insignificant, esteemed only as a market for Western manufactures. The Chinese were put down, as the Russians, always recognized as Europeans (despite suspicions about their "Asianness"), had never been. And the onslaught of greedy traders and arrogant seekers of concessions, backed by overweening governments, was readily susceptible of a Marxist interpretation.

Westernization was peculiarly traumatic for Chinese intellectuals. It was difficult enough for the Russians of the nineteenth century, despite their semi-European background and long tradition of Western contacts. The Chinese had a unified and settled culture very alien to the West; yet they had to become pupils of the barbarians, so obviously and imperiously superior in a material way. This seemed to require casting down the whole Chinese heritage, an idea which was unacceptable and impossible. Liberalism, individualism, and democracy were much more alien to the Chinese than to the Russian mentality, and efforts to graft them onto China seemed to promise further chaos.

The example of the Russian Revolution was accordingly thrilling in the narrow circles of students and teachers growing up in China. The prestige of the European world was shaken by World War I, and the Japanese had been making inroads on Chinese sovereignty, trying to use the weakness of Europe to make China practically their possession. The Japanese, as obvious inferiors who had gathered strength by assimilating Western technology faster than had the prouder and stiffer Chinese, were even more irritating than

104

the Europeans. That semi-Asiatic Russia could turn its back on the haughty Western powers and find another, presumably still more modern way to the future was electrifying, especially inasmuch as the Russians claimed that their way was universal, an answer to the afflictions of all peoples. The Russians proclaimed anti-imperialism, the downfall of capitalism, and the liberation of the oppressed; and they spoke to China as reformed sinners renouncing the evils of tsardom. Nowhere else was the resonance of Lenin's October so vibrant.

Nationalists in China had to be pro-Soviet, in the first years of Lenin's state, because they were anti-Western. Although he was no Communist, Sun Yat-sen, who is still respected by both Communists and Nationalists as a great leader of China's renewal, looked to Lenin and the Soviet state for assistance against the Western powers and the corrupt regime which they supported. He welcomed Comintern agents to advise his inexperienced Nationalist Party on organizational methods and revolutionary tactics.

The Chinese Communist Party was organized in the shadow of the Nationalist revolutionary movement. Bits of Marx's writings appeared in China after 1905, but they were taken seriously only in 1919 and after, when Marx and Lenin were made relevant by the Russian Revolution. Marxist study groups were formed; Comintern agents, speaking not to workers but to the nascent intelligentsia (teachers, students, writers, and journalists),[18] in 1921 started a tiny Communist Party, which the next year joined the Comintern. Marxism was welcome; as a young Chinese saw it, "in this age Marxism provides the only solution. . . . I feel that I have found the key to the contradictory problems which I was once unable to solve." [19] It ended self-doubts and gave a universalist, absolutist answer admirably fitting Chinese tradition. In China, unlike most non-Western countries, there was no religious bar to Marxism. It was easy for a Chinese patriot to turn from the traditional conflict of Chinese versus barbarians to the Marxian antithesis of proletarians versus exploiters, making the Chinese struggle part of universal history. The exploiters were primarily Western, while the wealthy and privileged Chinese were commonly involved with the system of concessions and accommodations with the European powers, and they stood in the way of a national revival. The Communists would count on the uncorrupted people to reunite and restore China.

Unlike Lenin's Bolsheviks, the Chinese Communists had virtually no competition on the left—no anarchists, agrarian socialists, or others as rivals. But they were troubled by the dichotomy in Soviet and Comintern policy, which wanted at once to support the non-Communist Nationalists as enemies of enemies of the Soviet Union and to encourage a party which fully accepted the Soviet model and would presumably remain loyal to the Soviet center. Consequently, the Communists were directed to subordinate themselves to the Nationalist Party (Kuomintang), a policy which they gladly accepted as long as Chiang Kai-shek and the KMT followed a strongly nationalist and anti-Western direction, and which helped them greatly to increase their numbers. In due course they believed they would be able to take the helm and push their allies into the trash bin of history; as Stalin said in 1927, the Nationalists were to be used, "squeezed dry like a lemon, then flung away." [20]

But Chiang Kai-shek, whether or not he heard of this proposal, applied the same logic to the Communists. On securing a solid base in Shanghai, he saw more to gain from cooperation with the more prosperous elements of Chinese society than with those who would join social revolution to civil war. He turned on his former allies and decimated their party. It endeavored to set off insurrections in the cities, but the result was only the complete destruction of Chinese Communism's urban base.

Mao then withdrew to the hills of southern China and built up a virtually new party on the basis of agrarian reform. This was not without support in the works of Lenin,[21] and the Comintern in 1928 realistically sanctioned guerrilla warfare in the Chinese countryside.[22] But guerrilla warfare was a strange thing for a Marxist party to promote. In theory, Marx had only scorn for the peasantry as a backward class; and Lenin, despite his pragmatic receptivity to peasant assistance in toppling the tsarist government, insisted on proletarian leadership and never made much headway in organizing the countryside.

Chinese Communism made much more progress among the rural masses (perennial mainsprings of rebellion in Chinese history) than it had with the lumpenproletariat of the cities. In 1931, Mao set up a Soviet republic in Kiangsi, and a year later the Central Committee of the party moved there. The chief business of the party was to fight off the military attacks of the Kuomintang, and the party became almost equivalent to the army; it remained so for many years, and even today is strongly under military influence. The proletariat in any meaningful sense was a trivial fraction of the population. Despite some thin pretenses of proletarian leadership, the Chinese Communist Party became essentially a peasant party with middle-class leadership. This was facilitated by the Chinese language, which translated "bourgeois" as "rich," and "proletariat" as "propertyless"; [23] as modified by Chinese semantics, the Marxian class struggle became the antagonism of landlords and poor peasants.

Military pressure from Chiang's forces became too great, however; and in 1934, Mao and his followers set out to move to a base more accessible to the Soviet Union. The Long March lasted a year and covered some 6,000 difficult miles. Militarily it was disastrous, because only about a tenth of the troops came through. But it made Mao formally head of the party, tempered and hardened the leadership, and gave Mao's party a background and tradition of heroism which has helped to sustain and unite it ever since.

Despite the appeal of Mao's agrarian reformism, he came to power by waging a nationalistic struggle. He was a nationalist before he was a Communist, and China has always been more important to him than world revolution,[24] although he was nominally wholly faithful to the Comintern as long as it existed. His opportunity came in July 1937, when the Japanese turned their peripheral creeping aggression into a large-scale attack on central China. As the fighting progressed, the Communists showed themselves the most capable organizers of popular resistance. The government of Chiang was driven into the interior, where it lacked solid backing, and the intellectuals turned to the Communists as the force most capable of defending and restoring China. Although not only American but also Soviet assistance went to the Nationalists, the Communists spread their network through well-directed guerrilla warfare until, by the time of the Japanese surrender, they could challenge the increasingly decrepit and corrupt Nationalist government. Finally, in October 1949, after nearly twenty years of fighting, Mao proclaimed the new People's Republic over all of Mainland China.

Having achieved this goal, Mao needed, like Lenin in 1921, the cooperation of non-Communists in rebuilding the devastated country. He accordingly launched the New Democracy, an idea developed during the years of fighting when the Maoists were grateful for any help they might get. It was a rather nondogmatic program reminiscent of Lenin's backstepping New Economic Policy. Like the NEP, this New Democracy encouraged the world to believe that the Communists were becoming moderates or "agrarian reformers," as many Americans saw them and as the Soviet Union portrayed them. In this "democratic dictatorship," sundry old parties were retained and given minor roles in the state on condition of total submission. As Mao wrote, "Our enemies are all those in league with imperialism—the warlords, the big bureaucrats, the comprador class, the big landlord class, and the reactionary section of the intelligentsia attached to them. . . . Our closest friends are the entire semi-proletariat and petty bourgeoisie." [25] Defectors from the KMT were welcome, and capitalists or merchants who were prepared to cooperate with the Communists were treated well, compensated for their property, and perhaps retained as state-paid managers of their enterprises. Class, insofar as it was taken into account, was based on wealth, an understandable but non-Marxist attitude. Class conflict was nothing absolute; contradictions "between the exploited and the exploiting classes have a non-antagonistic in addition to an antagonistic aspect," [26] wrote Mao, and they could be treated in any way that seemed desirable. "But in the concrete conditions of China, this antagonistic class contradiction can, if properly handled, be transformed into a non-antagonistic one and be resolved by peaceful methods." [27] Moreover, the view was adopted that the class character of people was alterable by education or reeducation. This was the ideological basis of the brainwashing campaigns for which Communist China became celebrated in the 1950s.

Nine years after the Soviet victory in the civil war, Stalin proclaimed the "Year of the Great Change" and pushed energetically forward with the transformation of Russia through industrialization and collectivization. Nine years after his victory, in 1958, Mao embarked on a parallel but even more extreme course of remaking the land. Possibly he was impatient with the policy of gradualism (although this was very successful); probably there were political reasons also, including a desire to assert Chinese independence in the already smoldering quarrel with the Soviet Big Brother. With an outburst of intense revolutionary ardor, the leadership proclaimed the Great Leap Forward. Stalin would build socialist industry in one country by force; Mao would utilize the manpower of China by coercion, discipline, and persuasion, the military methods by which he had won the civil war, to industrialize a backward country in a very brief time. Peasants were to build 2 million steel furnaces in as many farmyards; steel production was to be doubled, then at least tripled in one year. Grain production was likewise to be doubled or tripled. This was to be made possible by a new organizational form. The 470,000 collective farms established earlier in imitation of the Soviet kolkhozes were in 1958 amalgamated into 26,000 People's Communes. In these, life was to be as communistic as possible, with services performed by the community and complete submergence of the individual; in some, men and women were moved into barracks, the children into nurseries. Not only was China to skip from a preindustrial level over the capitalist stage; it was also to overleap socialism into communism, the highest condition of humanity, by the exercise of will and political leadership, leaving behind the slothful Russians.

At this time the contradictions between the two giant Communist states became more intense, leading toward their definitive split and the separation of Maoism as an independent variant or descendant of Marxism. The origins go back to Mao's reliance on the peasantry from the 1930s, which, in the subsequent Soviet interpretation, made his an essentially "petty-bourgeois" party. At least as early as 1936, Mao was looking to Chinese experience rather than to the Soviet model, and he received little from the Soviet Union except advice. Stalin does not seem to have anticipated or welcomed Mao's conquest of all of China. After his 1949 victory Mao frankly saw China as a better model for backward nations than the Soviet Union, hence at least potentially its rival; as China's leader, Mao saw himself as a fully qualified interpreter of Marxism.[28] He declared, however, that China must choose the anti-imperialist side,[29] and he was outwardly a faithful follower as long as Stalin lived, although the Soviets treated China shabbily in the Korean war. Only after Stalin died were the Chinese prepared to pull away.

Causes of the break were numerous. Mao declined to bow to Khrushchev as Stalin's successor and considered the denunciation of Stalin to be anti-Communist. China wanted more Soviet aid and saw no reason why this should go to non-Communist countries, especially to India, a rival. There were territorial differences. Russia was the only imperialist power retaining large areas taken from China in its time of weakness. And there were ideological differences. It seemed at the time that the biggest divergence was the greater militancy of the Chinese, who felt that the Soviet Union should press the worldwide battle for socialism, particularly against the United States, while the Russians saw the Chinese pushing them to risk nuclear war for the benefit of China, specifically the recovery of Taiwan. But the basic cause was that neither China nor Russia was willing to subordinate itself to the other in the world Communist movement. Pride and interests conflicted, and the supposedly shared Marxist-Leninist ideology was no real bond.

In 1960 the Russians, hoping to bring the Chinese to repentance, called home the experts who were assisting Chinese industrialization. They succeeded in helping to thwart the Great Leap Forward, which was already stumbling, as peasants tore up good steel rails to make worthless steel in backyard furnances. Production sagged dismally, and for a few years the government had practically to forget industrialization and concentrate on agriculture to feed the country. The pragmatists, led by Liu Shao-chi, gained predominance in the party; Mao was nearly relegated to a position of impotent divinity.

Under the Liu policies of relaxation and economic incentives, production recovered in a few years, and China again by 1965 seemed to be on the way to industrialization, albeit at a moderate tempo. But the aging revolutionary leader (Mao was born in 1893) was not content to sit back and watch the erstwhile utopian-revolutionary state become simply another bureaucratic structure subject to all the distortions and rotting of which not only Trotsky but Chinese history warned. To reassert the revolution and his own position, he called upon his charisma as founding father and supreme leader and applied the force of ideology against the dominant forces in the government and the Communist Party. Summoning the youth to renew its commitment to equality and the destruction of hierarchic orders, in the summer of 1966 he set in motion, with some difficulty,[30] the Great Proletarian Cultural Revolution.

The Cultural Revolution was a phenomenon singular in history: a revolution started and directed by the head of the state and made from below. The chief protagonists were very young people, the Red Guards, led by university students. Practically the first act of the revolution was the closure of the universities to release the youths; despite China's need for technology, for some years only elementary schools functioned. The Cultural Revolution was, in practice, a gigantic, although usually bloodless, purge of party and government ranks. Coming seventeen years after Mao's victory, it paralleled Stalin's purge-storm, which began in 1936, sixteen years after Soviet victory in the civil war; but it was much more ideological and popular. In essence, it was a dual protest, of the revolutionary old guard against newcomers usurping power and position on the grounds of practical ability, and of the young people against the failure, or betrayal, of the ideals of the revolution. Its motto was, "Better Red than Expert."

To set aside the "bourgeois" superstructures and to remove the inequalities that had grown up in the postrevolutionary calm, the Cultural Revolution practically dissolved the Communist Party organization and much of the state apparatus, including the economic planning administration. With fundamentalist fervor, it exalted "class" struggle, mass action, and manual labor for all. Its model was the Paris Commune of 1871; great cities declared themselves communes. In ideological fever (or delirium) it saw the past as worthless except for revolutionary struggle. Literature was discarded. Even technical journals ceased publication; hardly any books were printed except the works of Mao. The cult of his personality rose to fantastic heights, as everyone waved the Little Red Book of his quotations, spent many hours studying "Mao Tse-tung Thought," and attributed all successes to his inspiration. Yet Mao was not entirely in command; many conflicting groups outdid one another in claiming to be the best followers of the Great Helmsman without necessarily looking to Peking for directions. The Cultural Revolution also caused China to become isolated in a paroxysm of xenophobia such as no other great nation of modern times has suffered; nearly all ambassadors were recalled from abroad.

The call was for "continuous revolution," a variant of Trotsky's "permanent revolution"; but a revolution prolonged can only mean turmoil. As in the Great Leap Forward, the ideological upsurge upset industry and to a lesser extent agriculture. People wearied of marching, shouting, and demonstrating. The People's Liberation Army stepped in to restore order, under revolutionary committees dominated by military men. Normalization was accelerated by the Soviet invasion of Czechoslovakia (August 1968), and the promulgation of the Brezhnev Doctrine; the Chinese perceived a real danger and the need for sobriety to meet it. In theory, nothing was to be undone; but the country settled down, curbed the Red Guards, revived production, put the experts more or less in charge again, reopened foreign relations, and even came to a détente with the United States, which no longer seemed so fearsome when the Russian ex-comrades were menacing the Chinese border. Lin Piao, who had been a leader of the radicals, was removed allegedly for plotting against Mao; and relative normalcy returned under the guidance of the pragmatic Chou En-lai.

China remained, however, a more ideological state than the Soviet Union, just as it has been more extreme in most developments (except terrorism) than its Soviet predecessor. Ideology, in Mao's view, should be equivalent to culture. The people were far more permeated with the ideals of revolution and equality, which had been largely set aside in the Soviet Union fifteen years or so after the Bolsheviks' accession to power. The ranks looked and dressed alike, and pay differentials were small for a partly industrialized society. Everything was done to keep memories of revolutionary struggle against landlords and imperialists vivid. There was still much talk of the making of the "new man"—the old Marxist dream of human perfection in the perfect social order—an idea long since faded to a faint mirage in the Soviet Union. Manual labor was glorified. Soft-handed white collar workers, students, and officials of state and party were sent to work with the peasants to improve their political understanding, or to cadre schools, where the retraining was mostly physical labor, partly as education, partly as punishment. Soviet consumerism (what little there was of it) was derided as degenerate and petty bourgeois. Perhaps some day the people might have a life of ease and comfort; but for the time being, hard work and spartan standards were in order. It was constantly hammered into the public consciousness that there must always be struggle, that there were always enemies to overcome. And as perceived by foreigners, this campaign was highly successful; any Chinese citizen would eagerly assure the visitor that his chief desire was to help the state and the cause of the people under the guidance of Chairman Mao.

This is the core of the Maoist ideology, the duty to work better and fight harder; and the bulk of Mao's writings consists of variations on this theme. Maoism is mostly a mass of homilies and exhortations, hardly a system. As a theoretician he does not stand high; he may never have read Marx and Engels, and his more theoretical statements are likely to be borrowed straight from Soviet sources.[31] His writings, like those of Stalin, are simple, often vivid, but concerned with morale, organization, and discipline, not the finer points of dialectic. Mao has always been distrustful of mere intellectuals and concerned primarily with action; the cult of physical fitness is a revealing sidelight of his personality.

The corollary of exhortation to duty and abnegation is emphasis on the power of will; Maoism is much more voluntaristic than Leninism just as Leninism exceeds Engels's deterministic Marxism in this regard. Willpower practically takes the place of the economic base; the mobilized and politically aroused masses can do anything, just as Mao's guerrillas overcame materially superior forces. As Mao put it, "More people mean a greater ferment of ideas, more enthusiasm and more energy." [32] If China is poor, Mao wrote, "this may seem a bad thing, but in reality it is a good thing. Poverty gives rise to the desire for change, the desire for action, and the desire for revolution." [33] The right ideas move the world. "Once the correct ideas characteristic of the advanced class are grasped by the masses, these ideas turn into a material force which changes society and changes the world." [34] As shown by the *Parable of the Foolish Old Man*, one of the prime classics of Maoism, will and patience literally move mountains.[35]

Maoism leans on the people China possesses in superabundance, the peasants. It was peasant soldiers who raised Mao to power, and the factory proletariat remains relatively very small. Still more striking is that not even in theory are the factory workers the vehicle of the truth. The cadres are not sent to work with mill hands to restore their political purity and suppress "bourgeois" thought, but to absorb the ageless wisdom of the peasants in the fields.

Will and discipline come to the fore in revolutionary combat, and the largest contribution of Maoism—perhaps its most striking amendment of Marxism—is the theory of guerrilla warfare worked out in long years of practice by Mao. As he wrote in 1938, "According to the Marxist theory of the state, the army is the chief component of state power." [36] His most cited aphorism is direct and striking: "Every Communist must grasp the truth, 'Political power grows out of the barrel of a gun.' " [37] This is an unlikely idea for bookish Marxist scholars, but it would have seemed natural to Engels, who was called "General" and went fox hunting to keep in trim for the battles of the imminent revolution. By corollary, for Mao, unlike Lenin, the party is not sacrosanct. Mao continues apparently to think better of military than of civilian politicians; the army was not torn apart by the Cultural Revolution, and military men continue to hold a large share of top political posts. Mao chalked up his greatest triumphs as a military leader working much more with people than with matériel, and he carried this approach into his headship of the state.

To continue military methods and revolutionary struggle for many years after the original enemy has been destroyed requires that there be an ongoing conflict; consequently, contradictions must

113

exist even in socialist society. Perhaps because it relates to traditional Chinese modes of thought (the paired opposites of heaven and earth, order and disorder, yin and yang), Mao played with the concept of contradictions from early in his career; but it became operative in the 1950s. Today contradictions are seen everywhere, and the class struggle within Chinese society is reflected within the party. Hence the need to keep running to avoid going backward into revisionism and "bourgeois" vices. Contradictions may be antagonistic (resolvable only by force) or nonantagonistic; and they continually arise between the individual and the collective, centralism and democracy, bureaucracy and the masses; it is the role of the party to resolve them in the interests of the people.[38] According to the *People's Daily*, "In a socialist society there are classes, class contradictions, and class struggle. Class struggle will inevitably be reflected in the Party." [39] More than this, "class struggle" goes on within the individual, the mind being torn between good "proletarian" and bad "bourgeois" thoughts. "Class" has become a Hegelian ideal.

Mao Tse-tung Thought, which was officially consecrated as the sole guide for party work in 1945,[40] has thus gone far from what is usually understood in the West as the logic and spirit of Marx, and the social, cultural, and economic distance between China and the countries for which Marx was writing is enormous. Yet China claims absolute fidelity to the German master, and a remarkable amount of Marxism is mixed into the Maoist way. The present party constitution states that China is guided by Marxism–Leninism–Mao Tse-tung Thought. Huge portraits of Marx, Engels, Lenin, and Stalin are paraded on festive occasions, that of Mao usually standing alone. The vocabulary of Marxism prevails everywhere. More astounding is that the preferred reading of the cadre schools, as reported by American journalists, consists of Marx's *Critique of the Gotha Program* and *Civil War in France*, plus Lenin's *Materialism and Empirio-Criticism* and *State and Revolution*. Semiliterate peasants weary from hoeing cabbages are supposed to immerse themselves in these classics, as Soviet collective farmers do not.

In some ways Maoism is farther from the original Marxism than current Soviet Marxism-Leninism; in other ways it is closer. The idea of the classless society is much stronger in China, partly because of the distrust of Mao, the guerrilla fighter, for bureaucracy, complex organization, and the economic mentality. Marx would certainly esteem the continuing emphasis on revolution, on the dignity of labor, and on mass action. The Maoists take seriously the idea of bringing town and country closer together, and they look, in the style of the young Marx, to the rounded person, able to work on farm or in factory, to fight or write, as need be. They have made some effort to apply the principle of exchanging personnel in office,[41] a proposal put forward by Lenin in *State and Revolution* but not implemented in the Soviet state. Maoism takes dialectics more seriously than does contemporary Leninism; it not only dwells on contradictions, with progress through resolution, but employs the "unity of opposites." As Mao put it, with a certain Oriental cast: "Just as there is not a single thing in the world without a dual nature (this is the law of unity of opposites), so imperialism and all reactionaries have a dual nature—they are real tigers and paper tigers at the same time." [42] Like the Russians, the Chinese ignore Marx's writings on the Asiatic mode of production; with even more violence to rationality than in the case of Russia, Chinese history is squeezed into the slavery-feudal-capitalist framework.

It would seem that China could more easily dispense with Marxism than could the Soviet Union, because the former has no important problem of multinational integration, and Chinese nationalism can effectively serve to hold society together. It is also more difficult for China than for Soviet Russia to hope that its influence or power will spread through a world socialist movement. But nationalism in the Western sense is only nascent in China, and Marxism harmonizes with the universalist tradition. It was more satisfying for Mao, the hard-pressed leader of an agrarian rebellion, to see himself as representative of a higher cause, just as he must now wish to view himself not as simply another in the endless sequence of dynastic rulers but as the initiator of a new and better form of society, changing China from a laggard to a leader in the world. Marxism bespeaks a modern, scientific creed for a people who found the barbarians to possess a new and dangerous magic called science. It upholds values useful for modernization, including the honorability of labor in a society which once esteemed long fingernails more highly, and the equality of women in a land where their feet were once deformed. Most of all, it seems, a Marxist world view forms a useful backdrop against which to sustain the authority of the Communist Party and its leader as possessors of a correct, all-embracing, systematic doctrine, a rationale as suitable for today as the Confucianist theories of the universe were for previous ages.

For such reasons, China sustains a new and important variant of Marxism. The Chinese largely lack the organized channels through which Soviet Marxism impinges on the intellectual and political life of the world, just as they lack the weight which the Soviet Union carries in international affairs. China has given up the revolutionary rhetoric of 1959–1960, when it was calling for the "world village" (the peoples of the less developed world) to envelop and overcome through guerrilla warfare their exploiters, the capitalist powers of the "world city." This was counterproductive; the independent governments of Africa and Asia saw no need for new revolutions. But China has asserted a strong (non-Marxist) role as champion of the weaker states against the superpowers, of the poor against the rich, and to some extent of the darker-skinned peoples against the whites.

As the Soviet Union lost attractiveness, becoming more obviously a stale bureaucratic, elitist, and uninspiring state, Maoism offered a new and fresher inspiration for revolution, a rebirth of Marxist spirit.[43] The Great Leap Forward was thrilling, as was the Great Proletarian Cultural Revolution; socialists saw somebody actually trying to bring utopia closer, and they responded as they did to Stalin's First Five-Year Plan. Many guessed that China had found a key to the problems of the world, or at least to those of the Third World. Although the Great Leap went down in humiliating failure and the Cultural Revolution receded, the Maoists had real achievements to their credit. The standard of living was raised at the bottom; the malnutrition, beggary, and conspicuous disease of the old China were largely or, in places, entirely eliminated. There was a real attack on bureaucratic privilege, and China was at least outwardly the most equalitarian of societies. The Maoists spoke eloquently of the self-realization and self-government of the masses, and there was no one better for the anarchist-minded to believe.

Yet the Chinese example is not a sound long-term ideological investment. It is excessively imprinted with the personality of its leader, and its legitimacy and inspiration rest largely on his aging shoulders. When he and the few remaining comrades of the Long March depart, the Chinese Revolution will probably be over. It ages irrespective of his will or actions. The China of the 1960s was much more like the Russia of the 1930s than the Russia of the 1960s; and China, if it evolves peacefully, in all probability must follow approximately the same course. Maoist equalitarianism is already eroded; the pay of an industrial manager may be fifteen times that of a beginning worker. Excitement wears off; a second cultural revolution could be only a hollow echo, no matter how necessary it might seem, after a few years of quiet, to throw the country again into a maelstrom of "class" struggle. China has not found answers to the big questions of political order in a modernizing society, and the fact cannot be permanently disguised.

MARXISM FOR THE EXTERNAL PROLETARIAT

DESPITE the utility of Marxism-Leninism for uniting and governing a country bruised by the West, Communist success has been limited. Communists have tried cunningly to ride nationalist movements to power, but the tiger of nationalism has almost invariably been the victor. Nationalism is simpler and usually closer to the heart than Communism, and even good Communists have often reacted with passion when they saw the Soviet Union using the Communist parties for its own purposes. However anti-Western they may be, revolutionaries have not wished to subordinate their countries to Russian power unless, like Fidel Castro, they perceived a greater danger elsewhere. Religion has stood in the way of Communism; unlike the Chinese, most peoples of the Third World have a strong religious orientation, and Marxism-Leninism has been unable fully to dissociate itself from atheism. The economic incapacity of the Soviet Union has also checked the spread of Marxist-Leninist rule; the nations of Africa and Latin America, for example, cannot undertake to cut themselves off from the Western-dominated world market to the extent that Mao's China could. Insofar as states like Ghana, Guinea, and Burma have attempted to institute total controls over production, the results have been discouraging. Since the early 1960s the Sino-Soviet split has injected pluralism into a movement which can really prosper only if monolithic. It seems very difficult, too, for Marxist-Leninist Communism to come to power except as a result of a major breakdown of the social order, which in our age has meant a war; it was war that brought Communism to Indochina, as it did to China.

But Marxism is a very important part of the political atmosphere almost everywhere. Its terms are part of the language of politics of the discontented, and Marxist ideas have crept into the thinking of people whether or not they consider themselves Marxists or are even aware that the accepted truths are really debatable political propositions. Those loosely called intellectuals (lawyers, students, teachers, journalists, and planners), all too often impoverished if not undernourished, are especially prone to thinking in Marxist terms. Their condition resembles that of Russian intellectual circles in the 1890s, when Marxism was a general mode of thought, not an official dogma.

Reasons for the current prevalence of Marxist and near-Marxist ways of thinking in the less developed countries are broadly similar to those which commended the Marxist outlook to the Russians of the last century—namely, unpleasant relations with the industrialized "capitalist" West, and the strains of early industrialization. Compared with the industrialized countries, whose per capita incomes are equivalent to at least $2,000, the poorer countries, most of which have income levels of $200 or less, form something like a proletariat in the original Latin sense of those who produce only children. The disparity is as great as that between capitalists and factory workers. The preindustrial countries have little stake in the world order; they are the equivalent of Marx's workers with nothing to lose but their chains. Where income levels (held down by population growth if nothing else) fail to rise or trail far behind expectations, the Marxist theory of immiseration seems painfully near the truth. Such gross inequality cries out for an explanation that restores the self-respect of the impoverished and promises them some salvation. As the Marxist hymn, the "Internationale," has it, "We have been nought, we shall be all." Utopia is nearest in dreams when furthest in reality.

The less developed countries are subject to the social strains which originally produced the emotions and attitudes of Marxism (and other nineteenth-century socialisms): disruption of the social order by commercialization; growth of the market economy, eroding self-sufficiency; beginning industrialization and urbanization for which the nation is not prepared; resentment at the rise of a new class of those powerful through wealth rather than traditional status. Western culture is like a tornado in much of Asia and Africa, tearing down everything respected and venerated; and the upsetting of the old order is harder to accept because the new is foreign and implies the inferiority of those who are driven to change their ways. Hence the hurt outcry against "cultural imperialism," and hence a degree of alienation much greater than what the young Marx found to lament. Marxism, and even more the firmer line of Marxism-Leninism, are for the insecure, semi-Westernized persons who lack status in the traditional society. The leaders are those who have received some education but not the expected rewards; the followers are the uprooted masses.

Early industrialization makes more irritating the differences among social groups, even if it does not actually increase them. Class lines are clearer in the semifeudal societies, and stabilizing middle classes are weak. Modernization gives opportunities to those in a position to grasp them and makes a new bifurcation, which may be seen as the dichotomy of capitalists and exploiters. Even something so potentially beneficent as the Green Revolution, whereby yields of principal crops such as wheat and rice have been doubled or tripled by the use of improved varieties, fertilizers, and other modern inventions, has a backlash effect. Some farmers become relatively wealthy; the poorer peasants, unable because of poverty or ignorance to apply the new methods, may fall further behind not just relatively but absolutely, as the prices they receive for their crops decline. This whole unhappy syndrome Marxism proposes to undo. Thus, the Indonesian Communists, blaming capitalism for the loss of the feudal past, promised a return to the idyllic life of the villages, with a classless society and voluntary mutual aid under a "just king." [44] Ghana's President Nkrumah saw socialism as the way to restore pristine African communalism.[45]

It is easy to blame capitalism because its spirit and institutions are foreign as is the actual ownership of factories or mines by big impersonal, international, mostly American corporations. The wealthy of the world, who are nationally, culturally, and racially alien, are the exploiters, whose wealth rests on the poverty of the less fortunate. Small, local capitalists are frequently alien, too: Chinese in Southeast Asia, Asians in East Africa, Near Easterners in West Africa. Independence requires opposing capitalists and, by extension, capitalism in the world; even native businessmen may become anticapitalist in their desire for protection from the competition of foreign producers.

If "capitalism" is a bad word, standing for something which irritates and humiliates, "socialism" is good by definition, as it was for discontented Russians of the nineteenth century. It stands for the desired social goals of justice, rational guidance of the economy, and the necessities of life for all. It implies equality for a society in which old distinctions are outworn and new ones are repugnant. It means mobilization of the people for the affirmation of the state in an era of national self-assertion. It enables the intelligentsia to identify with the people, an almost religious need. Socialism stands for state-sponsored and hence supposedly rapid and beneficially directed economic growth. Hence in India, for example, nearly all of the many parties claim to favor socialism with varying degrees of fervor.

But being socialist is almost equivalent, in the poorer countries, to being Marxist. Marxism fits their needs by showing up the evil of the rich and foreseeing their annihilation, doing away with distinctions based on property, and stressing the industrial development which is seen as equivalent to wealth and power. Even if it were not so apt, Marxism is practically the only variety of socialism which Third World leaders know anything about. Such alternatives as Gandhism are futile because they reject the machine age. In the West, which the poorer countries must admire however they may dislike it, socialism is overwhelmingly Marxist in inspiration; the few non-Marxist socialists are muted and dispassionate.

Third World socialism is not only Marxist but also predominantly Leninist in spirit and doctrine, although its proponents usually decline to surrender their independence to a Leninist organization. Before World War I there was very little Marxism in the then colonial and semicolonial world. The Russian Revolution was a beacon of inspiration and stimulus to imitation. Not long after it, the Comintern began working to export Marxism-Leninism, Communist parties, and nationalist-socialist revolution to the less developed world, the exploitation of which supposedly caused the passivity of the Western proletariats. Whereas Europe knew Marx in social democratic form before Leninism, the Third World got its Marxism in Leninist guise.[46] The Communist parties have been the auxiliaries of the Soviet state in propagandizing its form of socialism. To this day it appears that Third World Marxists read Lenin and his exegetes but seldom Marx.

Stalin's disinterest after the failure of his policies in China in 1927–1928 reduced Soviet influence in the Third World; but Khrushchev attempted to revive Lenin's universalist inspiration and goals. Since then, the Soviet Union has assiduously courted Third World countries, identifying itself with their grievances against the industrial West and supporting not only socialistic but nationalistic causes. It has dispensed economic and, more effectively, military assistance. Many thousands from the Third World have been trained in universities and party schools of the Soviet Union and its East European protectorates, either as party leaders and propagandists or as professionals, engineers, or doctors. Soviet radio broadcasting offers abundant fare, as do a multitude of Soviet publications; *Soviet Land,* for example, is put out in thirteen of India's many languages.

The audience is generally receptive to Soviet attitudes, although not usually to specific doctrines. Marxism-Leninism goes to the Third World as a faith with the flesh and bones of power: Soviet material support, plus the impressive example of Soviet greatness. Intellectuals admire the formerly backward country—tsarist backwardness is exaggerated to make it appear that semi-Westernized tsarist Russia was on a level comparable to Ghana or Burma. If now the Soviet Union can challenge the United States militarily and in space, this must be because of Marxism-Leninism and the corresponding political and economic system. The Soviet Union claims to have a guaranteed method for rapid economic growth, social welfare, education, and elimination of crises and unemployment, all priority goals for the poorer countries. Against these wonders, the defects do not seem serious. If the Soviet standard of living lags, this is no matter for countries far poorer. If the Soviet government is undemocratic, this hardly hurts in the perception of countries for which democracy seems impracticable; at least the Russian dictatorship is dressed up with revolutionary and populist rhetoric. The Russian interpretation of freedom as access to economic necessities makes sense. If Soviet foreign policy has sometimes been ruthless, Russian expansionism has at least not crossed the ocean, as European expansionism did; dominion over Europeans is not imperialism in Third World definitions. The Third World does not care much about inhumanity in general—there is too much suffering at hand—only about the inhumanity of the West.

China contributes, also, to the storehouse of Marxist thinking, while reducing the ability of the Russians to convert the penchant for Marxism into political influence. The Chinese can boast no comparable success in world politics, and their resources for economic and cultural penetration are modest; but they are fellow members of the community of the deprived and nonwhite, and they offer a potentially more appropriate model of do-it-yourself socialist construction.

By contrast, the alternatives of democratic socialism or a more or less liberal, free-enterprise economic system are at a disadvantage. No one spends hundreds of millions of dollars yearly to promote non-Marxist systems in the Third World. Western governments at best feebly advertise their cultures; and corporations go in to make money, not to advance a cause. Western societies, and especially the American, are portrayed by Western media as racked by disorder, crises, crime, and other disabilities which are seldom mentioned in connection with the Soviet Union or China. The Western political model seems to mean inefficiency and corruption, and the Western economic model promises no glorious leap but at best a gradual accretion of capital and skills under the tutelage— some would say bondage—of foreign companies. The capitalist model offers no prospect of ever outdoing the West, but only, at best, of more or less catching up in fifty or a hundred years.

The example of Japan might seem persuasive, since it has shown a higher economic growth rate than the Marxist-Leninist states, having raised itself spectacularly from economic insignificance to world prominence, and has a much higher per capita income than the Soviet Union. But the Japanese propagate no ideology, are rather diffident about their methods, and have no simple formula to be copied. The Japanese do not go to Thailand as missionaries but as (often annoying) merchants and entrepreneurs. Moreover, intellectuals of the Third World find the Japanese way antipathetic because it retains traditional elites; the discontented are eager to be rid of theirs.[47]

Against the attractions of Marxism, its logical weaknesses are not decisive. If Marxism contains some pseudoscience, the poorer countries reek with less sophisticated and less systematic pseudosciences. In many, especially those of South Asia, even persons of more or less Western education take seriously the proposition that their destinies are determined by the positions of stellar bodies at the moment that they took their first breath. Education in the Third World is seldom rigorous and empirical but instead tends to be literary-theoretical, detached from local and concrete reality, cultivating a readiness to clutch at nebulous concepts. The atmosphere is laden with credulity and superstition; not only among the ignorant but also in so-called intellectual circles, many a pleasing myth finds widespread acceptance, from the secret sterilization of Indian women by the U.S. Peace Corps in Bolivia to the CIA's training of flies for espionage in Algeria.

Universities in the Third World are usually centers of radicalism because of their inadequacy, their part-time faculties and part-time students, and their ability to arouse discontent and confusion but not to promise employment conforming to expectations. The intellectuals produced are better prepared to speculate than to judge; alienated from their own societies, they cannot fully enter the Western mental universe. Thus, with one foot in each society, they have no place to stand. Their modernism is not derived from modern life but is an ill-digested abstraction.[48] Their discontent derives especially from the unemployment or underemployment which results from lack of correlation between needs of the economy and desire for education for social advancement. There are jobs for only about a quarter of Indian university graduates. Marx, too, and Lenin became radicals while unoccupied after leaving the university.

For unhappy intellectuals, Marxism is often a revelation. The young Stalin, loose in the Transcaucasus with an incomplete seminary education, found Marxism an intellectual marvel, since proletarian socialism flowed with scientific certainty from the incontrovertible truths of dialectical materialism. As Djilas observed, "it was the most rational and most intoxicating, all-embracing ideology for me and those in my disunited and desperate land who so desired to skip over centuries of slavery and backwardness and to bypass reality itself." [49] Those who turn away from traditional religions as too primitive and conservative are not emotionally prepared to be naturalistic agnostics. In Marxism they find a dogma bespeaking rationalism and modernism, an answer to backward superstition and a shortcut to scientific understanding. It offers a new order in a time of intellectual and emotional chaos, a basically different set of first principles for those whose societies are fundamentally unsatisfactory, while it claims as its essence the "concrete analysis of concrete conditions." [50] If the doctrines of Marxism are actually fuzzy, this makes it easier for the half-educated to speak grandly, endlessly, and effortlessly of the deepest profundities.

For the insecure, Marxism-Leninism means belonging to a vast and powerful world movement. Some people, like adherents of the Cargo Cults of the Pacific and the medieval millennialisms, hope for the miracle the distressed are prone to dream. In the midst of human degradation an Indian writes of Trotsky's vision of the superior race in communism: "The average human type will rise to the height of an Aristotle, a Goethe or a Marx." And, he continues, "Heart [sic] is almost electrified with joy at the vision (scientifically arrived at and based on a historical prognosis) of the man of the future communist society portrayed above." [51]

MARXISM AS ANTI-WESTERNISM

IF the Soviet Union were dominant in world affairs, it may be reasonably supposed that the numerous weaker countries would be ruled by Marxist-Leninist parties and that their dissatisfied intellectuals, insofar as they were free to express themselves, would be seeking alternatives to Marxist-Leninist dogma. But the current situation is just the opposite. The dominant powers in the world, especially in the economic contacts which form the bulk of interactions between states, are countries which generally subscribe to the idea of an open and competitive society and to the principle of a largely profit-guided economy. Hence the many weaker countries do not have Marxist-Leninist-type governments, and their dissatisfied intellectuals generally subscribe to a philosophy contrary to economic free enterprise or capitalism. Probably the strongest and most fundamental reason for the appeal of Marxism to the less developed world, especially in the postwar period, has been its singular and unrivaled anti-Westernism.

The question of questions for the Russian intelligentsia of the nineteenth century was the relation of Russia to the West; the overwhelming issue for the intelligentsia of the non-Western world today is not inequality of classes but of nations. This is subsumed in the word "imperialism." Differences in material wealth, although less than those indicated by statistics (because the real incomes of the poor are much understated), are enormous, humiliating, and unjust by ordinary ethical standards; hardly less irksome are differences in power and prestige, and the cultural predominance of the West. The poor countries have a heritage of rage from having felt themselves for many decades at the mercy of the more powerful forces in the world, used and misused, put down and scorned. To be a nationalist in Latin America practically means to be anti-Yankee, which is almost equivalent to being anticapitalist or Marxist. As D. A. Rustow wrote, "The appeal of Communism to the Near East . . . is based almost entirely on accumulated resentment of the West, and on the example of the Russian challenge to that same

124

West." [52] This may not be strictly in accordance with the logic of Marxian class struggle, but the battles of the poor countries are held to be Marxist because they are for equality of nations. [53]

Animosity is greatest not in the poorest countries, which may have most cause for complaint, but in relatively prosperous countries with more awareness of the outside world and with societies whose traditional framework has been loosened by industrialization. In Latin America, for example, Argentina, Chile, Cuba, Uruguay, and Venezuela have witnessed especially violent anti-Yankeeism; all are well above the average Latin American income level. Kerala, the Indian state with the highest literacy rate, has been the most receptive to Communism. Africans a generation ago saw Europeans as men of a different world and had no idea of equal rights; the result was indifference and passivity. Now they have sovereign states, equal in theory but very unequal in reality; the result is frustration and resentment. Education and travel facilitate comparison, and formal status gives a basis for complaint; thus, these countries have an increasing need for an explanation of their position. The radicalism of Third World leaders often derives from shocked awareness of poverty on returning from study abroad. The West teaches the big questions but fails to furnish big answers.

Marxism legitimizes envy, resentment, and hatred of the poor for the rich, cheers and consoles the have-nots, and makes their weakness and poverty into martyrdom and virtue. It offers hope, although of decreasing convincingness, for the hopeless. Such was not Marx's idea, however. He sometimes expressed sympathy for the exploited of British India, but his concept of the Asiatic mode of production implied that the backward peoples had no future unless or until colonized and modernized by Europeans. Marx and Engels had the sense of superiority common to most Europeans of the day. Thus, Marx wrote of "Croats, Pandurs, Czechs, and similar scum" and blamed Slavs for ingratitude toward Germans "who had taken the trouble to civilize stubborn Czechs and Slovenes." He found the domination of 8 million Slavs by 4 million Hungarians sufficient evidence of the superior "vitality and energy" of the latter. [54] In connection with the war between the United States and Mexico, Engels wrote, "In America we have witnessed the conquest of Mexico, and we are happy about it. It is in the interests of its own development that it henceforth be placed under the tutelage of the United States." [55] Through the nineteenth century, Marxists generally accepted the white man's burden of civilizing the heathen.

Marxism became relevant for the poorer and precapitalist countries through the theory of imperialism grafted onto it. Originally the product of a non-Marxist, J. A. Hobson, it was fleshed out by several socialists, was taken over and politicized by Lenin during World War I, and has been expanded since World War II. Its basic contention is that certain forces inherent in the capitalistic economy drive the rich nations to dominion over the less fortunate. This may mean that the capitalists, having piled up huge surpluses from their excess profits, find themselves unable to invest satisfactorily at home; thus, they need less developed territories controlled by themselves through their governments in which to invest as a way of getting rid of wealth. Another interpretation is that the monopolists find themselves unable to sell their products at home and so want protected areas abroad as markets for excess goods. A third is that the monopolists find profits declining at home, so they must reach out to exploit the defenseless people of the weaker countries. It may also be argued that the monopolists need cheap raw materials from the poorer countries. One or more such contentions may be brought up to explain a particular situation. It is not important that these explanations themselves may be somewhat contradictory: there is no market where there is no purchasing power, and too much profit and too little profit make equally persuasive reasons for imperialism. But the simple idea is gripping: the rich are rich because the poor are poor. As a Latin American writer put it, "The fact that the proletariat that produces the great prosperity of the United States is external, living on another continent, is most important. . . ." [56]

Some remarks of Marx and Engels point toward the theory of imperialism. For example, Marx wrote in 1847 of "millions of workers condemned to perish in the East Indies in order to procure the million and a half of workpeople employed in England in the same industry, three years of prosperity out of ten." [57] But the theory is grossly contrary to the main directions of Marx's and most Marxist thought. It brings to the fore a political action, the seizure of colonies. It looks away from the idea of surplus value unless the capitalists are setting out to industrialize the colonial lands, an intention not usually credited to them. The exploitation of raw materials is not exploitation at all in a Marxist sense; only labor is exploitable. The theory of imperialism shifts emphasis from economic factors to power and sets nation against nation instead of class against class. The exploitation of one country by another fits neither the scheme

126

of historical materialism nor the Marxian analysis of capitalism. It gives the proletariat and capitalists of the imperialist country a common interest; likewise the workers, so far as there are any, and the bourgeoisie of the exploited country. It was Lenin's view that socialist revolution " 'will not be solely, or chiefly, a struggle of the revolutionary proletarians in each country against their bourgeoisie—no, it will be a struggle of all the imperialist-oppressed colonies and countries, of all dependent countries, against international imperialism.' " [58] But this is a reversal of Marxism as known before the Russian Revolution.

The theory of imperialism, commonly called Lenin's because of what he made of it, is as logically and factually weak as it is politically potent.[59] It ignores obvious realities—that capital exports before World War I did not go primarily to colonies but to independent and, to a large extent, advanced industrial countries; that Britain, the chief colonizer, did not fence off markets but had a policy of free trade; [60] that at least one major imperialist, Russia, was an importer of capital, and that some rich countries, such as Sweden, had no inclination to get colonies. The theory ignores the fact that colonies may prosper; Canada and Australia, for example, progressed mightily before gaining self-rule, and even some African and other tropical countries showed rapid economic development, according to the statistics of which Marxists are fond, while being exploited by European powers.[61] For example, India acquired a first-class railroad network under British rule. The theory ignores many motivations for expansionism which rank alongside if not ahead of the corporate balance sheet, including the urge of politicians for glory and of officials for colonial posts, of armies for fields of activity and for causes and positions to be defended, of navies for bases and excuses for enlargement, of patriots for adventure, of missionaries for promotion for their gospel, and of do-gooders for the opportunity to enlighten and uplift the benighted savages. Instead, all credit is given to the foresight of industrialists wishing to stake out markets where buying power is negligible or to invest their funds where there is little infrastructure or trained labor.

Lenin adopted the viewpoint of the generals and superpatriots that colonies were a grand thing for the nation. He also went against Marx's sensible view that the cost of administering India exceeded revenues derived from it and that Britain was burdened to provide colonial positions for the upper classes.[62] Governments painted a bright picture of the wealth to be found in poor countries in order to induce capitalists to invest in them and assist in their development; governments pressed investors to go in more than investors pressed governments. Toward the end of the nineteenth century, Germany and the United States entered the colonial race; but neither, although these were the biggest capitalist nations, acquired territories of economic value. From the point of gain and loss, the whole episode of tropical colonialism in the nineteenth century was a melancholy misadventure, the costs of control and development nearly everywhere outweighing the gains.

Nationalism and the common human weakness for asserting power are more convincing explanations for imperialism. It was the Japanese army which pushed the civilian government into Manchuria and China in the 1930s, not the great commercial houses; and no one has found evidence that Hitler was moved by investment or commercial needs to plunge into war. Likewise, the Soviet Union today probably profits very little by control over its satellites but is resolved to keep that control for military and, above all, prestige and political reasons. There was plenty of imperialism in the world centuries and millennia before capitalism became important; states which had power to do so plundered, subjugated, and possibly enslaved their neighbors.

To the contrary, maturing economies advanced in the nineteenth century from crude robbery to more responsible tutelage. In our day, states (except for noncapitalist Russia) have practically given up the idea of administering alien peoples even for their supposed benefit. Instead of scrambling ever more desperately for the last scraps of colonizable territories, as Lenin's theory required, the capitalist empires have been dissolved with very little violence, largely voluntarily and without damage to the economies of the ruling powers. The Netherlands, stripped of almost the only really profitable colonial real estate, the East Indies, has risen to new prosperity, while Japan, deprived of colonies, has performed the greatest of economic miracles. Nonetheless, the Leninist theory of imperialism, slightly retouched, has gone on to greater popularity and acceptance than in the best days of the empires.

To save the theory, colonialism has been renamed "neocolonialism," something slippery and undefinable. From Lenin's point of view, colonies were colonies, possessions to go to war over; but a "neo-colony" is little more than a country unhappy in its relation to a stronger power, most often the United States. It is no longer possible to point to colonials being commanded by the officials of a distant state, so the argument becomes more nebulous, revolving around the terms of trade, monopolistic practices, or undue influence by the capitalists. Even the contention that the supposedly sovereign governments are really subject to the hidden controls of the foreign capitalists is not very satisfactory, because the governments of the Third World very much wish to consider themselves independent and frequently make an effort to demonstrate self-will by thumbing noses, figuratively speaking, at the leading Western states.

But the failure of independence to bring the expected prosperity and glory and the persistence (sometimes increase) of material misery and relative backwardness require explanation. Since troubles earlier were ascribed to foreign domination, it must be that this domination has continued in such disguised and subtler forms as the capitalists are clever enough to devise.[63] Neocolonialism is even more dangerous than colonialism because it is more insidious. The influence of the capitalists is still present and visible in their merchandise and enterprises; wholly inspired by greed, the capitalists must be responsible for the poverty of the poorer lands. As a Guatemalan revolutionary, Luis Turcios, stated it, "I saw the misery of our peasants, the misery of our Indians, the exploitation—and behind each one of these I saw North American imperialism." [64] It is assumed that the monopolies and their governments conspire to cheat the weak. Foreign aid, too, is seen as an accessory of neocolonialism, to maintain dependence.

It is impossible to know how much reality lies behind charges of neocolonialism—that is, how much Third World countries are cheated in their dealings with the industrial countries. It is clear that corporations go into less developed countries in order to make a profit, but this does not mean that their activity may not be beneficial to the host countries. It is desirable, from a simple economic point of view, that capital, skills, and management flow to areas where they are relatively scarce; there they can exploit otherwise underutilized manpower and resources, not in the pejorative sense of meanly misusing them, but in the sense of making them productive. It is not easy to weigh returns garnered by foreign businesses in the Third World against what they may contribute to employment, taxes, the balance of payments, government coffers, and modernization. It can hardly be claimed that business in poorer countries is extraordinarily lucrative. American and European capitalists generally prefer to make large investments in developed countries, except when seeking resources located by nature, especially petroleum. No large part of the wealth of the rich countries can be drawn from the poor ones, because they do not produce enough.

The huge companies have advantages in dealing with weak and backward countries. They can shift earnings to minimize taxation, over- or undercharge for products transferred, and so forth.[65] On the other hand, sovereign governments, even though poor, have advantages of police power and can decree taxes or the hiring of nationals; the chief recourse of the multinational corporation is to threaten to withdraw. To the extent that the less developed country gets the worst of the bargain, it is probably mostly because of lack of sophistication in requiring the foreign corporation to serve national purposes even while making its profit.

Experience has shown that ownership is not equivalent to control, and contemporary governments are inhibited from rushing to the rescue of investors abroad. Gunboat diplomacy has been replaced by considerable respect for the sovereignty of states quite lacking in military power, even when these nationalize valuable properties, insult superpowers, or subsidize international terrorism. Many successful foreign businessmen in the Third World enjoy no governmental protection. In Latin America, for example, many Arabs, Jews, Italians, and Germans have made their fortunes without external help; so too have Chinese in Indonesia and Malaysia, and Indians in East Africa. Foreign corporations generally pay much better wages and treat workers with more consideration than native enterpreneurs. In most Latin American countries labor unions have consistently left Communism to the intellectuals.[66]

Irritation in the dealings of the powerful with the weak is a fact, however. Rightly or wrongly, people in the less developed countries are practically compelled to believe that they receive less than their share because they are weaker; there is no other explanation for the enormous gap between the poverty of many and the wealth of few. The gross differences cause psychological problems no matter what the conduct of the Western powers.[67] The less hospitable the social order is to modernization, the more need to admit foreign enterprises, and the greater the dislike for them. In conditions of gross inequality, any contact, from charity to robbery, is likely to be injurious to the psyche of the inferior party—and the representatives of the capitalist West in poorer countries are seldom models of tact. Experts, managers, or officials of a Western power in a developing country readily take on an elitist mentality, often leaving morals behind, ignoring sensitivities and enjoying the superiority they can hardly escape feeling. Their very presence is an insult.

Thus, effects of unequal contact are coupled with effects of modernization, giving Marxism relevance to the less developed world because it interprets the misfortune and injury of the many as the result of the greed and riches of the few. But the intellectuals of the Third World have not pursued this Marxist line on their own; they have had strong and probably indispensable support from outside. The Soviets, who have themselves been guilty of sharp practices, such as speculating in Egyptian cotton and Burmese rice, have done all they could to support the conviction that the troubles of the poorer countries are entirely due to the rapacity of the imperialists. It is at least equally persuasive that many Western intellectuals tell the world that Marxism-Leninism is essentially right; they blame their countries for the unmerited inequality in the world, speaking stridently to rouse their countrymen to take action against the unjust extremes of abundance and penury and the dangers they may pose to the international order. Radical leaders of the developing world need only cite what they learned in American or British universities.[68] In the view of Western Marxists, the theory of imperialism is to be retained, even if the facts are admitted to be dubious, because of its exceptional political utility in providing a basis for Marxist action in the less developed countries and for international socialist solidarity.[69]

For such reasons, it seems axiomatic for most intellectuals of the Third World, who generally lack historical perspective, to regard imperialism as an outgrowth of capitalism, and capitalism as potential, if not actual, imperialism. "Virtually all prominent African leaders appear to accept in varying degrees the Leninist analysis of imperialism." [70] Marxism lays bare the evil essence of Western power; it merges into nationalism, and for the radical nationalist the guilt of capitalism is unquestionable.[71] Fidel Castro expressed this well in a December 1961 speech: ". . . the more we dig deeper and uncover the bloody claws of imperialism, the miserable exploitation, the abuse they commit in the world, the crimes they commit against humanity, the more, in the first place, we feel sentimentally Marxist, emotionally Marxist, and the more we see and discover all the truths contained in the doctrine of Marxism. . . ." [72] Marxism has thus become for a large part of the world virtually equivalent to anti-Westernism. The message of *Capital* is not

131

the theory of value but the description of poverty in the West and the forecast doom of the arrogant foreigner; the downfall of capitalism signifies the rise of the precapitalistic states, and independence is to be consummated by revolution. The struggle of Latin American students or Indian peasants becomes part of a universal and surely victorious fight of idealists against the corrupt old world, and Marxism even becomes a vehicle of racial resentment.

The specific ideas of Marx—the movement of history by class struggle, the role of the proletariat, and socialism as the outcome of capitalism—could hardly be less suited to the less developed countries. But it may be that the intellectuals of developing nations who see in Marxism primarily a repudiation of the values of Western capitalist-industrial civilization are good, even excellent followers of Marx and Engels. Looking beneath the surface of the protean, multiform agglomeration called Marxism one finds again a deep ambivalence. Marx respected material progress and damned the society associated with it. He exalted technology and hated its results. This appears most vividly in the *Communist Manifesto,* in which Marx's tribute to the achievements of the bourgeoisie ("The bourgeoisie, during its rule of scarce one hundred years, has created more massive and more colossal productive forces than all preceding generations together . . . what earlier century had even a presentiment that such productive forces slumbered in the lap of social labor?" [73]) is discordant with his damnations of it ("has stripped of its halo every occupation," "unfit to rule because it is incompetent to assure an existence to its slave," "its existence is no longer compatible with society"). Marx, the Hegelian, was in favor of progress but despised the social order which was by his own analysis progressive.

Marx, like Lenin and countless other radicals, was an intellectual of an economically less developed country. England in the first part of the nineteenth century was the only industrialized land. It was the most forward, most productive, and richest nation of the world; and it was an affront to the continental countries which lagged behind, not least Marx's sleepy Rhineland. The attractiveness of Marxism for less developed countries is also appropriate historically. Marx from his youth was reacting to the breakdown not of capitalism but of the semifeudal order in a precapitalistic, unindustrialized Germany, injured by British competition. After 1815, many small textile mills and other industrial plants sank under the irresistible economic might of more advanced England; Germans complained of English penetration much as peoples of the Third World today complain of neocolonialism.[74] Marx had to both admire and hate capitalism, which meant in effect British economic power, as is shown by the curious adjunction of praise and damnation for capitalist society in the *Communist Manifesto*. The pained expressions about the damage to idyllic relations from the new commercialism are also laments for the traditional order, in the same spirit as the outcry of nationalists today against the "cultural imperialism" of the West. To combat the evil, Marx wanted a revolution in Germany, a replay of the wonderful French Revolution which would spare Germany the ills of capitalism, in the same way that the Slavophiles and Lenin wanted Russia to skip or at least greatly abbreviate the capitalist stage of development, and much as Marxists in China and other unindustrialized countries seek a shortcut to the blessed state of socialism. Marx was even prepared to claim special revolutionary capacities for the Germans because of their philosophic background and quite specifically because they were economically backward.[75] The chief difference between the Germany of 1848 and the Russia of Lenin's day was that in the latter the breakdown of the traditional order was more traumatic and the assault of commercialism, capitalism, and the West was more injurious and more of an insult—all of which makes Bolshevik extremism understandable.

Lenin, when he visited England as a young man, was pleased to observe the poverty and class differences there,[76] although these ills were much more apparent in many lands, including his own. When Engels went to England, he was so struck by the sufferings of the workers there that he forthwith wrote a book on the subject; his commentaries on the poor of Germany, who were evidently rather poorer, are missing. Marx likewise at tremendous length and with purple passion wrote about poverty in Britain, the most prosperous country in the world, with hardly a word about the deprivations and sufferings of any other people. He was saying, in effect, that cocky England with its industrial prowess wasn't so great after all. The Soviet press similarly informs its people in detail about the sufferings of workers in the leading capitalist states, while in its eyes the poverty within less developed countries is unimportant if not nonexistent.

Marx went to England because he could not express himself freely in Germany or France. But there he failed to receive the appreciation due a scholar with a German doctorate. Academically,

economically, and socially he was a nonstarter. He was never natu-
ralized, legally or spiritually, never fit into British society, and
always remained an expatriate. Not surprisingly, he scorned the
British. As Engels wrote of them, with some bitterness and envy,
"The Ango-Saxon race—these damned Schleswig-Holsteiners, as
Marx always called them—is slow-witted anyhow, and its history,
both in Europe and America (economic success and predominantly
peaceful political development), has encouraged this still more." [77]
Marx spent most of his life attacking his land of residence, which in
his day was practically equivalent to capitalism. The unspecified
"bourgeoisie" who did the great deeds and committed the crimes
laid out in the *Communist Manifesto* were the admired but annoying British. It is no wonder that his theories, distorted and twisted
for changed circumstances, appeal deeply to present-day intellectuals resentful of the preeminence of the West, and especially of
the United States. Marxism is a satisfying way of rebelling against
the leading sector of civilization.

MARXISM AS AUTHORITARIANISM

FOR the intellectuals of the less fortunate countries, Marxism gives
a framework in which to see the relation of their countries and
themselves to the advanced industrial countries. But having talked
endlessly and having convinced themselves of great truths, they
wish to act politically; often underoccupied, they seek to apply
their superior knowledge to the real world. Lawyers gravitate even
more strongly toward politics in the less developed countries than
in the United States because they are in oversupply—a legal education being prestigious—and prepared to assume authority. (Lenin,
it will be recalled, had a legal education.) Other professionals, such
as doctors and engineers, are also drawn to political action, especially in Latin America, because of the weakness of other potential
leadership groups, of aristocracy, bureaucracy, or business.[78] The
more frustrated they are, the more extremist they become, seeking
by political action to find an outlet for their energies and passions
and a role in the real world.

The intellectuals in less developed countries cannot be less
progressive than those of the most modern countries, but would be

more so; and Marxism, with more or less of an admixture of Leninism, promises them a leap into the future. Better still, it implies that this leap should be under their direction, for scientific socialism is to be built by experts. It enables leaders to combine the pursuit of power with the idealistic pursuit of social justice, to claim legitimacy for new power where old power is discredited. It sanctions tutelage over the people in the name of serving the people. Marxism is useful for power seekers and power holders in roughly the ways it served Lenin and his successors: by legitimating, uniting, isolating, and moralizing new authority amid the weakness or breakdown of more traditional means to these ends.

For those who are prepared to go along with the Moscow-led movement, the Soviet political example is at hand and Russian techniques of party rulership are ready-made. They can then hope for moral, political, and probably economic support; moreover, they have a principle of unity against the fissiparous tendencies which beset radical movements. Even if they are not prepared fully to accept Soviet leadership, proponents of change are likely to be impressed by Soviet methods and discipline as better suited to their countries than the slacker ways of the West. Their problems are more like Soviet problems: need for rapid industrialization, the potential for national disunity, and vulnerability to the politically and culturally corrosive effects of Western influences. Even if they are anti-Communist, if they are Marxists, they probably see the Soviet Union as a socialist state and correspondingly relevant for their institutions.

Marxist or Marxist-Leninist thinking joins with the Soviet example to justify the rule of a self-chosen elite which may consist of bourgeois intellectuals but has often consisted merely of men with guns. For many reasons, democracy has not thrived in the Third World; one of the few things the hundred or so nations have in common is an absence of it. Some have dabbled in it, but their limited experience has not been satisfactory. It has, moreover, a foreign odor, as of something the capitalist powers would like to fasten on client states to make them more amenable, an instrument of economic if not political domination. The word itself is good, because the people are good; but it is better to speak of "one-party democracy" or "democratic dictatorship," allegedly popular rule by a vanguard party leading not the proletariat (an idea which generally does not appeal) but the nation, the will of which is incorporated in a Sékou Touré, a Kwame Nkrumah, or a Castro.

Marxism, decreeing the primacy of economic over political institutions, rationalizes control as necessary for the welfare of the masses. "Socialism" legitimizes rule by anyone. A junta of Somali officers, making a virtue of expropriating a few banks and other businesses, calls the country a "democratic republic" and the regime "socialist," thereby raising itself above ordinary military dictatorship. The promise of redemption through political action for the masses suffices. Despite liberal traditions, Marxism makes it possible to set aside democratic imperatives. The Marxist president of Chile, Salvador Allende, stated on the eve of elections, "We will never change our program, whether we get a million votes or one." [79]

Marxism is the chief theory for full or partial state management of the economy. Transfer of the economy from private owners to official managers appeals as the substitution of rationality and direction for chaotic individualism. Only the state has the resources and purposefulness for development. [80] Private production permits profiteering and creates new privileges. [81] Socialism stands for native against foreign interests and defense of the nation in the face of neocolonialism. As Sartre put it, "In order to triumph, the national revolution must be socialist; if its career is cut short, if the native bourgeoisie takes over power, the new State, in spite of its formal sovereignty, remains in the hands of the imperialists." [82] The socialized or closely managed economy, making the people the theoretical owners and the political bosses the practical owners, suits intellectuals, for whom it is a realization of theory and a kick at capitalists; for politicians it represents power; and for bureaucrats, jobs. Marxism stands behind efforts to put people to work, to check luxury consumption in the name of equalitarianism and general welfare, and to hold back trade unions' and workers' demands for the sake of the broader class interests of the workers, thereby permitting more capital accumulation in the hands of the managing elite. Economic needs seem to preclude democracy, if this were otherwise possible; democratic socialism is problematic in the most developed countries of the West. But in the Marxist view, "bourgeois" freedoms are of little value, and the transfer of economic assets to the people, as incorporated in the vanguard, is the essence of democracy.

While rationalizing control of the economy, Marxism serves as a fitting backdrop for social change. It gives generalized sanction for an attack on traditional aristocracies and privileges, from landholders to tribal chiefs. Revolutions are made by force, and Marxism gives the leadership the self-righteousness and self-confidence necessary for coercion of the historically bypassed classes. It is in this spirit that Chilean leftists of the Allende years (1970–1973) were determined to make their partial revolution "irreversible" by the destruction of the middle classes. Marxism at the same time calls for and justifies the reshaping of mores, a process which is to correspond to the remaking of the economic order. This may mean an attack on such customs as the segregation of women, who are to be treated as equals and brought into the modern labor force. Almost all evil ways may be attributed to capitalism, deemed an immoral and foreign influence. Prostitutes were reformed in North Vietnam, it is said, by being shown that vices were the heritage of colonialism, which made people into commodities. Marxism, making the superstructure responsible to the base, authorizes the control of opinion—the exclusion of hostile class influences—which is essential for social, economic, and political transformation.

As in the case of the Soviet Union, Marxism also serves less developed countries as a cement for a shaky or synthetic natural unity and as a protective wall against disruptive external influences. Many states of Africa and Asia are split into a multiplicity of linguistic, religious, or tribal groups; a Marxist or semi-Marxist ideology may be able to override their differences and antagonisms. It is hardly fitting to attempt to exalt class over nationality, as the Russians do, but a Marxist approach at least furnishes common goals and an ideal to defend against foreign "bourgeois" influences. Various Third World leaders have raised a foreign threat to whip up unity behind their own rule—for example, Sukarno of Indonesia and Idi Amin of Uganda. In this case, the foreign danger is associated with colonialism (as in Sukarno's "confrontation" with Malaysia) or capitalist America (as in President Amin's charges of interference by the CIA).

Marxism is thus an accessory of the authoritarianism which seems unavoidable in the Third World. The fact which requires explanation is that Marxism is not very thoroughly used; these hundred-odd states have almost unanimously shied away from the political realities of Marxism-Leninism, although they may, as in the People's Republic of the Congo, have adopted many of the trappings. Even if socialistic, they do not outlaw private production in principle; they do not try to guide opinion in the Soviet way; and if they have single parties, these are not narrow elite groups but are open to all. Lenin's goal—to restore authority in a modernized form in a society dislocated and bruised, and to save the threatened unity of the state—is their goal also. Against the commercialism and individualism of the West, Marxism is the handy prophylactic. But while leaders are angered against the West, few are prepared to give up as much of indigenous values, including religion, as full-blown Marxism-Leninism requires. In the nations striving to achieve a national identity, even an artificial nationalism seems to appeal more than proletarian internationalism. They are eclectic; of Marxism-Leninism they like the theory of imperialism, the idea of party (which can be equivalent to individual) leadership, and the planned economy. The concept of class struggle, however, does not fit the less developed world, although class struggle is the lifeblood of Marxism as politics. Without an acceptable means of demarcation, such as racial difference or membership in a disliked economic class, it is probably impossible for leaderships to destroy large elements of their society. The developing nations have been more concerned to unite various groups than to set them at odds.

There has been no lack of ambitious dictators on every continent. But it has not been possible to take the idea of class warfare very seriously, and thereby to impose a Marxist-Leninist type of totally controlled state, except where the governing group has seen itself at war, or virtually at war, with powers that could be called capitalist. The war against foreign forces identified with the bourgeoisie made it possible to install in Russia, Yugoslavia, Albania, China, Vietnam, and Cambodia the full panoply of controls over the economy and public opinion, and a system of political organization as perfected by the Leninists; in the case of Cuba there were minor hostilities (the Bay of Pigs), years of "imperialist blockade," and a felt threat. Once the Marxist-Leninist state is established, it is self-maintaining, at least for a considerable period, since it has systematically eliminated all bases for opposition. But without war or its equivalent, the myth has never been compelling enough to secure real power.

VARIATIONS ON THE THEME

THE many countries of the non-Western, non–Marxist-Leninist world are diverse; they do not even share poverty, since some are, through oil, among the richest of the world. They have nothing in common but the sense of injury by the West. They not surprisingly harbor a rich diversity of interpretations or applications of the teachings of Marx. All call for socialism, but the content is variable so far as definable. Some are violent; terrorists make themselves respectable by calling themselves revolutionaries and Marxists. Palestinian guerrillas are of Lenin's professional revolutionary breed, but their tactics have usually been reprobated by Leninists. The urban *guerrilleros* of Brazil (crushed in 1969), Uruguay (repressed in 1972), and Argentina are another aberrant species.

Many are more tame. The ruling coalition in Sri Lanka (Ceylon) in 1973 joined independent Marxian Socialists, Trotskyites, and Marxist-Leninist Communists, but it took no extreme measures. An important Burmese leader once spoke of Marxism as "the same in concept" as Buddhism.[83] Brazilian Catholic bishops, without acknowledging Marx, accused the military government of multiple abuses "to guarantee the functioning of their capitalist system." They used Leninist terms in charging that "the social and economic structures in Brazil are built on oppression and injustice that evolve from a situation of a capitalism dependent on the great international centers of power." [84] Similarly, many reformist parties, such as Acción Democrática in Venezuela and APRA (Alianza Popular Revolucionaria Americana) in Peru, have taken Marxist or near-Marxist positions, while dictatorships such as that of Perón in Argentina and Getúlio Vargas in Brazil have paid the compliment of imitation with their spurious ideologies.

The variegated colors of Marxism are mostly new. Marxists in the 1920s through the 1940s generally followed the line of the Soviets or the Comintern, which was largely responsible for spreading the Marxist word, organizing, encouraging, and supporting Communist parties and related groups. The Soviet example was compelling because of its promise; and it was alone. But the defection of Yugoslavia in 1948 and the proclamation of Castro's Cuba as a Marxist-Leninist socialist state in 1961 opened the door to deviants. Yugoslavia cultivated relations with Third World nations and purveyed its independent socialism as a better model for nonaligned countries. The Castro government, despite dependence on Moscow, went its own way to exalt immediate revolution. Still more important, when China broke away from the Soviet bloc it became an impressive alternative, whose leaders seemed more innovative, action oriented, and impassioned than the graying Soviet bosses. While the new models were thrusting themselves forward, the old Soviet beacon lost much of its glow. The Soviet Union has ceased to be revolutionary and offers neither new ways nor new ideas, only power; and foreign power is often irritating to revolutionaries.

While Third World Marxism has divided into innumerable eddies, there are some common characteristics. One is that it tends to be highly emotional. Interpretations are developed more or less ad hoc for the peculiar circumstances of place or time, generally with little theoretical sophistication, as in Tanzanian President Julius Nyerere's simplification: "Karl Marx felt that there was an inevitable clash between the rich of one society and the poor of that society." [85] Books embodying the passionate but confused outpourings of a Frantz Fanon or the inconsistent arguments of a Régis Debray quickly become classics of the genre. Despite intense emotions, the convictions of Third World Marxists sometimes seem a little shallow; there is not much of the messianism of the Russian and Chinese revolutionaries. The old theory of the advantages of backwardness lurks here and there, but there is little confidence that the backward country is truly to be pioneer of the new social order.

Some theoreticians can see revolution in their own country as helping socialism everywhere; when capitalism is undercut by the defeat of neocolonialism, revolution in the advanced countries will bring universal liberation. But usually the enemy is less capitalism than imperialism, and the goal is not revolution in the old sense but liberation.[86] Latin American Marxists seem to hope not for the victory of the Soviet Union but for the defeat of the United States. Instead of class struggle, they cheer the struggle of poor versus rich nations; instead of proletarian revolution, they look to "wars of liberation" or anticolonial or anti-American violence. Guerrilla action takes the place of economic evolution; there is no faith in the automatic demise of capitalism, but joy in battling against it.[87] Exploited races as well as exploited nations take the place of the proletariat. So far as there is a relation between economic development and socialism, it is negative; the conservative working classes of the advanced countries are corrupted by complicity in the exploitation of poorer countries. In the divorce of Marxism from economics, the neo-Marxist left objects almost as much to "cultural imperialism," such as the prevalence of American television programs on the national airwaves, as to alleged economic exploitation. The affront to national dignity is the essential insult.

Communist parties gained a role in many countries by joining in the fight for independence. For example, Burmese Communists made a place for themselves first in the war against the Japanese and then in the drive for independence. But when independence was achieved the alliance of Communism and nationalism was broken. Except where the Communists were able to gain supremacy, as in China, they generally lost ground; the Marxism which appeals to less developed countries is not the Russian variety but their own.

In most of Africa, Communist parties, which were mostly started by Europeans, never had a real chance. They have remained weak or nonexistent. But neo-Marxist thinking is prevalent. States call themselves "socialist," although the share of national income controlled by the government may be smaller than in the United States or Western Europe. The People's Republic of the Congo uses a full set of symbols of socialist revolution, including a flag patterned after the Soviet model, but depends economically on French assistance.

A neo-Marxist with theoretical pretensions was Kwame Nkrumah, ruler of Ghana from its independence in 1957 until 1966. Having become acquainted with Marxism as a student in the United States and Britain, he returned to his homeland to agitate against colonial rule; in due course he became the chief leader, president, and semideified "Liberator." In several books he applied to Africa a simplified theory of imperialism, blaming this for all troubles past and present. With greater originality, he expounded in his book *Consciencism* a complete ideology of the same name. African religiosity notwithstanding, Nkrumah theoretically based his ideology on philosophical materialism, giving a long discussion of categories and concepts from Thales and Heraclitus (whose ideas of impermanence are cited as support for revolution) to Wittgenstein, apparently to establish Nkrumah's credentials as a scholar and thinker. He equated socialism with virtue and capitalism with imperialism and slavery, to be destroyed by nationalistic revolution. The inevitability of the victory of "the African Hercules," a being of higher spirituality, was proved by an elaborate pseudomathematical calculus. This parody of Marxism served fairly well. Nkrumah became a venerated despot until mismanagement, corruption, and multiple failures led to his overthrow by the military while he was touring in China.

A French West Indian revolutionary, Frantz Fanon, who espoused the Algerian fight for independence, gave a different twist to neo-Marxism. Particularly in his *Wretched of the Earth*, an eloquent book unsullied by logic, he made the colored races the proletariat and gave them the historic mission of replacing the corrupt capitalist-colonialist order.[88] "In the colonies," Fanon wrote, "the economic substructure is also a superstructure. The cause is the consequence; you are rich because you are white, you are white because you are rich. That is why Marxist analysis should always be slightly stretched every time we have to do with the colonial problem." [89] More humanitarian than Marxist, Fanon saw factory workers as a narrow "aristocracy" and was concerned instead for the truly wretched, the rural poor and the urban lumpenproletariat whom Marx scorned. He was indignant at the smashing of native cultures and social forms, and his strongest message was the catharsis of violence to purge the souls of the colonial subjects of their inferiority feelings. His motto was, "Natives of all underdeveloped countries, unite."

Fanon mixed Freud and Hegel with Marx and did not consider himself properly a Marxist.[90] On the other hand, Fidel Castro, whose doctrines are equally far from classic Marxism, for political reasons saw fit to proclaim himself Marxist-Leninist. For Castro, as for Fanon, Mao, and other Third World Marxists, the proletariat has virtually disappeared as the moving force of history, replaced by the peasants as makers of revolutions. Castroism, a hybrid of Marxism and Latin American populism, began as a middle-class, democratically oriented revolution, without support of the established Cuban Communist Party. Two years after victory it became "socialist" by its leader's fiat. For the Castroites, revolution was a military question to be solved by peasant guerrilla warfare. Its Marxian character was a matter of will; in a slightly different way from Mao, Castro wished to push his country into instant communism.

The chief ideologist of Castroism was Ernesto "Che" Guevara, an Argentine of bourgeois origin who achieved martyrdom trying to revolutionize Bolivian peasants. He wanted to declare a revolution and then bring it about by courage and violence. As he deduced from the Cuban experience:

> 1. Popular forces can win a war against the army. 2. It is not necessary to wait until all conditions for making revolution exist; the insurrection can create them. 3. In underdeveloped America, the countryside is the basic area for armed fighting.[91]

He saw the peasant desire for land as the mainspring of the struggle, and conceded in principle that popular support was necessary.[92] However, he tried to do without it in Bolivia; and when it failed to appear, he tried to mobilize it. As he wrote in his diary, ". . . the peasant base is still not being formed, although it seems that through planned terror, we can neutralize most of them; support will come later. Not one person has joined up with us . . ." [93]

The most literary exponent of Castroism and Third World Marxism is Régis Debray, a product of France's elite École Normale Supérieure. Generalizing from Castro's revolution, Debray found the city actually bad for the revolution, "a cemetery of revolutionaries and resources." [94] The true proletarian was the guerrilla fighter, while the industrial worker with a stake in society was really "bourgeois." It was not even necessary to have large-scale discontent; the revolutionary core could organize a *foco* anyway; and the guerrilla *foco* was not an instrument of the party but the center of the movement.[95] If the Communist Party failed to make the revolution, it should be set aside. Latin American Communist parties, having shown themselves impotent, were to be replaced by those who really want revolution, who are ipso facto a vanguard no matter what their social class: *"The guerrilla force is the party in embryo."* [96] There was no need for a guiding party. On the contrary, "the best teacher of Marxism-Leninism is the enemy in face to face confrontation." [97] Combat made proletarianism: ". . . a proletarian morality was already being defined and incarnated by the Rebel Army—a morality which was later to reveal itself as *also* a proletarian policy." [98] Debray thus vacated Lenin as well as Marx.

In accordance with these ideas, Castro tried to promote guerrilla insurgencies wherever possible in Latin America, thereby coming into conflict with the staid, city-based, orthodox Communist parties. The Castroites regarded the Moscow-directed Communists as gradualist cowards, while the conservative Communists regarded Castro and his crew as adventurers and spoilers. There was much bad feeling; the Bolivian Communists were even suspected of contributing to the capture and death of Guevara. But Castro abated his revolution mongering, since it failed to cause more than minor annoyance to target governments, and the Cubans had to conform to their dependence on the Soviet Union.

The common ground of anti-Americanism and general discontent was sufficient to enable both revolutionaries and moderates to join in a coalition behind Allende in Chile in 1970. Thanks to the union of the left and the split between moderates and conservatives, Allende was elected president with a little over a third of the votes cast. On this narrow basis and despite the domination of the

Congress by the opposition, he tried to bring Chile to socialism by legal or semilegal means. He had the ardent good wishes of leftists, Marxists, and Communists around the world, either because of the setback for the United States in its onetime sphere of influence or because the Allende example showed that socialism might indeed come by constitutional means.

For a few months the experiment prospered, as the Popular Unity government raised wages, nationalized foreign and Chilean-owned industries, and mobilized the workers. But because of the preference for ideological over economic goals, production sank and inflation surged wildly. Allende was making a virtue of necessity when he said, "There are things that are more important than a piece of beef or a kilo of potatoes." [99] Opposition grew; Marxists even lost control of most of the universities. The government was plagued by strikes, which it met with police action and strike-breakers. Violence sputtered, supported on one side by the CIA, on the other by Cuba and Soviet-bloc states; and it became evident that the government could not go forward by legal means. Its ideology prevented retreat, and the coalition could not sufficiently contain its radicals to compromise with moderates who desired to keep the constitutional order. Amid shortages and the virtual breakdown of the productive apparatus, the armed forces seized power and ended not only the Marxist episode but also democratic government in Chile.

The radicals were thereby encouraged to insist that the ruling class or American imperialism would not permit socialism to come peacefully, hence that violent revolution was necessary. But revolution did not seem much more promising; the years passed without successes on its scorecard. Marxism in the less developed countries struck a wall of economic reality. The Soviet Union was not itself sufficiently productive to offer much support for like-minded states, while less developed nations which tried to build socialism on their own were unable effectively to control and manage their own economies. However attractive Marxism was as an answer for problems of injustice and maldistribution of wealth, it seemed to be more slogans than program, more a basis for indignation than a blueprint for ameliorative action, more potent as a defense of national sovereignty than as a means of economic and social reconstruction.

144

CHAPTER

V

——

Marxism in
the Western World

THE MESSAGE FOR THE OVERSHADOWED

MARX did not deal with inequality except between factory workers and owners, and this he did not so much explain as describe. Nonetheless, any group which perceives its welfare or self-respect abused or threatened can express discontent in Marxist terms.

This is most clearly true of the less developed countries, and particularly of their alienated intellectuals. But degree of resentment and propensity to a radical philosophical explanation depend less on the reality of injustice than on how that injustice is perceived. Inequalities may appear larger to relatively prosperous countries; there is no simple correlation between poverty and social radicalism. Moreover, people in wealthy industrial countries may share a similar bitterness insofar as they feel their own nations and cultures to be overshadowed and dominated by America, the center of world capitalism, and their economies penetrated and presumably exploited by huge American corporations. Vexation against the American world role, against the American military, cultural, or economic presence, can breed Marxism anywhere. Of all major powers, the United States is not only the strongest and richest but also the most capitalistic in its mentality and folkways; anti-Americanism thus tends to be Marxist in tenor if not in specific content.

In the 1970s, American preeminence has been conspicuously receding. With the growth of Western Europe and Japan the American share of the world economy has shrunk; American technology is challenged; the dollar, although still in the lead, is no longer king of currencies. In world politics, the United States began a broad retreat with the winding down of its Vietnam involvement between 1969 and 1975. No longer do big American corporations seem to have the field virtually to themselves; now they jostle with European and Japanese firms, which draw their own share of hostility. No longer does it seem that American money and entrepreneurship are taking over the earth; Servan-Schreiber dramatized this danger at the time that it was beginning to ebb.[1]

However, the anti-American reaction has strongly influenced European intellectuals and will not soon disappear, even if the U.S. should become lamb-like and inoffensive. It rose in the aftermath of World War II, when the United States, a victor which had hardly shared the sufferings of the Old World, loomed so mightily over stricken Europe. However welcome the Marshall Plan, it was a balm to European self-respect to aver that American aid was basically selfish, designed to relieve the capitalist economy of unsalable surpluses or to fasten American economic dominion on the victims of the war. In the cold war, many felt that Europe was being turned to an unnecessary or at least exaggerated hostility toward the Soviet East for American purposes; the reaction to American anti-Communism was sympathy for Communist and Marxist views.

This has been most conspicuous in the case of France. American influence seemed antinational to a country attached to the grandeur of the past, independently of de Gaulle's appeals to national pride. Americanization—the flood of English expressions into the French language, the invasion of American literature and styles— was deeply offensive to French intellectuals. Marxism, mixed with the native revolutionary tradition, provided the easiest refuge.[2] As a result of the wartime and postwar experiences, the main ideas of the left, of revolution and the proletariat, became semisacred.[3]

Revival of nationalism and self-assertion in Germany likewise has implied pro-Marxism. In the first postwar decades, the prestige of victorious and subsequently helpful America, plus antagonism toward the dictatorial Marxist-Leninist regime of East Germany and its Soviet protector, sufficed to minimize Marxist tendencies in West Germany. The Social Democrats even reversed their commitment of 1891 and officially renounced Marxism in 1959, although retaining respect for the name of Marx. But by the end of the 1960s the cold war policies of negotiation from strength and the use of pressure against the division of Germany seemed to be played out; the only hope of reducing the barriers between the two parts of the German nation apparently lay in accommodation with Moscow and East Berlin. Anti-Communism appeared sterile and perhaps contrary to German national interests, as the threat of Soviet aggression or internal Communism appeared to have largely or entirely disappeared. At the same time, American prestige was reduced by the Vietnam war; America seemed no longer the noble protector of freedom but the maker of war against a small, poor country which could not possibly threaten the West. Defeat in World War II had delegitimized ruling structures in the eyes of students and intellectuals, while Marxism offered a "class" explanation of Nazism, divorcing it from German character and relieving the German nation of guilt. Hence a large part of the German intellectual establishment found itself anti-American in spirit and sympathetic to a Marxist outlook as a vindication of Germany and a declaration of independence from American tutelage. Marxism, a German tradition from its beginnings, seemed to betoken not subordination to a Russia becoming less menacing but resurgence of a Germany thinking for itself. German Marxists would have their country again playing a great role on the world stage, a consummation envisaged as possible only by dissociation from America.

Annoyance with an overbearing United States seems likewise to have been the principal stimulus for Marxist attitudes in Scandinavian universities, especially during the Vietnam war. The Russians were no apparent threat; America seemed to be the arrogant menace to cultural and economic nationhood. For Eastern European elites, resentment of American success and exasperation at being regarded as poor relations is probably one reason why Marxism continues to have considerable appeal, even when the countries have broken with the official ideology. On the other side of the world, Marxism has been a means of self-assurance for many Japanese who were irked by the long period of American control and then domination, followed by continuing dependence on the United States. The intense nationalism of yesteryear is no longer possible, and a new vocation must go counter to the strongest power impinging on Japan from overseas. Some may accept the banal effort to find a Japanese destiny in productivity; others wish at least to season this with the universalist flavor of Marxism.

When the target of protest is anti-Marxist, antisocialist, and capitalistic in orientation, protest and rebellion easily take on Marxist colors. This is true not only of groups outside American society, but also of groups within it that are or feel more or less excluded from power. American Negroes have long been remarkably deaf to the blandishments of the Communist Party because of a sound feeling that the white-led party was more desirous of using than helping them. But in the upsurge of radicalism of the late 1960s and after, a substantial fraction of black radicals sought the intellectual respectability of Marxist thought and equated racism with capitalism, seeking allies among the white majority by calling (as did the Black Panthers) for battle against "exploiters." It is non-Marxian to speak, as did Du Bois, of the Negro exploited by the white proletariat as well as by the white capitalists.[4] But there has been a strong undertone of anticapitalism in the concept of black liberation,[5] which is seen as contingent on "a movement to upset the delicate machines of corporate capitalism." [6] Conversely, the struggle against racism is seen as a precondition of the broader revolution.[7]

It is possible to relate racial discontent to Marxism on the ground that the less favored race is economically exploited, although Marx suggested no reason why colored workers should be paid less than white. The relation of Women's Liberation to Marxism is more tenuous; it should be desirable for capitalist exploiters to have women competing with men for jobs, as Marx believed, and sexes are not Marxian classes. But Engels, endeavoring to generalize, once wrote, "*The first division of labor* is that between man and woman for the propagation of children. . . . *The first class oppression* coincides with that of the female sex by the male. . . ." [8] An important aspect of socialism for Social Democrats before World War I was to release women from patriarchal dependence, which was part of the traditional (that is, capitalistic) order. The Marxist-Leninist states claim to have freed women and have certainly brought them into the labor force, including the skilled professions, although women have no more political power in the Soviet Union than in the United States. Male self-assertiveness has to do with the accumulation of property, and Marxists associate masculine domination with private ownership. Thus, the United States Socialist Workers Party blames "bourgeois" psychologists for assigning women a lower role and states (in its 1971 program) that "today the patriarchal nuclear society remains the basic economic cell of class society." In it, "obedience to the father and to the norms of the monogamous family unit help to prepare the child for acceptance of the ideology of class society." [9] As two radical women would have it, "a strategy for the liberation of women, then, does not demand equal jobs (exploitation), [but] meaningful creative activity for all; not a larger share of power but the abolition of commodity tyranny. . . ." [10] Women see themselves in a situation of inferiority, and Marxism is again called upon to account for apparent injustice.

Insofar as Marxism is associated with Women's Liberation, it is not only because some discontented women gravitate toward the teachings of Marx, but also because organized Marxist groups wish to annex any sort of protest to their cause. Similarly, some Marxists welcome homosexuals as allies. Radical presses publish Gay Liberation books, and Gay Liberation, like Women's Liberation, is hailed as an attack on the basic structure of "bourgeois" society.[11] Any fault of the so-called capitalistic society can be linked to its evidently primary institution, the private ownership of the means of production.

FAILURE OF LIBERAL CAPITALISM

MARX AND ENGELS looked to crises and the breakdown of the market economy to drive the middle classes into the proletariat and radicalize the workers to revolution. Whenever the wheels of capitalism fail to mesh properly, so that sellers cannot sell and buyers cannot fill their needs, Marx seems to have been vindicated. Unemployment, the tragic and unnecessary wastage of lives, and idle productive faculties show up basic irrationalities which are more persuasive than the logic of Marx's arguments. To prove capitalism wrong, it appears in practice, is to prove Marx right.

It was in the depression of the 1930s that Marxism penetrated the American consciousness; those years saw a flurry of books on socialism and related topics hitherto little noticed. Votes for U.S.

Communist Party presidential candidates rose from 49,000 in 1928 to 103,000 in 1932 (subsiding to 49,000 in 1940). To be mildly pro-Soviet was modish in the first administration of Franklin Roosevelt; like Russia, the United States was looking for new ways of managing the economy. A number of American labor unions became sufficiently leftist tinged to alarm conservatives; it was a novelty in American experience that unions began talking of political action on behalf of the working class.

Marx seemed in the early 1930s to have predicted what was happening in the capitalist world; many perceived Communist Russia, with booming production and a labor shortage, to be much more the way to the future than directionless capitalist America. In subsequent years, the Soviet economy looked less inspiring and the American less hopeless. But converts to Marxism have usually been moved less by economic suffering than by a sense of moral outrage, and even in times of prosperity the capitalist economy has been afflicted with many sins or shortcomings. In all countries, many of the intelligentsia are likely by temperament and outlook to be disturbed by the irrationalities and injustices which they perceive. They are, hence, at odds with the power structure, and, in the wealthy industrial countries, skeptical of capitalism and more or less pro-Marxist.

The very word "capitalism," derived from "capital," or money, has a bad odor of greed and selfishness, while "socialism" has a connotation of social (that is, unselfish) action, or organization for the benefit of society. Marxism is heir to the ancient feeling that the love of money is the root of all evil. The free enterprise economy is subject to criticism as being based on greed for possession, a more obvious evil than yearning for power; the latter is ordinarily presented as devotion to the people. Private ownership seems to imply that the goods of earth are for the grasping if not the unscrupulous, and selfish owners deny the use of wealth to the needy; milk should be for children, not for profit. Private property in land has placed huge estates in the hands of persons with no particular skill in farming; immense corporations, with power over the well-being of hundreds of thousands of people, are controlled by manipulators of paper. Capitalism invites the owners to pay their workers as little as possible and to charge as much as possible for sometimes inferior or unneeded goods; sometimes it seems that those who are most ruthless in doing so are the most rewarded. A business cannot much weigh the social effects of its policies if it is subject to competition from companies that are less inhibited. People want General Motors to think of the general welfare, but its economic imperative is to think only of the welfare of General Motors. In a sense, capitalism is, and perhaps must be, almost synonymous with lack of social vision. Business interests commonly oppose almost everything which idealists favor, from safety standards for labor to pollution controls, because they all affect the balance sheet. Those who strive to improve society almost inescapably, like Ralph Nader, run head-on against corporate interests and call government to the rescue.

Capitalism seems to mean commercialism, crass and sometimes corrupt values, the distortion of human relations whereby, as the *Communist Manifesto* put it, there remains "no other nexus between man and man than naked self-interest." It may entail political corruption of some kind or degree, as business interests use economic power to forward their interests; it may appear that the tycoons rule by wealth where the people should rule by votes. The intellectual sees himself victimized by something like the McCarthyism which swept the United States in the 1950s, or he finds American foreign policy designed to protect American business interests everywhere at the expense of the people. If cultural output is dictated solely by dollars and cents, capitalist style, one must expect more crude pandering and cultivation of grosser instincts than fine art. Capitalism seems to mean environmental problems and waste of natural resources, as each enterprise is led by the logic of its bookkeeping to make maximum use of public resources while giving minimum attention to social values.

Worst of all, perhaps, and most offensive to the sensitive, is the inequality generated by economic freedom. It is hard to argue that the inequalities of private property in any Western country correspond closely to merit or contributions to the general welfare. Wealth to a large extent generates wealth. It is the large landholder (perhaps an heir who knows nothing of farming) who is likely to be able to buy more land, the small holder who may be forced to sell, the big corporation that can swallow the little one. Corporate executives, more than any other group in Western society, set their own salaries and set them high, particularly in comparison with the earnings of journalists, professors, and the like. It is the wealthy who can best bend the laws to their benefit. Despite efforts of government to level, inequality persists even in a semisocialistic country such as England; and differences of wealth make social snobbery. Equalitarianism is the prevalent mode in the democratic countries, yet it is forever frustrated. The chief drive for socialism is not the vision of utopia but indignation at undeserved poverty amid unjustified riches.[12]

For all these vices, capitalism, and with it liberal democracy, has no better defense than that there is no better system. It stands on the unexciting proposition that it is less imperfect than the visible alternatives; but Marxism promises, vaguely, perfection. To those who feel guilty, like the Russian "superfluous men" of the nineteenth century, for consuming without producing, Marxism commends itself as the only philosophy unequivocally opposed to the established order.[13] The ideal of power for the working masses is like a beatitude ("Blessed are the poor, for they shall inherit the earth") at a time when men believe that poverty is unnecessary and may be blamed on the system.

Marxism unequivocally assigns to the less fortunate the right to a larger slice of the world's material blessings and ascribes a special virtue to them; the middle-class intellectual ("bourgeois"), sated with material goods and thereby guilty of depriving his fellow creatures, agrees that the riches of some rest on the deprivation of others. He may romanticize the manual labor antithetical to his way of life; college presidents in America sometimes take laboring jobs for spiritual renewal. Sympathy for the plight of the less developed nations deepens anger at the failure of the capitalist-dominated world system to provide a decent existence for the majority of humanity. There is a certain obscenity about the frivolous luxury of some Americans in a half-starving world—and this is a more persuasive argument for Marxism than all three volumes of *Capital*.

Outrage at the wrongs of the prevalent order merges into alienation from it, the sense of lacking a suitable place; and doubt and despair lead to Marxism.[14] Intellectuals are apt to be estranged from society and prone to generalize their plight. There is no need to be a Marxist to resent alienation, and Marx neither invented, significantly developed, nor consistently adhered to the idea. But the figure of Marx himself is suggestive; no one was more alienated from the unappreciative "bourgeois" milieu, and rejection of the world of his day was his lifelong theme. He was an excellent model for alienated intellectuals because of his unbending persistence in his life-style and because of the ultimate success which crowned his labors. Anyone who feels himself neglected or lost, at odds with contemporary values and societies, can find in Marx a kindred soul and fellow sufferer whose defiance was ultimately vindicated and rewarded. Ironically, the failure to find satisfaction in material goods nourishes Marxism in the affluent—ironically, because Marx's was a utopia of material abundance. Modern mass society is seen as industrial slavery; capitalism, with whatever abundance of material goods it may supply, so fails to inspire that intellectuals may see themselves and others as exploited and dehumanized even as they are materially satisfied.

It is the virtue of Marx in this respect to teach that the social order is the cause of woes. As individuals we are potentially perfect and not responsible for the ills about us, which are to be cured in the most agreeable of all possible ways, by casting down the covetous, selfish, and powerful. The way out is simple and alluring: smash the system. Marxism legitimizes the resentment against authority which smolders in nearly everyone.

MARXISM AS RELIGION

THE DARWINIAN revolution has done its work, and the faiths of older generations have been sadly eroded. Yet myth and mysticism are perennial; for example, America has some 200,000 astrologers divining occult meanings from the angular positions of celestial bodies. The 1970s have seen a revival of witchcraft, demonology, and Satanic cults, along with mysticism and trance. Humanity has never been really science minded, and there has been in the United States a turning away from exact or hard sciences and a disillusionment with reason: the real is hidden within us; our perceptions are distortions; happiness is to be sought not by work but by direct communication with the spiritual universe.[15] As the world becomes more baffling, the longing for simpler answers becomes more intense.

Yet science is the magician or the villain of the hour, bringing marvels from nuclear missiles and laser beams to interplanetary probes; and the new faiths are especially attractive if they are scientifically dressed and present, or can seem to present, a challenge to conventional "establishment" science. For example, astrology uses elaborate symbolism and an esoteric jargon borrowed from astronomy, genetics, and psychology. A theory that Venus was once a comet born of Jupiter, paid a visit to the earth in historic times, provided manna for the children of Israel, briefly stopped the earth's rotation, and then went on to its present orbit, all in complete defiance of the laws of mechanics and physics, has found many a true believer.[16] This hypothesis of catastrophic celestial miracles has been made popular by factors like those which have helped Marxism: the single-minded persistence of the author, his erudite citation of many more or less relevant myths, his claim to answer mysteries ranging from the causes of the ice ages to the uses of Stonehenge, and the charge of a conspiracy by the establishment to repress his audacious heresy.[17] As with Marxism, a wish fostered belief—in this case, the hope of finding confirmation of the literal truth of biblical accounts.

Rational inspirational truth is not easy to find; the phrase is perhaps self-contradictory. This age has seen devotion to inflated charismatic personalities, tin gods with resounding rhetoric, and movements such as fascism which are not only intellectually sterile but inhumane. Democratic theory is timid, unexciting, and unpromising; the troubles of the Western world result from a system which calls itself democratic. More than material poverty, confusion and anxiety make Marxists nowadays,[18] in much the same way that confusion and anxiety generated socialist thinking in Marx's day.

Marxism appeals particularly to persons—especially the so-called liberal intellectuals—who have respect for science but are not trained in exact science, who are primarily interested in ideas and have limited direct contact with reality. Marxism is simple enough to make one feel he understands it with minimal study. For the discontented it may be little more than resentment against the ruling classes. Marxism is a reductionism; all the issues of society are reduced to one principle, the basic contradiction between capital and labor, in practice between rich and poor; and the basic morality of happiness through equality is charmingly simple. This suffices. As Blumenberg notes: "For the most part, little was known of Marx's theories. But that little was enough to exert a magical power on the workers, leading them to withstand the enemy. To find comparisons for the effect of these doctrines, one has to look to the history of religion." [19] Best of all, Marxism eliminates the need to analyze how we get to the utopia of socialism and what we make of it when we get there; history, with some push from the right-minded, will take care of us.

Yet for those who wish sophistication, Marxism offers endless possibilities. Marxism is by far the most elaborate and systematic of modern ideologies; fascism, Tolstoyism, Gandhism, monarchism, and others are not in the race. Much is vague and suggestive, admirably lending itself to theory building. For example, the "negation of the negation" in itself means nothing, but an indefinite mass of meanings can be read into it. It is always a challenge to make Marx intelligible. Marxist theory or a vaguely Marxist approach is excuse enough for disquisitions in almost any branch of sociology, anthropology, or philosophy, where novelty is otherwise hard to achieve. The abstract concepts and special vocabulary lend themselves admirably to scholasticism; one can read many pages of Marx, Engels, and their followers without stumbling on a single concrete fact. Ideas of alienation, theory and praxis, will and inevitability, and the neat interlacing of thesis, antithesis, and synthesis—these all, like the magical circle from primitive communism through the long maze of class struggle to utopian Communism, fascinate the metaphysical bent of some scholars. Not surprisingly, we read that Marx's "particular blend of philosophy, history, economics, social psychology, and politics is so remarkable an achievement that most of us are only able to come to grips with fragments of it." [20]

The suppositions of Marxism are piled together to form a grand structure of definitive truth. "It works as a closed system," writes Kurt Sontheimer, "which has a broad answer for all questions, a system of thought that seems always applicable, a mental construct the inner rationality of which is linked to the irrationality of the wish for a general model encompassing all phenomena." [21] It purveys a controllable universe in which everything is related and whatever does not fit can be dismissed as unimportant.[22] It is "a complete and coherent theory, which cleared up more mysteries of the past, simplified more complications of the present, and opened up into the future a more practicable-appearing path than any such theory which had been hitherto produced" [23]—or since, it may be added. "And it is precisely the interconnection and intertwining of this threefold formulation of the problem, the economic, the social, and the ideological, that gives to Marxist ideas their singularly penetrating quality." [24] The result is sometimes marvelous: "The new light seems to pour from all directions across the skull; the whole universe falls into pattern like the stray pieces of a jigsaw puzzle assembled by magic at one stroke. There is now an answer to every question. . . ." [25]

Marxism holds the key to the answer, if not the actual answer, to all problems. It is an argument for dialectical materialism that no other theory explains everything; hence, to deny Marxism is to deny the possibility of a complete social science.[26] The Marxists can therefore comfortably take a strong and unequivocal stand on almost any issue, from American involvement in Vietnam to overthrow of the Chilean government. Thus, from a Marxist perspective, the illegal U.S. campaign practices of 1972 were a simple result of monopoly capitalism.[27] "Only by dealing with the class structure of society in the capitalist world and the system of imperialism which supports it can we in any meaningful sense provide an environment in which humankind will be able to flourish." [28]

The Marxists congratulate themselves on being scientific where conventional science is unable to tread: "But Marxists are scientists. They possess the basic principles of a science capable both of explaining and effecting social change." [29] They have a built-in advantage, because their critics are ipso facto backward apologists for the established order, not only misguided but also evil, not so much to be answered as to be "unmasked." The Marxists, however, are exempt from determinist theory, "liberated" from "bourgeois" prejudices to stand as the historically correct side. They can even enjoy the pride of sacrificing their own class interests for their ideals, claiming to be guided not by pious wishes but by objective analysis. This enables them to take over new ideas indefinitely, while "bourgeois" thinkers remain blind to Marxist truths.[30]

The best reason for belief, perhaps, has been the promise and vision of the new world, something infinitely desirable and foreordained to come, yet which men can have the glory of struggling to accomplish. Revolution means entry into the Kingdom of Heaven. Many others sang hymns to the beauties of socialism, but Marx claimed, in a union of mysticism and logic,[31] to *prove* that unhappiness would vanish. Optimism in Marx was unlimited, for "mankind always sets itself only such tasks as it can solve" [32] —a dictum the medieval alchemists would have welcomed. The dissonance between cynicism about present society and hope for the future is appealing, and the contradiction between the fated march of history and faith in human action leads to firmer dedication. Predestinarian Calvinists were the best moralizers.

Marxism offers salvation not only in the future but also in the here and now, by making life relevant and by furnishing a deeper purpose for the personality. Men need religion not only for assurances of future reward but also to relate their lives to the meaning of the universe; Marxism puts any life into the grand framework of history. Suffering becomes significant, a purification for those so unfortunate as to be of "bourgeois" origin, as society awaits the purgatory of revolution. The déclassé intellectuals have always needed an escape from loneliness and insecurity; from their beginnings in Europe, they have been believers in a cause.[33] Marxism is wholehearted, a total program, sometimes a total commitment. Isaac Deutscher confessed, "I cannot think otherwise than in Marxist terms. Kill me, I cannot do it. I may try; I just cannot. Marxism has become part of my existence." [34] It was said of Bertolt Brecht that he "was not attracted by the workers' movement—with which he was never acquainted—but by a profound need of total authority, of total submission to a total power, the immutable, hierarchical Church of the new Byzantine state, based on the infallibility of its chief." [35]

Intellectual Marxism becomes a deeper commitment (and the personality more submerged in it) when it becomes political action, as it surely must if it is taken quite seriously; Marxism is most effective when it finds expression in an organization, mixing authority with truth. The intellectual fellowship of Marxism receives firmest expression in Communist parties, the visible vanguard of the workers. Joining the Communist Party is a dramatic dedication by which the individual is incorporated into a greater being, as into an army, subordinating his will to the will and superior wisdom of the party. The mingling of faith with action (theory and praxis) is therapeutic; there is an emotional release in accepting the scriptures and higher authority, even though the supreme leader may be a Stalin. In 1920 and 1921 hundreds of thousands of European socialists, intelligent and usually skeptical observers of politics who had previously been dedicated to freedom from authority, were willing to subject themselves to the Russian-dominated Comintern and subsequently to permit themselves to be used as tools of Stalinism.

The attractions of belonging to the party may well be primary, the Marxist-Leninist ideological position coming after.* Within the fold one finds order, discipline, and certainty, as well as moral and, if necessary, economic support. The party man is part of a tremen-

---

* Whittaker Chambers gives an account of the adventure of joining the party and the trauma of divorce. See Whittaker Chambers, *Witness* (New York: Random House, 1952), p. 192.

dous worldwide organization which is sure to march indefinitely forward to the revolutionary transformation of society. Everyone has his duty and his place under the wing of the wise and powerful party, which is Marxism incorporated. For such reasons, the Marxists and the Communists have usually been more energetic and disciplined than their rivals; they have been more desirous of action and readier to subordinate their own opinions to the needs of the cause or party. Hence it has been possible for a small minority of convinced Communists to sway big unions, just as it was possible for a small Leninist party to take charge of the Russian empire.

Yet the attractions of the faith are limited. In tranquillity and relative prosperity, its message loses excitement, and questioning intellectuals fall away. It has a certain grossness, and facts cannot indefinitely be squeezed into its procrustean bed of theory. The materialistic outlook palls, and the association of truth and virtue with wage earners is not permanently satisfying to many. The idolization of the proletariat wears away in direct contact. Becoming Marxist or Communist is like falling in love, an essentially emotional commitment. One does not unlearn a great truth, but one may fall out of love. Hence Communist parties have always been suspicious of the unreliable intellectuals, although ready to use them.[36] This attitude even antedates Lenin's distrust of "bourgeois" intellectuals. Engels wrote that "one of the greatest services which the Anti-Socialist Law did us was to free us from the obtrusiveness of the German intellectual who had got tinged with socialism." [37] Sooner or later the teacher, writer, or thinker is likely to remember freedom and liberal values; hence the universities are rich with ex-Marxists.

POWER TO THE INTELLECTUALS

AROUND THE TURN of the century a Polish socialist, Waclaw Machajski, theorized that socialism represented the interests not of manual workers but of the intellectuals who would use them as a means to power, to construct a state capitalism to be run by and for the educated.[38] These ideas were soon forgotten, but they were realistic. In effect, the social function of Marxist and socialist theory is to give intellectuals a role and a mission appealing at once to idealism and ambition. For any vision of realigning the levers of society implies an elite to operate the levers. Whether or not the workers like to be told that they are being crushed down, sinking when they want to be rising, helpless when they want to be strong, the self-appointed leaders of bourgeois origin feel that they are coming to the rescue of the oppressed. The very fact that Marxism is not very attractive for workers attests to the superior insight of the intellectuals who would guide them.

Marxism is in practice less a theory of society than a claim to power: "Out of the brooding and laboring thought comes an instrument that is also a weapon in the actual world of men." [39] The initiates can tell the downtrodden that their hopes will become reality, and show the way to the New Jerusalem. One of the most pregnant of Marx's well-turned aphorisms was that "the philosophers have only interpreted the world in different ways; the point is to change it." [40] Somewhat more directly, he stated the roles of intellectuals and workers: "*Philosophy* is the *head* of this emancipation and the *proletariat* is its *heart*." [41] It is the duty of the intellectuals to mobilize: "The task of socialists' mass practice is to connect the 'little wheel' of socialist theoretical consciousness to the 'big wheel' of a political class. It is in that process that every potential Marxist socialist has the opportunity to play a decisive role in the making of future human history." [42]

Marxism is unique among philosophies for its activism and consequent relation to political power. The planned and rightly ordered society has to come under the leadership of the initiates; emphasis on theory confirms elitism. The doctrines, capable of indefinite esoteric elaboration, set off the leaders from the crowd; theory serves its masters. The moral relativism of Marxism also favors the possessors of the truths, who define the right in their own terms. Like Plato, Marxism would have philosophers be lawmakers and kings. As Stuart Chase noted in 1932, "Why should the Russians have all the fun of remaking the world?" [43]

Marxism invites the thinker and analyst to be a doer and political guide. It suggests to people who ordinarily possess no power over other persons or things that they, too, can swing their weight. The "egghead," possibly doubtful of his masculinity and relevance to the practical world, sees a way of leaping out of passivity into "instant heroism," conceivably to real power, as Lenin did. Identification with the proletariat is largely abstract, but the intellectual may delight in the idea of brawny workers marching under his com-

mand.[44] *"Communism will make a man of you."* [45] The professor
with a frustrated will to power may also thrill at the idea of violence
(which Marxism sanctions against the oppressors and for the supreme goal), even if he would shrink from the reality. Marxism sets
aside inhibitions against at least daydream vengeance for the
slights and injuries inflicted by the rich and strong upon their intellectual superiors.

It cannot be admitted that groups such as students and scholars
are really claiming power for themselves; for this reason the critique of Machajski was reprobated by socialists and cast into ob-
livion. Theories such as James Burnham's that managerial bureaucrats are the heirs of industrial society are politically sterile, as are
ideas of an engineering technocracy. The Marxist class approach in
theory completely excludes rulership by an intellectual "class."
But a substantial fraction of the highly educated may well perceive
themselves as a deprived class worthy of taking power. Aware that
they know more than the merely rich, brainworkers may convince
themselves that they should earn comparable salaries and wield
equally obvious influence. Largely excluded from high-level decision making (in the United States since the end of the Kennedy administration), subject to economic and political superiors who are
intellectual inferiors, they can feel exploited, with more to gain
than to lose from a reordering of society. They especially resent the
wealthy, whose superiority is laid to greater greed. Doing away
with the power of money means enthronement of reason. Marx was
a déclassé, resentful, unrewarded intellectual; it is not surprising
that he appeals to many vexed by status not corresponding to their
gifts.

For many Marxists, hatred for the rich and powerful seems to
be the backbone of the faith; the rest is gloss. Their purpose is not
so much, in reality, to change institutions to socialism as to overturn
elites, to reverse the peck order of society. We, the unjustly deprived, will knock down the proud rulers and take their places—as
more equitable rulers, to be sure, but in unchallenged authority.
Marxism rationalizes such a reversal; the present-day owners and
aristocrats are disqualified from improving the state, while the new
elite cannot be accused of power seeking because the basic motivations are economic and propertyless intellectuals are pure.

That Marxism is for intellectuals is not an incidental but a fundamental fact of the movement. As Plamenatz wrote, "The most
powerful ideology of our time, the Communist ideology, which

owes as much to Lenin as to Marx, is conspicuously not a class ideology. It comes closer to being an ideology of the *déclassés* who for one reason or another have come to hate the established order, or an ideology of a ruling party imposing its decisions on all social groups." [46] The logical conclusion is a frank but inexpedient call for rule by brainpower. A neo-Marxist concludes that the way of the future is not the expansion of the proletariat, so that it may take over society, but its abolition by technological progress. In that event, "neither manual workers, whatever they call themselves, nor capitalists can be the basis of a new society. It has to be based on people who use their brains." [47] Nonetheless, whatever the hopes of the intellectuals, wherever the rich have been overthrown and the means of production have been taken over by the state, the thinkers have become more the servants of the party bosses than they ever were of the capitalists.

AGAINST WAR AND FASCISM

IF it is a myth that opposition to Marxism is moved by selfish interests only, it is nonetheless true that Marxism and Communism have gained respectability and credit from the discredit of their most vocal enemies. In the late nineteenth century it was the chauvinists and militarists who most violently attacked the Social Democrats. In the interwar period the bitterest enemies of Marxism and Communism, the fascists who would allegedly save their nations from those social diseases, were their most effective friends. They made anti-Communism intellectually disreputable in many circles, and they enabled the Marxists, despite the considerable bellicosity of Marx and Engels, to present themselves as partisans of peace and friendship among peoples.

Nearly everyone in our day has claimed to be for peace, even to willingness to fight for it, but no other political movement has been able so effectively to promise peace as the Marxist. This has been a major, perhaps dominant appeal to intellectuals, who are most inclined to be internationalists and to abhor conflict. It is easy to believe that the cause of war must be the prevailing social order. Capitalism, with its disorder of ruthlessly competing—that is, warring—private interests, seems prima facie disposed to war. In practice, however, certain noncapitalistic societies, such as the nomads of Central Asia and the feudal powers of medieval Europe, have been much more conflictual than any capitalist society. When commercial societies, such as Holland of early modern times or Venice of the late Middle Ages, have engaged in war, it has been a moderate warfare for commercial (hence limited) stakes, unlike the total warfare of military states for power and dominion. The agricultural Spartans, not the commercial Athenians, were the champion warriors of classical Greece. It is a fair supposition that those who manage wars, political leaders and generals, have been most responsible for starting them, whereas merchants and industrialists are more influential in peace and prefer stability and tranquillity to the unknowns of war. In no war since Marx began to write—including the Crimean and Franco-Prussian wars, the two world wars, the Korean and Vietnam wars, plus various miscellaneous and civil wars—has there been a clear economic cause to set over political rivalries. But if one believes that the capitalists run the state, then they must be held responsible for its misuse for mass slaughter.

It was Marx's sensible view that the internationalization of capital was a deterrent to war; but modern Marxism, especially the Leninist variety, finds war inherent in capitalism. In this view, political conflicts at all levels are a reflection of economic conflicts and class struggle, so that for the abolition of war it is necessary and sufficient to abolish private ownership of the means of production. In the new era of justice and abundance, war would be an absurdity which no one could conceivably desire. By corollary, nationalism in the Marxist interpretation is a "bourgeois" phenomenon, due to fade to harmlessness in the era of socialism.

Whatever the theory, war has been more advantageous to revolutionaries than capitalists, and the young Marx and Engels took a cheerful view of the prospects of European war in the 1840s; they hoped for a grand conflagration that might promote radicalism in Germany, much as the wars of a half-century earlier had pushed the French Revolution (temporarily) to Jacobinism. In the Russia of 1917, Lenin's strongest rallying cry was immediate peace; this more than anything else led the weary soldiers to support the Bolsheviks and so made possible their seizure of power. In the West, too, many of the war-disgusted were led to Marx.[48] Max Reimann, onetime president of the German Communist Party, was converted by Lenin's call to peace.

Through the 1920s the fear of war receded; but the Bolsheviks, who were anxious for peace to restore their devastated land, made the most of pacifism. They were the most forceful advocates of nonaggression pacts and disarmament, and they embarrassed the Western powers in disarmament conferences by making striking proposals for complete disarmament and asking when the other powers were going to do more than talk about disarming. On this basis they regained much of the prestige lost through futile subversion by the Comintern.

The issue became serious with the rise of chauvinistic German fascism. The Soviets had not been notably antifascist by principle; relations with Mussolini's Italy were quite as good as those with other Western countries. But Hitler came forward as savior of Germany (and Europe) from Marxism and Bolshevism; the Communists thereby became worthy opponents of the anti-intellectual, anti-Semitic, militaristic Nazis. The languishing French Communist Party sprang to life in 1934–1935 and became for the first time a mass movement.

The Spanish civil war, beginning in 1936, was widely seen as the defense of republican freedom against the aggression of the generals, supported by the fascist dictators Hitler and Mussolini. The noninterventionist attitude of the Western democracies seemed cowardly and hypocritical; the limited assistance of the Soviet Union to the Spanish republic earned admiration, and many a young idealist risked his life for the ideals at stake in Spain, which increasingly became the ideals of Marxism.

Successive international crises, coming atop the economic depression, turned large numbers of intellectuals in Europe and some in America toward Marxism, Communism, or some degree of pro-Sovietism. For many, the old order and old ways of thought had failed; the choice must be between fascism and Communism, an idea which both fascists and Communists propagated as best they could. The choice was not difficult; compared to Hitler's *Mein Kampf* or Rosenberg's *Myth of the Twentieth Century*, Marx's *Capital* was a model not only of humane thinking but of scientific clarity. The fascists were self-proclaimed hypernationalists who glorified heroics and war; Communism was bookish, internationalist, and at least overtly progressive and pacifist. The Soviet Union was calling more emphatically than any other power for collective action to defend the peace against fascism, a call to which the leadership of the Western powers was largely deaf. Nazism became more menacing year by year, and its image was blackened by the growing persecution of the Jews, who carried their tale of troubles as refugees across the world. The far more murderous deeds of Stalin, the liquidation of millions of peasants and the purges, were screened from the outside world; to believe the scandalous reports was, in any case, to put oneself on the side of the fascists and warmongers. Almost anything was to be pardoned, in any case, on grounds of the defense needs of the workers' state. It was better to believe that someone was standing up for human decency. An intelligent man like György Lukács remained in the Communist Party, denounced his own previous views, and wrote panegyrics to Stalin because it seemed necessary in order to combat fascism. In 1938, Britain and France showed willingness to compact with Hitler at Munich, desirous, many believed, of turning Nazi expansionism against the Soviet Union; numerous intellectuals, in disgust, decided that Marx was basically right or that Marxism was the only alternative.

Stalin outraged all but unconditional adherents by his compact with the Nazi devil; by aggrandizement at the expense of Poland, the Baltic states, and Romania; and, most of all, by his war on Finland in 1939–1940. But the Soviet image as champion of peace was restored by the unprovoked Nazi attack and the hardfought defensive war. It became possible to excuse the misdeeds of 1939–1940 as necessitated by strategic needs against Nazi Germany, when the Soviet Union was the Allied power doing most of the fighting and bleeding in the contest with the fascist menace. It became respectable again in Europe (briefly in the United States) to regard the Soviet Union as a hope, perhaps *the* hope of the world.

In the time of the cold war, especially between 1947 and 1962, the Soviet Union again sought to don the mantle of peace in opposition to American bases and military alliances and the dangers of nuclear war. There were numerous Communist-sponsored "peace appeals" and Soviet disarmament proposals. Many on the Western side declined to believe that Soviet expansionism was the sole villain responsible for tensions, placing part or all of the blame on American neo-imperialism and militarism, which were explainable as outgrowths of capitalism. It was contended that capitalist—in this case, American—industry needed markets abroad which were to be kept open for exploitation by American political and military domination; moreover, the capitalist economy could avoid crises only by large military expenditures and so had to sustain international tension.

Many who were disinclined to accept such arguments became more receptive as they were repelled by the crudity and stiffness of American anti-Communism, the effort to make the United States a guarantor of any repressive regime which would certify opposition to the alleged Communist conspiracy. The United States seemed to be a world gendarme against popular movements which were a threat not to American security but possibly to corporate profits. The bipolar U.S.–U.S.S.R. confrontation took on appearances of a Marxist-type class conflict, the rich against the people on a world scale.

Fears of nuclear war contributed to openness toward Marxist-Leninist ideas. To reduce dangers of unspeakable catastrophe, it seemed necessary to come to an understanding with the Soviet Union; this meant a friendly approach to Soviet ideology, increased tolerance and a full hearing for the advocates of Soviet Marxism. Some would go further in the dilemma and accept the lesser evil: "Better red than dead."

As people grew weary of the cold war and less afraid of Communist aggression, they tended to take the Marxist world view more seriously. If there had been a danger of Russian invasion of Western Europe or of takeover by totalitarian, Soviet-backed Communist parties, this faded from sight after the 1962 missile crisis when, faced with superior U.S. power, the Soviets backed down. After Nikita Khrushchev was deposed in October 1964, his successors were much more discreet and less blustery about the inevitable victory of the Soviet way. World Communism ceased to be a monolith, fractured most seriously by the Sino-Soviet split. Many intellectuals in France, Denmark, and elsewhere came to believe that the real threat to the independence of nations was not the Soviet Union but the more powerful and visibly more expansive United States. Maybe the Marxists were right, they said, in claiming that the chief reason for the cold war was the infinite appetite of American munitions makers, supported by the compulsion of American corporations to make the whole world their oyster.

The feeling that capitalist America was more dangerous than socialist Russia rose as American assistance to South Vietnam was converted, in 1965, into large-scale participation in the war. The reaction against anti-Communism, and hence the popularity of Marxism, reached a high pitch in the United States and elsewhere throughout the Western world. It became more and more difficult, as thousands of tons of bombs turned into millions and as the desolation and slaughter dragged on, to accept the picture of powerful America fighting in Vietnam to halt a Communist monolith bent on world domination. Marxist Russia and China were not making war on a weak, preindustrial country; to the extent that people turned away in disgust from the American pretension of acting as savior of freedom through napalm, they saw idealism in the positions of the Marxist-Leninists. Antiwar movements turned into antiestablishment movements, and the conviction grew that warfare was built into the American system; hence the Marxist alternative gained acceptance as American involvement deepened and came to seem more futile. Not only did capitalist America seem morally wrong; it was impotent and presumably decadent. Anti-Communism had led into the grand mess; therefore Communism was presumably at least partly right. It was indicative of the change of American attitudes that from 1966 to 1971 the percentage of the public expressing confidence in big business dropped nearly in half (from 55 percent to 27 percent), the decline being sharpest among college graduates.[49]

By the end of the 1960s and the early 1970s, American intellectuals had come to protest strongly against what they saw as the American capitalist propensity to violence. As Herbert Marcuse had it, in disregard of the cruelties of history, "If anything has become clear in capitalism it is that purely external violence, good old-fashioned violence, is stronger than it has ever been." [50] Well-placed academics were prepared to call the United States a fascist country responsible for the world's woes, to berate technology as a cancer, to exalt the institutions of Communist states, to denounce democratic procedures as fraudulent, and to regard subversion of American institutions as liberation. In place of the myth of American spotless virtue, revisionist historians consecrated a myth of American guilt, of American imperialism for profit. This was inevitably merged into a Marxist or Leninist analysis of the failings of capitalism in the land of its greatest flowering.[51] Or the United States found itself compared by its uninhibited domestic critics with the model monstrosity of the modern world: "The society most similar to ours in this respect [institutionalization of war and racism] was that of Nazi Germany, whose massive destruction of six million Jews . . . was unparalleled in history. . . ." [52] Only a minority took such an extreme position, but it would be no exaggeration to state that Marxism permeated a substantial part of the relevant American professions, including economics, political science, and sociology. The American universities were (partly and temporarily) radicalized by Vietnam, as the French universities had been radicalized by the Algerian war a decade earlier. It was no longer true, as once appeared, that the American political mind was firmly set against Marxism.[53]

The greatest victory which the Vietnam war won for Marxism was the radicalization of a large part of a generation of American youth, those who attended universities from 1968 to 1971.[54] Youth has usually been rebellious, but students are an odd substitute for the proletariat. They issue from the elite and are due to become the elite, and few of them take much interest in the conditions of labor. With some reason, Engels had a low opinion of student radicals of his day.[55] In interwar Europe, students were perhaps the readiest of all major groups to embrace fascism. It was said in Italy in 1921 that "student youth, today in large measure composed of enthusiastic followers of fascism and supporters of its antisocialist action, in the previous generation made a large contribution of intellect and fervor to the socialist movement." [56] German students likewise joined the ranks of Hitler's followers with little dissent.[57] But where a more or less capitalistic state has been the adversary, as in Russia in the late nineteenth century, in China in the 1920s and 1930s, and in many countries of the postwar Third World, the students have been the best revolutionary "class." They have been much more energetic in opposition to the ruling powers than factory workers have been, whether because students' idealism is greater or because they have more leisure and fewer responsibilities. There is always a generational conflict to add to other grievances.[58]

After the conformist 1950s, American young people found many reasons for restiveness, from failures of the nuclear family to urban deterioration to the irrationalities of the cold war. The idea of "alienation" gained popularity; as Mario Savio, leader of the Berkeley Free Speech Movement, orated in 1964: "Somehow people are being separated off from something. . . . The students are frustrated; they can find no place in society where alienation doesn't exist, where they can do meaningful work. . . ." [59] But opposition to American intervention in Vietnam was already focusing and energizing the protest. The leading bearer of radicalization was the SDS (Students for a Democratic Society). Before 1965, SDS was a tiny organization, chiefly concerned with civil rights. In the fall of 1965, as American troop strength in Vietnam was rising rapidly, it was not yet Marxist, although it was anti-anti-Communist. But it undertook an active antiwar protest and gradually, as protest met frustration, turned more ideological and more violent. By the fall of 1966 its language was studded with Marxist terms and it was advocating socialism. "The feeling grew that what SDS lacked was a series of engraved ideological tablets along its organizational walls and a bearded nineteenth-century portrait over its hearth. And the inevitable result was a turn toward the traditional standby, Marxism." [60]

Marx promised change and action, showed up the falsity of the older generation, and offered alliance with the supposedly irresistible force of the proletariat; youthful opposition to gerontocracy is a near equivalent of opposition to wealth. Membership in SDS rose steadily from 1,000 in June 1964 to about 80,000 by November 1968.[61] By that time, SDS and many students who thought like it were talking in Marxist jargon and trying to provoke police violence to arouse revolutionary counterviolence. Around the world, too, from Tokyo to Paris, students echoed the American students' roar of indignation and added the Vietnam war and denunciation of American imperialism to local complaints; Vietnam was associated with antiquated classroom procedures in provoking the May 1968 riots which shook the French government.

As the American withdrawal progressed in 1969 and 1970 and the military draft receded, the SDS withered, but a committed core became more radical. The Weatherman faction degenerated into a cult of violence, given to such insanities as exulting over sadistic nonpolitical murders and discussing whether it might not be correct to kill white babies as potential "pigs," [62] finally winding up with the real violence of an explosion which destroyed the house in which explosives were being manufactured. But a large wedge of Marxism had been driven into the brains of millions of young Americans.

This was somewhat ironic. The Vietnam war was peculiarly poor evidence for the Marxist analysis of war and capitalism. Wealthy persons were much more apt to be dovish on Vietnam than the poor; the industrial workers were the most solid supporters of the military policies of the administration. In the Democratic primaries of 1972, affluent suburbs voted for Senator McGovern, who promised immediate and unconditional pullout. At the same time, it required a very strained interpretation to see American intervention in Vietnam as the expression of corporate or financial interests;

the American stake in Vietnam was negligible, and in all the analysis of decision making there has been no indication of intervention by business spokesmen.

Yet the issue was not logical. War is irrational, unless it can be justified in terms of supreme interests of the community; and war is harder to justify in an age of mass media which bring images of devastated villages and corpse-strewn fields into the living room. A bad war discredits the system, delegitimizes authority, and turns people toward the obvious alternative, the promise of a perfect reordering based on a systematic analysis attributed to, but perhaps only nominally following, Karl Marx.

THE WEIGHT OF POWER

MARXISM is a very special creed. A thinker may owe more or less to Plato, Kant, John Dewey, Hobbes, or Locke, but he is unlikely to lay much stock on being a true follower. One is not likely to emphasize how closely one's thought interprets Hume or Hegel; instead, even while acknowledging the debt, one will probably stress one's own improvements. Marxism is semireligious; adherence to the real meaning of Marx is seen as virtuous per se, and social radicals of diverse strains feel it incumbent to regard themselves as true Marxists. Leninists, Maoists, Social Democrats, leftish liberals, Trotskyites, and Third World rebels, however they may be at war with one another, all claim to be Marxists.

The present-day force of Marxism is to be explained less by the persuasiveness of the theory than by the power of the countries which have made it their official mythology.[63] Marxism is intellectually important and must be taken seriously in large part because it is politically important. For this reason, intellectuals must analyze it and dig out and elaborate its profundities even if they are not positively awestruck; one assumes that there must be something to a creed which has stirred so many and which nominally governs a third of the world's people.[64] Understandably, although not entirely logically, the need for knowledge about Marxist-Leninist states quickens interest in Marxist sociology.[65] Taking the doctrine very seriously usually implies accepting it as at least partly true; even for the sophisticated, the backing of great powers gives

Marxism great credence. In political affairs no argument is half so persuasive as success, and it is difficult not to be somewhat awe-struck by Marx, whatever the cogency of his analysis, because of all that has been done in his name.

It is another of the anomalies of Marxism that, while seeking to reduce politics to economic terms, it is peculiarly directed to the struggle for political power. Thus it "provides the foremost intel-lectual drama of our day, intellectual because its doctrine is used politically. For the same reason, it is the foremost political drama. In Marxism, ideas confront politics: intellectuals, politicians, pas-sions, the coldest analysis, the hottest moral considerations all meet." [66] Modern Marxism centers on the Soviet Union, and the several varieties relate to it, positively or negatively. Feelings about Marxism are inseparable from feelings about the Soviet state and other powers which claim the backing of Marx, as impressions of grandeur mingle with sympathies for the underprivileged and hopes for social revolution. Hopes of pro-Soviet Marxists rest al-most entirely on the Soviet state; even those critical of the Soviet Union as a distortion of Marxism see it as a great anticapitalist force. The general image of Marxism in the world has also been made largely by the Soviet Union, both by its example (secondarily joined by those of China and other powers) and by the torrent of propaganda flowing out of Russia for these many decades. Enthusi-asm for Lenin, Stalin, or Mao means enthusiasm for Marx.

Marxism was validated politically by Lenin's premature "so-cialist" revolution, which made Marx into the patron saint of the largest state.[67] Elsewhere, socialism was only a long-frustrated hope; in Russia the faith took on airs of reality and seemed to have found its focus. It was a great discovery. As W. E. B. Du Bois wrote in 1933: "Yet until the Russian Revolution, Karl Marx was little known in America. He was treated condescendingly in the univer-sities, and regarded even by the intelligent public as a radical agita-tor whose curious and inconvenient theories it was easy to refute. Today, at last, we all know better, and we see in Karl Marx a colos-sal genius of infinite sacrifice and monumental industry. . . ." [68] The utility of Marxist-derived ideas for revolution in disordered Russia taught the world the truth of Marxism.

Since Lenin had succeeded so brilliantly, it seemed a guaran-tee of authority for parties which had long struggled in vain now to call themselves Marxist, and a surety of success to affiliate with the Leninist party and mimic its tactics. However the conditions of

Russia in 1917 differed from those of postwar Western Europe, a large part of Western socialism placed itself voluntarily under the discipline of the Soviet-centered Communist International in 1920 and after. It was not decisive that the sins of the Soviet system— censorship, terrorism by the secret police, and the disbanding of the democratically elected Constituent Assembly—were visible from its early days. As the Webbs wrote, "Much is subsequently forgiven to a revolution which succeeds." [69]

Most nonsocialist intellectuals of the West took little note of the Russian Revolution at first because it was remote and isolated— the Entente blockade was lifted only in early 1920—and because hardly anyone believed it could maintain itself. However, the Allied intervention cast the Soviet state as a victim of aggression in a war-weary world; the Western world was impressed with the staying power of the new Soviet system. Many came to see it as the alternative to the prevalent structures of the West, a hope incarnated in political reality. Early visitors to the abysmally poor Russia of the early 1920s were caught up by the infectious enthusiasm of the Bolshevik builders of tomorrow, by the exuberant equalitarianism and dedication, the eagerness to innovate, the casting away of prejudices and distinctions—in short, by the richness of spirit in the midst of material poverty.[70] Best of all, perhaps, they saw the Soviet Union as a new order dedicated to the science of society and run not by old-time aristocrats but by people like themselves—idealists, economists, social workers, and the like.[71] Neglected in materialistic "bourgeois" society, they envied the privileges and prestige given to artists and writers in revolutionary Russia. As Trotsky put it, the leftist intellectuals became attached not to the working class but to the victorious revolution.[72] Even in England, where Marx was little regarded, British Labour Party leaders felt they could hardly attack the Soviet Union. When faults were perceived they were excused as transitory defects in what nearly everyone regarded as a workers' state, a state striving toward humanistic values.

Magnetism increased as the Soviet Union grew stronger. Stalin, a cunning man but a graceless, murderous tyrant, received more adulation from free men of Western democracies than the relatively original, idealistic, and charismatic Lenin.* Stalin's Second Revolution of collectivization and planned industrialization coin-

* For an essay on the willingness of educated people to believe power good when it claims to be good, see Caute's *Fellow-Travelers.*

cided with the onset of depression and, a few years later, with the growth of a new menace of war in Western Europe. While the capitalist industrial states were sinking into the quagmire, the Soviets were loudly proclaiming with mountains of statistics, which much of the world was believing, the superiority of the new way of planned industrialization. The high growth rate, far above any previously recorded (except perhaps the Japanese, of which few were aware), made the Soviet Union seem the wave of the future, due in fairly short order to outgrow its incompetent rivals. Negative information could be discounted as coming from "class hostile" sources; if the Stalinists were indeed employing force, was it not to set humanity free? If there were perversions, these were the fault of the West, which had failed to follow Russia into socialism and so condemned it to isolation, or of the fascist menace, which made democracy impossible in the Soviet Union.[73]

Much of what now seems to have been credulity toward Soviet pretensions was in essence indirect criticism of the regime at home. Fellow travelers, while adoring Russia from a safe distance, knew little about it except that it was different and hence supposedly better, and they had no desire to see its political institutions copied in France or Britain.[74] Their attitude was faintly like that of the French philosophes who criticized the Old Regime by idealizing the Chinese autocratic-bureaucratic system, of which they had only the vaguest knowledge and which they certainly would not want to have seen installed in their own country.

The gullibility of good minds was, in any case, phenomenal. Needing to see hope somewhere, many an idealist could persuade himself, as long as Stalin was visibly changing Russia, that the change must be for the better and could undo all wrongs. If the road is to utopia, we can bravely ignore the jolts on the way. In the language of poetry: "Yes, why do we all, seeing a Communist, feel small?/ There fall/ From him shadows of what he is building . . ./ It is the future walking to meet us all." [75] The Soviet Union was the singular incarnation of the technological and scientific spirit applied to society, with its constructive feats not only in heavy industry but in education and health. The pseudo-democratic constitution of 1936 was generally received as proof of democratic intentions if not practices; Stalin at least pretended to democracy, while Hitler ranted against it. The leading British socialists, Sidney and Beatrice Webb, declared in the mid-1930s that Stalin was a modest servant of the people, that the Soviet Union (where a hint of opposition to Stalin was virtually a death sentence) was the freest of nations, that the actions of the political police were wholly justified, that Soviet citizens enjoyed full freedom of speech, and that the promise of the future outweighed any defects of the present.[76]

Even intelligent Westerners of considerable acquaintance with the Soviet Union persuaded themselves (or permitted themselves to be persuaded) that Stalin was something close to a saint. Harold Laski and Sir Bernard Pares, an eminent historian of Russia, judged the purge trials to be quite just. Outstanding scientists bowed to Stalin as a high authority on science.[77] America, with its relative immunity to Marxism (until the 1960s), was less affected; but here, too, as *Partisan Review* put it, there was "already a tendency in America for the more conscious social writers to identify themselves with a single organization, the Communist Party. . . ." [78] The part played by Marxist theory in rallying people to the Soviet side was secondary. The contrary was usually the case: men became Marxist because of adherence to the Soviet model.[79] Stalin was able to decree mental gymnastics not only for his captive audience but for foreign Communists and a host of non-Party members as well.

The prestige of the Soviet Union as builder of a new way of life shot up to new heights in World War II, when the Soviets claimed and widely received chief credit for the defeat of fascism. Soviet victories from Stalingrad to Berlin were hailed as victories of socialism—that is, of Marxism-Leninism-Stalinism. As an American economist wrote, "it is the Soviet Union's military success in the war against Germany which more than anything else has convinced the world that socialism really works." [80] Communist parties throughout Europe earned and received enormous credit in the resistance movement, and Soviet armies expanded the area where it was imperative to subscribe (or at least pretend to subscribe) to Soviet Marxist doctrines. Farther west, "the Russian army indirectly imposed the study of Marx in France." [81] Adulation of the wonderful leader reached its zenith abroad as in Russia; for example, Nobel Prize winner Frédéric Joliot-Curie saw Stalin as a "great genius" of science.[82] Even the postwar Stalinist attack on any trace of liberalism or Western influence in Soviet literature and art (the "Zhdanovshchina") had little effect. Shortly afterward, the victory of Communism in China added a fifth of the earth's population to the Marxist-Leninist camp; it was a reasonable surmise that to be Marxist was to be on the winning side, and that one should look for the truths in the Marxist way.

In the years up to the end of the 1950s, Marxism profited by the high economic growth in both the Soviet Union and China, evident confirmation of the philosophy's effectiveness and vitality. As long as the Soviet Union and the parties which it patronized abroad seemed menacing and the United States provided economic assistance, Marxism did not prosper much in Western Europe. The death of Stalin, however, left a better-looking Soviet Fatherland of the Workers, and the loosening of the Soviet bloc broadened the Marxist rubric; Marxist thinking both in the Soviet bloc and in other Marxist-Leninist countries became more flexible and varied. There were setbacks: destalinization and bloody intervention to fasten the benefits of socialism on Hungary in 1956 shook even faithful adherents. But a Soviet sputnik initiated the space age, and Khrushchev made the most of successive feats: the first man in orbit, the first rocket to hit the moon, the first photographs of the moon's other side, and so forth. Marxism-Leninism had evidently brought a relatively backward country to the forefront of technology and power. Projecting, as usual, much more unity and purposefulness than it possessed, the Soviet Union seemed well on the way to becoming the dominant world power within a decade or two.

The real Soviet achievements were of themselves powerful arguments for Marxism-Leninism, but they were magnified and supplemented by propaganda, flooding the world with Soviet views and Marxist-Leninist ideas, approaches, and vocabulary. Organized large-scale political propaganda in peacetime is a Soviet innovation and remains a Soviet specialty. Propaganda was deemed an adjunct of war, and the Bolsheviks declared ideological war on the "capitalist" world.

From the beginning of his political career, Lenin attributed much importance to the press; in 1902 his proposal for a party newspaper was secondary only to his desire for a disciplined party. The Bolsheviks made a systematic study of the art of persuading and mobilizing the masses, and the well-supported party press contributed greatly to putting them in the lead in 1917. After gaining power, the Leninists saw themselves at first as propagandists of world revolution more than as rulers of a state. They immediately began speaking to peoples instead of governments, hoping to save themselves from the Germans by igniting the revolution smoldering there. They also hastened to publish works of Marx and his adherents, thereby starting the modern literary ascension of Marx.[83]

174

In the civil war, propaganda was a chief weapon of the Bolsheviks, who had a message and knew how to wield it.

Propaganda became an essential part of the Soviet system, the means of giving effect to ideology, a pillar of Soviet power. The Soviets shaped attitudes, negatively through stringent censorship, positively through the use of all means of communication. At all levels, the ruling party still has divisions for agitation and propaganda, commanding an army of lecturers and professional propagandists supported by a host of amateurs. Their numbers have swelled into many millions, and a large network of schools trains specialists. To this day, in Soviet literature, press, cinema, and broadcasting, there is in principle little place for the purely entertaining; everything should improve production or political outlook.

The will to propagandize abroad has not been less than at home; the logic of a universalist creed required and requires that it be spread universally. The means available abroad have been much less, but the Soviets have made full use of them. At first, the Leninists could reach the outside world chiefly through radio, and they were the first to perceive the potential of this medium. From its inception, the Soviet Union has outbroadcast all competitors. In the early 1920s the impoverished Soviets had the world's most powerful broadcasting facilities and first shortwave station. By 1942, Soviet radio beamed 400 hours weekly to the world; by 1973, 2,100 hours weekly. Directly or through Communist parties and related organizations, the Soviet Union has been responsible for a host of publications, dozens of periodicals in all major languages exported from the Soviet Union, plus a myriad produced locally in important countries. In the United Kingdom, for example, Marxism-Leninism found expression in theoretical journals and periodicals for labor, youth, teachers, and so forth, with others specializing in cultural affairs, history, international relations, and science.[84] Soviet books are sold below cost around the world; the Soviet Union also has publishers abroad to produce books for political rather than commercial value. Many a book publishable only by courtesy of the Soviet state finds its way into university libraries, if not the general marketplace. Lenin is not a very thrilling author, but as Brezhnev has pointed out, "the works of no other man have been so widely read as are those of V. I. Lenin. They have been published in 117 languages of the world. Lenin's books have been printed in hundreds of millions of copies." [85] The Marx-Engels Institute in Moscow has done much to make those writers readily available. Numerous works of Marx were first published by the Russians, and some are still available only in Soviet editions. Any student of Marx is likely to find himself working largely with Soviet-supplied texts.

There are many other means of propaganda, such as the free services of the Soviet news agency, TASS, along with Novosti, whose offerings may be welcome to impecunious newspapers of the Third World. Nearly everywhere there are associations for friendship and cultural relations with the Soviet Union, such as the Japan–Soviet Association, or the France–U.S.S.R. Association. Many a writer or potentially influential person has been given a guided tour of the Soviet land; numerous writers, wined, dined, and flattered for a week or so in Russia in the 1930s, came home to exude faith in the new Soviet world. Students go cost-free to Lumumba University in Moscow, and from time to time the Russians throw big parties, such as the 1957 World Youth Festival, which may have cost some $200 million.[86] The large majority of Communist parties abroad, supported by the Soviet Union, serve to propagandize their patrons and Marxism-Leninism.

How much the Soviet Union may have spent to spread its message abroad is pure guesswork. For 1962, direct expenditures were between $100 million and $1 billion; whatever the figure may have been, it was much increased by expenditures through various front organizations.[87] For the beginning of the 1970s there is an estimate of $2 billion yearly, involving half a million persons.[88] Marxism, Soviet-style, has been systematically forwarded and subsidized as no other doctrine in history.

Other nations, especially since the advent of the Nazis (who in this as in many other respects copied the Soviets), have engaged in image building abroad. But the stream is mostly one-way. The Communists have continued to devote a larger percentage of their resources to it than their more easygoing opponents, and they are practically compelled to do so because of the universalist nature of their ideology. They take propaganda much more seriously. They are very aware of the usefulness of names; Soviet-style Germany baptizes itself "Democratic" and other satellites call themselves "People's Republics"; not everyone will remind himself each time he uses the name that "Democratic" or "People's" is doubletalk for "dictatorial."

The Communist effort is purposeful and coherent. American books and magazines are more widespread in the world than Soviet publications, with insignificant official support; but they are as often critical as laudatory of the United States. Soviet propaganda is reinforced by a strong self-righteousness. The image is marvelously simple; the Soviet state never errs and has only minor and temporary blemishes, just as Marxism-Leninism is without fault. Soviet successes are associated with ideology; victory in war, economic growth, and victories in international sports are taken as tributes to the Soviet way and to the ideology which allegedly guides and inspires it. Soviet propaganda, moreover, is served by discrediting the "capitalist" order, a message which finds ready hearers everywhere.

Propaganda can do little without some basis in fact, and Marxist-Leninist ideas have prospered on the basis of two world wars, the Great Depression, fears of fascist aggression and, later, of nuclear war, and the Vietnam conflict. The Soviets have made the most of the issues—very largely in connection with war and fears of it—and turned them to their own benefit, thereby bringing many people to the Soviet view of world affairs. But the effects of Soviet propaganda have been much broader. Even where it has failed to make converts or to change opinions on any particular issue, it has gradually and cumulatively made Soviet and Marxist-Leninist concepts part of the intellectual atmosphere, breathed in by those opposed as well as those sympathetic to the Soviet system. Its opponents have inevitably accepted some of its premises and adopted much of its vocabulary. Such terms as "socialist" (Marxist-Leninist), "proletarian dictatorship" (instead of oligarchic or autocratic rulership), "wars of liberation," "imperialism" (in the sense of Western influence, not conquest generally), "bourgeois," "class struggle," and "capitalist" (as adequately descriptive of pluralistic societies), together with the idea of "capitalist" and "socialist" states standing in opposition on the world stage, have become common coin, accepted categories for educated discourse. Even non-Communists widely accept that the Soviet Union is somehow representative of the proletariat. Likewise, it is at least partly a Soviet achievement that many students strain to find economic causation in political affairs, and that the adjective "middle-class" has become rather pejorative in most of the world, equivalent to narrowminded and selfish instead of solid and respectable, as it implied a generation ago.

Preposterous slogans become conventional wisdom if sufficiently repeated. If a superpower were to spend hundreds of millions of dollars to promote practically any faith—for example, a modernized Confucianism—it would be taken very seriously in the world. It would represent a respectable alternative philosophy for rebellious youth, a different outlook and basis for a critique of society; writers would feel it necessary to give its proponents a hearing and to analyze its meanings in detail, finding in it ideas on which to build. Political arguments would have to take neo-Confucianist viewpoints into consideration; by habituation, if not by intellectual usefulness, its concepts and terms would suffuse the vocabulary of social studies. Any theory backed by great power has, ipso facto, validity.

Fascism furnishes a more realistic example. If Hitler had been more prudent, like the bombastic but basically fairly cautious Mussolini, and had determined to assimilate his early gains and conquer the world by propaganda, Nazi racial mysticism might well have become a major intellectual current. The scholarly resources of Germany would certainly have been able to produce racist doctrines comparable in plausibility to those of Marxism; Gobineau and Houston Stewart Chamberlain were as influential in their day as their contemporaries, Marx and Engels. Social Darwinism would be a major political philosophy, and students would diligently seek racial explanations for almost everything in history, from the rise and fall of the Roman empire to the technological backwardness of Afghanistan. Others would analyze the subtleties and deeper meanings of Nazi teachings, while still others would spend their time in refutation of racial-genetic interpretations. The scientific spirit would require weighing both sides and withholding judgment when (as often happens) the evidence is dubious.

In actuality, the Nazis repelled many by their blatant antimodernism and their exaltation of brawn and daring over brain, in contrast to the insistence of the Marxist-Leninists on being the most modern and scientific. Nonetheless, the strength and early successes of Nazism did fascinate many; not a few outside the Third Reich saw some variant of Nazi theories, crude as these were, as a "wave of the future," a cure for the woes of the liberal-democratic order. Mussolini, it was said, made the trains run on time, and Hitler gave German youth a vocation.

No one can fully separate validity from success, especially when dealing with philosophies; power engenders pious attitudes and credulity in intellectuals as well as others. Persons of great authority, from presidents to generals, are not to be judged by the standards of ordinary folk. Awe of the mighty figures largely in religion; many examples are to be found in the Psalms. It is human to find virtue in power; it is essential, oftentimes, to do so in order to harmonize reality and ideals. Emotional attachment is easier to awesome objects; as one adherent of Marxism-Leninism, Anna L. Strong, said, "If I must have a lifelong boss, let it be a big one." [89] Especially for social scientists, who are always mixing policy with knowledge, power is a mighty argument.

Since Marxist analyses and dreams are backed by a large chunk of world political power, there is some tendency, even in a strong and independent country such as the United States, to approach Marxism with at least a little piety. So far as Marxism "works" as a method of making history, it must be in some sense true.[90] Though one may believe that Lenin (and, even more, Stalin) perverted Marxism, it was a winner in Russia. Marxist slogans have proved such mighty weapons of politics and revolution that one must look for the truth in them, and even skeptical intellectuals feel they should be tolerant of Marxism because it is the state religion of so many people. Logically, one might well discount self-serving and politically useful statements. Rather than suppose a creed is true, in effect, because it is supported by a state, it would be reasonable to guess that it is propagated purposefully because it is not true in a factual sense. But few are so intellectually self-willed, and it is easy to assume that the Soviet creed is upheld because of its philosophical appeal, not just because it is a useful instrument for party rulership of the Soviet domains.

Intellectuals, concerned with ideas and words, are impressed by words. They have been commonly willing to credit the Soviet state with good intentions because it has long and loudly professed them. In politics it often happens that words speak louder than deeds. Political systems are judged by their ideologies; the capitalist-run world press has given much more space to political prisoners in ideologically conservative Brazil than to their counterparts in revolutionary Cuba, although there were thirteen times as many, in proportion to population, in Castro's prisons.[91] For many, the United States is to be judged by its bad deeds, the Soviet Union by its good intentions.

Unless there is a means of refutation, anything backed by the Soviet Union is likely to be taken seriously—for example, tales of men purportedly 150 or more years old who have all the vigor of healthy septuagenarians but who are too delicate for medical examination. The officially sponsored Soviet (or other Marxist-Leninist) view of an issue is to be at least analyzed respectfully. It demands a fair hearing; and those with faith in objectivity will give it one, although the Soviet side feels no need even to pretend to give a hearing to "bourgeois" views.* In a symposium or book of readings it is found suitable to give equal time to Soviet and Western statements, although the former are compulsorily directed toward a state-serving view and the latter may strive themselves to give a more or less balanced point of view. The "fair-minded" person will then add up the Western and Soviet viewpoints and divide by two in order to arrive at an estimate of truth.

The West is more susceptible because it is self-critical, oftentimes weary of its own achievements; and the Russians have done their best to encourage doubt and protest. The pluralistic society is unsteady, intellectually more revolutionary than Soviet society, and sometimes given to self-flagellation. In enlightened circles from San Francisco to Paris and beyond, it has long been hoped that even though appearances may be discouraging, the Soviet Union, as exponent of a different social philosophy, may represent somehow a new departure, a means to the happiness which eludes Western man—a longing, basically, for the Leninist experiment to succeed. The Soviet Union, to the contrary, considers itself engaged in permanent ideological warfare by whatever method, with stronger hopes for the destruction of the enemy fortress than for the building of its own paradise. The ideological warriors are not strong enough to win the ideological war, but they have battered the brains of their less resolute opponents.

LATTER-DAY MARXISMS

IT MAY BE a sign of both political success and intellectual decay that Marxism has become a broader movement, more diffuse and less coherent. This has been the tendency of the movement from its inception. Around 1890 it was fairly well understood what it meant to be a Marxist. Soon revisionism and revolutionism began pulling

---

* For example, *Asian Survey* gave its March 1974 issue entirely to the presentation of the Soviet viewpoint; the fifteenth edition of the *Encyclopedia Britannica* had a Soviet editor write about Soviet culture and a correspondent of Novosti Press Agency describe Soviet political institutions.

in opposite directions, as different groups reacted differently to the failure of revolution to appear. In the interwar period the Soviet state, with its officially propagated Marxism-Leninism, served as unifying center; but there remained a fundamental split between adherents of the Comintern and their rivals and opponents. The latter, too, were divided into the moderates and the more anarchistic activists.

Now the Communist movement has become polycentric, without a generally recognized fountain of orthodoxy, while the actual words of Marx are less applicable than ever to practical affairs. Reinterpretation has gone ever farther, and uncontrolled reinterpretation means divergence. The Soviet state remains the chief official support of Marxism, but the political needs of other Marxist-Leninist states are different, and their ideologies consequently deviate from the Soviet line. The Russians have been able to keep most of the Eastern European countries fairly well in line, but Poland and Hungary have shown some divergence, and Yugoslavia has long propagated independent views. Meanwhile, revolution in the Third World frequently runs against Soviet design. The Chinese, with prestige of numbers and enthusiasm, stand sharply opposed to the Soviet Union. The Soviet Union itself, although it continues to attack capitalism, has ceased to be an inspiring model. Instead of leading the way to socialist abundance, it lags in economic growth and depends technologically upon the "capitalist" West; instead of showing the way to a new social order, it has become stiffened, bureaucratic, domestically more conservative than Western states, and patently elitist. In the United States and Western Europe, increasing numbers rejected the Soviet model in the late 1960s and early 1970s, forming neo-Marxist splinter groups or joining the "New Left," which is more of a tendency or set of tendencies than a movement.

Hence, while the prestige of the name of Marx continued to rise through the 1960s, Marxism became more fragmented than ever; it was like a spreading plant which sends runners roundabout while the center withers and dies. Only the name, much of the vocabulary, and the emotions which moved Marx—desire for revolution and hatred of the ill-defined bourgeoisie—hold the diffuse tendencies together. It is held virtuous in leftist circles to revere Marx as an inspired prophet, even though one may not take seriously any specific utterances except a few slogans. There is a feeling that in order to rebel against the obvious evils and unhappiness of modern (that is, capitalist) society, one should be "Marxist"; there is, after all, no other evidently successful philosophy of revolution. If history has proved Marx's doctrines wrong, it has also proved them fruitful. People still call themselves Marxist, think of themselves as such, and use Marxist language to criticize society with little reference to the real Marx, much as people think of themselves as Christian with little reference to the person of Jesus Christ.

One can find the heart of Marxism to be logically defective, yet continue to cherish the soul. Many, such as Max Eastman and Sidney Hook, conceded the uselessness of the dialectics yet considered Marx very great and important. C. Wright Mills listed seventeen main points of Marxist thought and found them all to be unclear, misleading, or simply wrong; yet he preferred to consider himself a Marxist.[92] Laski regarded Marx's theory of value and surplus value, the central plank of his economics, as technically wrong but morally valid.[93] Radicals uninterested in the proletariat speak of Marx and ignore Bakunin, to whom they stand much nearer. Even critics who find no truth of importance in Marx and little sense in the system are rather apologetic in their estimations, conceding his greatness, finding suggestions of deep truths, and allowing that if he answered nothing he at least asked great questions. Lukács insisted that Marxism was primarily a method of proletarian revolution, independent of the truth of any or all propositions—a definition which separates Marxism from Marx, who had no particular method but claimed to have discovered great truths. Others say that Marxism must be strengthened by new methods and concepts.

Thus, Marxism becomes much less a doctrine than a phenomenon—a prophecy, or a secular religion for persons who have lost supernatural faiths. The theory of society fades into a political drive: "What remained in Marxism was the hard core of moral purpose." [94] It is an indefinite promise of human improvement, a name and rationalization for the emotions indispensable for radical action.

Consequently, Marx is credited with many great insights. For example, such a non-Marxist as Zbigniew Brzezinski sees Marxism as vital "in the maturing of man's universal vision," promoting an "intellectually rigorous method," "in its time the most advanced and systematic method for analyzing the dynamic of social development," and so on.[95] According to Alfred G. Meyer, "we are all Marxists whether we know it or not or whether we call ourselves that or not," [96] because we accept ideas of alienation and determinism in social science, although Marx neither originated not rigorously developed either concept. Scholars who cannot make useful sense of

Marx's works do not simply drop him but earnestly endeavor to find meaning behind the words. Hence Marxism is kept intellectually alive by continual revision—that is, by transformation which keeps the symbols and claims that the revision brings us closer to the "true" meaning. This may even be rather ethereal: in the preface to the 1970 edition of his *Marxism,* Meyer admits to having inadequately appreciated the poetry present in every major work of Marx, an author ordinarily thought so dry that his followers seldom read him. One does not speak of "Darwinism for our times," or of developing a purer and better Darwinism (Darwin hypothetically having turned out to be wholly wrong in his specific ideas), but of learning more about the workings of evolution. Kolakowski, for example, admitting that the actual teachings of Marxism have proved unhelpful, would put together a "better" Marxism.

One way in which modern Marxisms adjust to reality is by the more or less open abandonment of reliance on the proletariat. Marxism has always been much more for the intellectuals, a class more interested in theory and more internationally oriented than manual laborers are; but it could be assumed (as Marx did) that the working class was growing and would be the grand force for socialism and the remaking of society. Sartre could still speak somewhat mystically of "the proletariat as incarnation and vehicle of an idea," [97] and the "workers" have had a semisacred aura in the minds of many European intellectuals. The radicals of SDS in 1969–1970 felt it their duty to carry the word to the factory workers, however unattentive these were to the emissaries of another world; but the students retreated in failure. It is excessively obvious that the industrial workers are neither increasing in numbers nor suffering increased deprivation nor becoming more revolutionary in temper in industrial countries. As Marxist economists Paul Baran and Paul Sweezy concede, ". . . as monopoly capitalism develops, the demand for unskilled and semiskilled labor declines both relatively and absolutely . . ."; thus the diminishing proletarian minority becomes ever better integrated into society.[98] For the New Left, the workers in advanced countries, spoiled for revolution by the consumer society, are perhaps the most reactionary class of all.[99] In return, the factory workers tend to distrust those who would radicalize them.* The capitalists, too, have partly receded as the target, because militarists and politicians plainly share responsi-

---

* United Auto Workers President Leonard Woodcock is quoted as saying, "The workers are the victims of the social snobbery of the liberal intellectuals" (*New York Times,* August 8, 1972, p. 31).

bility for the ills of the day; the enemy becomes no particular class but the "establishment."

If the idea of revolution by the exploited proletariat must be dropped, while uprisings in the style of the French Revolution are outmoded, one might ask what remains of Marxism. Passé in its revolutionary outlook as in its economics, it would belong to history if it had not made history. Marxists must find other tools to make the new society. Lenin made his revolution by discontented middle-class intellectuals leading peasants and soldiers as well as factory workers. Neo-Marxists in the less developed countries look to peasant guerrillas, and many in industrial countries identify with them as far as possible. For such a product of civilization as Régis Debray, Marxism meant escape and the excitement, comradeship, and purity of guerrilla war. Others have seen the best possibilities in underprivileged racial groups. Herbert Marcuse and his fellow thinkers would lay hopes on the "liberal bourgeoisie," students, radical women, blacks, or perhaps any other discontented sector of society. Fanon spoke for the outcasts and racial outsiders. Some would retain the idea of the proletariat by defining this class in terms of faith instead of economic condition. There is a sort of managerial Marxism, which sets aside illusions about lower classes and sees the new class of technicians and executives as makers of the future.[100] There are also democratic Marxists, whose faith is in the people as a whole. They more or less deny most of the basics, including the immiseration of the proletariat, the increasing severity of crises in capitalism, the need for violence, and the internationalist commitment, while stressing "bourgeois" democracy and the gradual transformation to a vaguely defined socialism, which does not mean total state control of the economy. They are, of course, highly critical of the Soviet state and its politics.[101]

New variants of Marxism need new heroes and new models. The staleness of the Soviet state, its self-serving diplomacy, and its preference for stability over revolution alienate enthusiasts for revolution; although not prepared to deny that it is socialist, radicals recognize it as bureaucratic and oppressive. Trotsky and his Fourth International, Leninists who idealized the international proletariat but rejected Stalinism as a perversion have retained adherents to a remarkable extent, despite the success in 1940 of Stalin's axe man; there are Trotskyites, Trotskyite parties, and Trotskyite publications around the world. Newer figures have even more appeal. When China was preaching violence and supporting the Communists in Vietnam, Mao was idolized by many who knew little about his theories and practices. Castro, an aging but belligerent ex-student and the paragon of opposition to "American imperialism," was exalted mostly by students. Che Guevara, who died in the service of his cause, allegedly at the hands of the CIA, became a saint. Ho Chi Minh was similarly venerated. Somewhat ironically, the New Left and radical students, while calling for freedom and detesting military dictatorship, identified not with moderate Communists but with dictatorial ones who inspired not by their thoughts but by their deeds. These leaders were more symbols of self-assertion than teachers.

The so-called New Left, which between 1966 and 1972 surged like a tidal wave over American and Western European universities, was interested in action, not theory. Action was directed primarily to a specific and concrete end, opposition to American "imperialism" everywhere. This was an extension of the swing away from the cold war before 1965, and it coincided with the revisionism that blamed the United States for starting the confrontation with the peace-loving Soviet Union, spreading hundreds of military bases around the world, and allegedly making the "free world" into a sort of American empire. The chief villain was not capitalism but the "military-industrial complex," a phrase made famous by its insertion into President Eisenhower's farewell speech. The battle against American interventionism in Vietnam broadened into espousal of the cause of the developing nations, any or all of which might someday struggle valiantly against the oppressors, just as the Vietnamese people were doing with remarkable success. The guerrilleros were the heroes and the true revolutionaries. American capitalism, driven to expansion by the nature of capitalism, fed on the hunger of the poor; and American students, in revulsion at their share in the guilt, reacted against Western civilization in general.

To oppose the war, students could hold meetings, protest, and agitate pacifically; but pacific means produced no immediate results. In frustration, the New Leftists developed a cult of violence. There was no hope for the early ripening of revolution, so the radicals wanted to shock society into awareness, to bring polarization without reckoning the consequences. Socialism became the affirmation of one's humanity in the struggle for a better society.[102]

The antiwar movement was fused with other protests: civil rights, students' rights, and Women's Liberation, among others. Specific protests merged into general revolt against the unresponsive society. Since the prevalent order was so thoroughly bad and so refractory, it had to be rejected in toto; if some became revolutionaries, others withdrew to communes or simply turned inward to unconventional life-styles (hippyhood and its variants). If America was liberal, liberalism was damned as domination by the corporate establishment.[103] Rationalism was bad because it undermined activism.[104] If the extremists were tolerantly allowed to express their views, tolerance became repression, in Marcuse's famous dictum, and democracy became disguised totalitarianism. The moralistic New Left snorted at the gadget society and the "welfare state." Welfare, in fact, caused spiritual dullness and was a deterrent to the prescribed revolutionary action. When French radicals gained control of student government at the University of Strasbourg, they immediately closed the psychiatric service: students should feel their impotence and maladjustments.[105] The university was bad; manipulated by the capitalists, it had sold out to the war machine and was a training ground for servants of the establishment.[106] Since the university was the nearest thing at hand, many extremists, with the SDS in the lead, began their assault on the campus.

To reject the corrupt society was to feel alienated from it, and the New Left was happy to find in Marx a treatment, although hardly an analysis, of this beautifully foggy concept. For those who saw no prospects of proletarian revolution and had little patience for scientific socialism, this was a great discovery in the works of the celebrated philosopher. It made unhappiness from almost any cause the fault of the wrongly ordered society; for those who were bored, weary of the rat race, overwhelmed by the complexity and impersonality of industrial society, or simply disgusted with the amorality of war, "alienation" became a mark of superiority, of spiritual vocation in the midst of philistinism.[107] Contrary to Marx, the new radicals found alienation to result more from prosperity and leisure than deprivation and coercion. "Indeed, there is evidence to suggest that the more affluent society becomes and the more leisure time that workers enjoy, the more does the process of alienation take root." [108] (By this measure, Marx's communist utopia would be the most alienated of all.) In compensation, rebellious youth sought refuge in community, liberated life-styles, and meaningful work, which could mean anything from trying to tear down the old order to engaging in handicrafts.

The student movements hence found the central meaning of

186

Marx in alienation,[109] in what may be characterized as "groping efforts toward intellectual maturity." [110] However, it may be questioned whether the New Left should properly be called Marxist. Alienation does not fit the political essence of Marxism because of its implications of individual rebellion and rejection of all authority, including the theories of Marx. From the Marxist-Leninist point of view, the New Leftists were anarchistic spoilers. Althusser gave theoretical grounding for this view by rigidly separating the early from the "scientific" Marx.[111] The New Left in return blamed the Soviets for lukewarm support of North Vietnam and the Vietcong, indeed for neglecting or misusing the Third World in general. In a Soviet confrontation with American "imperialism," the New Left would side with the Soviet Union. But it would also side with those within the Soviet bloc seeking more democracy or freedom, attacking dictatorship from the perspective of Marxist "humanism." The French student leader Daniel Cohn-Bendit called his book *Leftism, the Remedy for the Senile Disease of Communism.*

If Marx turned Hegel on his head, the New Left has gone far toward upending the mature Marx. It has spoken for ethical, not scientific socialiam; decried oppression, a political concept, not exploitation; and seen change of consciousness as the cause of change of society, instead of the reverse. "Hostile to all forms of economic determinism," it would restore *"human consciousness, human subjectivity, to the heart of Marxism,"* [112] reversing Marx's achievement of making philosophy "objective."

Marxism having become the fashion in the late 1960s, it extended pseudopods, like a gigantic amoeba, in many intellectual directions. Marxism was amalgamated, chiefly at the hands of Jean-Paul Sartre, with existentialism and its condemnation of the meaninglessness of modern life. The Catholic Church, which once with reason execrated Marx as antireligious, adjusted to modern trends and turned tolerant; theologians sought dialogue with Marxism and Communism, while village priests, especially in Latin America, took up Marxist concepts and terms in speaking for their unhappy flocks. It was assumed that Marxism and Christianity both were striving for salvation, albeit in different ways. The Vatican recognized Christian values in the thoughts of Mao.[113] Although Marx and Engels had little to say on art, serious exegetes developed Marxist aesthetics.[114]

Especially interesting is the rather extensive effort to ally Marxism with Freudian psychoanalysis by a liberal interpretation of both.[115] Outwardly and logically, Marx and Freud are opposites. The one sought causation in material means of production and the social relations arising therefrom; the other looked to emotional drives, mostly those buried in the unconscious and doubly remote from the material world. Yet there is a deeper resemblance. Both developed relatively simple answers for complex issues facing modern man. Both sought to give clear and systematic or scientific interpretations, and neither adhered to scientific method or heeded the requirements of rigorous investigation. Marx based his theories on general ideas of philosophy and economics, with illustrations picked out to suit; Freud developed subjective understanding from his clinical studies, interpreted in the light of a broader model, without measurements or controls. Freud, like Marx, used undefinable concepts, such as ego, libido, and id, and built on nineteenth-century mechanisms, using psychic energy as analogous to mechanical energy. More vital, however, is the fact that both men were able expositors of shocking views, enemies of middle-class complacency, unmaskers of "bourgeois" falsity. They are the big guns of modern times directed against the bourgeoisie; hence a Marxist may feel attracted to Freud, and a Freudian may find Marx of interest, and both would find it very satisfying to bring them into harmony. For this purpose, it is possible, for example, to equate Marxian alienation with Freudian neurosis, and the exploitation of the masses with the inhibition of instinctive drives; the cause of emotional ills is "capitalist" society.[116] The psyche is to be released from repression as society is liberated from exploitation.[117]

Modern Marxism has become virtually a style of discontent—a channel for antiestablishment expression, as incapable of refutation as it is of exact formulation, and tied up in words laden with emotive meaning but nebulous in operative significance. It is most intoxicating for the youthful and idealistic; it is for wielders of words. Above all, Marxism is for those who believe they should be happy and cannot understand or forgive that they are not.

CHAPTER
VI

■

The Debt to Marx

THE LENINIST STATE

BEFORE the Russian Revolution, Marxism was of no special importance in European politics, much less Western culture. Consequently, to ask what the world owes Karl Marx (and Friedrich Engels) is mostly to assess the Russian Revolution, the effects of the Soviet Union and other Marxist-Leninist states, and the influence of their political ideas and methods on the non-Communist world. But on such matters judgments are as diverse as the judges. There are far too many unknowns to weigh; values are subjective—how is political freedom to be weighed against security of employment?—and one must thread one's way among the might-have-beens of history. We cannot guess what alternatives to Bolshevism a Russia without a tsar might have found, or what the state of Western political thought would be if there were no Marxism. But it is legitimate, or at least common practice, to weigh issues intuitively. Historians have not hesitated to assign blame or guilt to conquerors or prophets.

It is fair to give Marxism a large share of blame or credit for the events of recent generations. There is no reason to quarrel with Lenin's assertion that he had to have a revolutionary ideology to build a revolutionary party. No leader can set up a political program

189

without a basis in accepted ideas; he cannot simply invent these but has to pick them out of the intellectual environment. There was nothing around but Marxism with which Lenin could rationalize the kind of party he desired: a disciplined organization determined to turn Russia upside down. The concepts of class war and the dictatorship of the proletariat and the goal of historically determined socialism were indispensable; only on a modified Marxist basis could Lenin forge his party and equip it with what otherwise would have been the incredible effrontery to push aside all other parties and seize power in 1917. Marxism then helped Lenin to victory in the civil war, as suggested above, and gave a rationale for dictatorship. Russia could hardly have become a democracy in any event, but the self-righteousness of Marxist goals and categories made it possible to undo with remarkable rapidity the liberalizations introduced by the February revolution and to make controls stronger than under the tsars. Censorship was restored almost immediately. Terrorism was introduced against individuals in little over a month, against enemy classes within nine months after the Bolsheviks took power. Such measures rested on the claim of the Bolsheviks to represent a class which was automatically right; without such a rationalization they could not have been acceptable to the country, nor would Lenin have had followers prepared devotedly to carry these impositions out. Without Marxism, probably no Russian ruler could have conceived of total state control of the economy, without which there might be authoritarianism but not totalitarianism.

Marxism cannot be said to have dictated Soviet behavior—the Leninists took what they desired from Marx—but it facilitated Soviet actions. History offers no better example of ideology turned into a tool of despotism than Stalin's triple revolution. It became right, in a Marxist framework, to enserf the peasants in the name of progress and socialism; it became class justice to liquidate millions of those who had the temerity to oppose, or potentially might oppose, the party of the proletariat. Finally, the workers could be required to work for bare subsistence (a condition Marx had ascribed to capitalism) because the socialist purpose was guaranteed by the theory, which left the dictator free to use the means which suited him.

Economic absurdities, ruthless terror, and reversion to political primitivism under Stalin were mediated by dogma in the name of faith, destiny, and unchallengeable historical forces; it may even be stated that the excesses were intended "to prove the truth of dogma." [1] Backwardness, isolation, almost unexampled self-righteousness of the elite, and a party attuned to despotism made possible the madness of Stalin's purges. The theory of morality as class interest destroyed restraint.[2] Intelligent Bolsheviks were too imbued with the view of the party as representative of the working class, their only theoretical basis of morality, to stand against a Stalin who could manipulate party votes; and their only ambition was to continue in the career of building socialism. Hence they abased themselves, and Stalin trampled on them.

The very failure of Marxism contributed to the fearful decade of Stalinism, 1929–1939. The revolution had brought almost none of the promised glories. Unless the leaders were willing to admit that the theories were in error—which would have been to admit that their lives had been misspent and that they should bow out in disgrace—they had to lay the blame on failure to proceed strongly enough to socialization (hence collectivization and planned industrialization) and on class-hostile sabotage or personal evildoers (hence the purges).

The controls and much of the Stalinist mentality remained necessary, and with them the need for ideological justification. This pillar of the Soviet state is as essential as ever; and if the state seems at times a trifle unsure of itself, the enfeeblement of the ideological foundation seems most responsible. Ideology is primary; only with good reasons for conformity, or a framework within which persuasive reasons can be formulated, does it seem possible to maintain the regimented Soviet state. The very utopia of Marx, wherein men are to work without pay and rewards furnished by the collectivity (that is, the state), admirably lends itself to total despotism, which can use its powers to persuade people that they are free. And the Marxist replacement of political by economic categories frees the rulers from accountability.

Marxism has thus been something like a sledgehammer, helping the party to reshape Soviet society. Under its blows, the Soviet state has achieved much at great cost; we do not know whether, under less ideologically powered leadership, the cost might have been less. Growth in the last tsarist decades was proceeding apace; it was the success of industrialization which set the stage for bolshevization. Soviet growth rates were for a long time higher, even without the benefit of the foreign investment which was prominent in tsarist Russia. On the other hand, the people received little more than the satisfaction of rising graphs and self-congratulation. The standard of living, which recovered under relatively relaxed policies after the civil war to reach the prewar level in 1927–1928, sank sharply under the weight of Stalin's second revolution. It was not until well after World War II that material standards, especially for the peasant majority, climbed back to the level of forty years before. In the last decades, they have risen fairly steadily; but the standing of the Soviet Union among the nations of the world in terms of output per capita has hardly changed since tsarist days. The rewards have been so modest in relation to effort and sacrifices that one must suspect that ideology and structure have been substantially counterproductive. They have certainly been in some ways; for example, the refusal, politically motivated but Marxist rationalized, to permit small-scale private production is obviously hurtful to consumers.

The material achievements of the Soviet Union are more creditable in terms of state-furnished services, especially health and education and economic security, than in terms of consumer goods. But the promise of Marxism—and of Lenin's revolution—was much more social justice than material abundance. Inequality is less conspicuous and so less irritating than in tsarist Russia and in most nonsocialist countries. But inequality of power has been institutionalized in the rulership of a self-selecting elite, and political privilege seems increasingly to be converted into material privilege, exemplified by special stores open only to the new class.

Whatever the material achievements, the price paid has been high. Estimates of the cost in human lives vary, but tens of millions certainly perished prematurely for political reasons. Stalin is credibly held accountable for about 20 million victims in a single decade, 1929–1939, most of them casualties of the labor camps.[3] As the Soviet dissident Roy Medvedev commented, what the last tsars' political police accomplished in a year, Stalin did in a day. Under the banner of Marxism, Stalin caused suffering on a scale without historical precedent.

On the debit side must also be entered the loss of political and cultural freedom. Compared to the Soviet Union of Stalin's time or even our own, tsarist Russia in its last decade was a free country, with competing political parties and a press which, though checked by censorship, spoke out fairly freely. (*Pravda* was published in the capital beginning 1912.) Stalin left the Soviet peoples uniquely beaten and cowed. More than a decade after Stalin's death, a tiny minority was showing some revival of independent spirit; but conformism and compulsions remain strong. Nowadays, Soviet citizens are supposed to do nothing but work for the state and amuse themselves in approved ways; a person who wants to do something outside his profession, albeit nonpolitical, is reportedly suspected of psychiatric disorder.[4]

The Russian mind has been shrunken and compressed for half a century. The immediate result of the hopes and inspiration of the revolution was an outburst of creativity in the arts, producing works of some originality if little depth. But relative tolerance of divergence within a socialist framework was followed by the effort to harness art and literature to the uses of the state, and Soviet Russia became an aesthetic desert. To this day, little of interest is produced except in opposition to the regime—a situation like that of nineteenth-century tsarist Russia, except for the fact that opposition then was much easier and more rewarding. Soviet science has been much more productive than have the arts, but it too has suffered from the ideological straitjacket. Not only have semi-Marxist strictures played havoc with Soviet genetics (Lysenkoism), but other sciences, such as psychology and anthropology, have been cramped by the need to adhere to Marxist views, especially those of Engels. For example, Soviet psychologists have been tied to the Pavlovian conditioned reflex, a means of analyzing the personality strictly as a product of the environment.[5] Sociology has been narrowly limited to studies useful to the state, while philosophic thought has been prostituted. The only sensible course for Soviet citizens is to avoid unnecessary thinking, submitting to the categories and absolutes of Marxism as interpreted by the superior wisdom of the party.

Marxism-Leninism cannot escape the indictment that it has incapacitated the Soviet Union for change and reform. There is no legitimate free inquiry into essential questions of the organization and purposes of society. A self-selected rulership inevitably becomes self-serving, and there is no way within the system to renew leadership. The Soviet state has become static, the revolutionary élan worn out. Corruption has returned, and dedication has faded.

A weighing of other Marxist-Leninist countries would yield similar results: some material benefits from centralization, against the material costs of overcontrol and the psychological or spiritual costs of nonfreedom. The Soviet-controlled countries of Eastern Europe, starting from a higher level, had more to lose than the Soviet Union, and there the balance may be more negative. On the

other hand, Westerners are more leniently disposed toward
Maoism and the Chinese experiment, because the Chinese had less
to lose. If the people have become more strictly disciplined and
conformist than the Russians, the well-nourished and fairly neatly
dressed masses of today are a happy contrast to the hungry and tat-
tered people of yesteryear. Intellectually, however, China has been
even more straitjacketed than Russia. Not much is left, for better or
worse, of the cultural heritage of the Middle Kingdom. When a
would-be industrializing country can go through such aberrations
as the Great Leap Forward and the Great Proletarian Cultural Revolution and shut down its secondary and higher education for many
years, or can reserve its presses for the turgid works of Chairman
Mao, the outlook for its long-term development is not bright. China,
moreover, like the Soviet Union and other Marxist-Leninist states,
seems totally unable to come to grips with the biggest problem of
its future, the allocation of political power.

INTERNATIONAL MARXISM-LENINISM

WHATEVER the effect of Marxist ideology on the peoples of the
Communist-ruled states, the West is more immediately concerned
with its projections abroad through official state and unofficial party
policy. Soviet diplomacy has usually been prudent, although ready
to pick up gains where feasible, but this has been practically a con-
tinuation of the tsarist approach for which Marx bears not much obvious responsibility. Marxism has been conducive to some Soviet
misestimations, such as expecting attack from the capitalist democracies in the 1920s and appreciating belatedly the German Nazi
menace. Recently, Marxism has not prevented détente with the
United States and other Western powers. Yet it is an unhappy reality that ideology and/or social structure prevent any real understanding and trust between the Soviet Union or China and the chief
industrial powers (the United States, Western Europe, and Japan)
in an age when it is necessary not just to avoid combat but to cooperate effectively in meeting global problems.

The indirect, nonpolitical influence of the Soviet example has
also been ambiguous. In their proclaimed purpose of leading a
crusade for a more just society, the Russians have provided theory

and vocabulary for the discontented and have called attention to many a real evil. Soviet propaganda, although exaggerated and unfair, has spurred the conscience of the West to cope with unemployment, racial and social discrimination, and colonialism, and to accept more responsibility for alleviating poverty. Particularly in the period when Khrushchev boasted of burying the West by surpassing it, Soviet competition has stimulated the West to improve education and economic growth. It is salutary to have a sharp critic ready to call the attention of the world to shortcomings. On the other hand, the Soviet example of intolerance, repression, and falsification may be assumed to have been poisonous, however difficult to assess; the actions of a great power are never without effect, especially on those compelled by military realities to be respectful of it.

Regarding the ideological impact of the Soviet state upon the West—the sponsorship of Leninist-style political parties to work for power or to destroy the "bourgeois" social system—it is easier to reach a negative appraisal. It is inherently unlikely that the intromission of the politics of a semibackward empire, although made possible by an originally Western creed, would be helpful for Western society and civilization. Nor are many Communists likely to claim that their parties' have helped the West. That has not been their purpose; and their achievements, so far as they count any, have been toward either gaining power for themselves or helping their patron state by hurting its rivals. A good Communist cannot favor anything which helps the industrial nations to reform or improve their societies, achieve social harmony, or make "bourgeois" democracy a reality. There is no reason, aside from propagandistic or opportunistic considerations, for revolutionary Marxists to cooperate in any civic endeavor or to do anything toward alleviation of sufferings or raising the satisfactions of the "bourgeois" way of life. And if any group strives mightily and persistently to thrust staves in the spokes of the social order, it cannot fail to do damage.

Marxists have usually not been so consistent in devotion to theory. Marx and Engels themselves on occasion welcomed reforms which could only make revolution less likely, and their followers in Western Europe became increasingly disposed to regard the overthrow of the social order as a nice dream. But the action-oriented Leninists scoffed at any improvements which did not bring the revolution nearer. Consequently, the first effect of the formation of the Comintern in the beginning of the 1920s was to split the Social Democratic or leftist parties of the West and to thrust into their politics a struggle of Communists versus moderates which detracted from and often overshadowed the struggle for reformist socialism or improvement of the workers. By insistence on his Twenty-one Conditions, Lenin made sure that the new Communist parties would be authoritarian, subversive, and Russian dominated—that is, foreign oriented in their homelands. For Lenin, obedience was more important than truth, indeed, more important than effectiveness; better a weak but subservient party than a stronger but independent one. Failures led Lenin only to demand more discipline, purges, and stricter obedience to his unsuitable model. Yet because of the attractiveness of a real revolution and a program of action, the Communist parties drained activists, especially young ones, away from the socialist parties, leaving them staid and unimaginative.

The chief business of the Communist parties was to fight and discredit the socialists, those who rejected Leninist and Russian leadership, and to destroy them as competitors for the loyalty of the laboring masses. This struggle was moderated in line with the ideological retreat of the Soviet Union between 1922 and 1927; but it was raised to new intensity with Stalin's rerevolutionizing of the Soviet Union from 1928 onward. The battle against the "social fascists," as Social Democrats were called, was raging furiously just when real fascists were reaching toward power in depression-stricken Europe. It was played down when Stalin saw the desirability of joint action after 1934, and was forgotten while Stalin was at war with Hitler; but the split of the left remains to this day unbridgeable except for occasional tactical arrangements, such as those reached by French Communist and Socialist parties.

By insisting on revolution Russian-style, for which there was no possibility, and by scorning gradualism the Communists seriously undercut possibilities of reform in interwar years. They confused issues on the left and displaced the moderate socialists to the right; radicals were faced with a choice between a Soviet-oriented party and a set of compromisers with the "bourgeois" order. Where influential, the Communists alienated middle-class idealists from the labor movement. That part of the leftist labor movement which came under Stalinist direction was bureaucratized, rigidified, desiccated, and subjected to purges and the fluctuations of the Soviet line. The lower the intellectual level, the more loudly did the parties claim a monopoly of truth. Yet they were too strong to be ignored or simply set aside in the democratic state.

The Marxist-Leninist parties introduced a new disorder and a heightened intellectual dishonesty into Western politics of the 1920s and 1930s. They misused key words of Western political thought, such as "freedom," "elections," and "democracy." Lifted above conventional morality by the dialectic of history, they promoted authoritarianism and ruthlessness beyond the traditions of the modern West. Like Lenin (and to some extent Marx) they gloried in violent language and extremist positions: "With relentless selectivity, the Communist machine has winnowed out the grain and retained only the chaff of Western culture." [6] With their demands for total commitment, they changed many a personality; an ex-Communist was not the same as a non-Communist. They sought not to use Western political institutions even for the benefit of their own clientele, as did more normal parties, but to make democracy unworkable and to destroy it.

Thus the Communists in many countries practically guaranteed power to conservatives or rightists. Not only did they divide the left and burden it with the question of subjection to Soviet leadership; they also frightened the middle ranks and gave the authoritarians of the right their best argument, the need for strength to forestall Bolshevism. The Communists contributed mightily to the recession of democracy. Shortly after World War I, every country of Europe west of Russia had a democratic constitution; by 1937 only the western and northern fringes of Europe (plus Czechoslovakia) could be called democratic. Economic problems and the resurgence of authoritarian traditions after the euphoria of the end of the war which was to make the world safe for democracy contributed to this ebbing of what had seemed a glorious tide. However, Soviet-inspired authoritarians, along with fears of Bolshevism, did more than their share to swing the balance to dictatorship.

This is the responsibility, primarily, of Leninism. But it is also the responsibility of Marxism, a philosophy more given to anger and antagonism than reconciliation and moderation, a creed which cultivates hatred ("class consciousness") more of a class of people (the "bourgeoisie") than of abstract injustice. It is purposefully extremist and conducive to violence in thought and action. The Leninist parties only heightened and exaggerated tendencies previously inherent in the Marxist-inspired movement—tendencies which it was moving away from before World War I. The question of reform is always difficult for the thorough Marxist; since reform means patching up something which should be torn down, it is not logically to be welcomed unless it adds to revolutionary capacities, an unlikely condition. Marxism, partly for political convenience and partly because of the Hegelian idea that an antithetical class could execute the transformation of society, tied the socialist movement to an outworn vocabulary, obsolete economic notions, and a mythical history. It made it harder for labor unions to adapt to modern ideas.[7] By stressing class and class struggle it unnecessarily associated socialism with a minority interest and with an unwinnable conflict. Marxism made socialism divisive, rejected potential allies, and alarmed many who might welcome a less truculent and abrasive doctrine.

It also appears that "Marxism has been the opiate of Marxians." [8] Democratic socialism has not been so barren as authoritarian Communism, but the entire Marxist movement has been singularly lacking in original or creative thought since its beginnings. This is not surprising for a set of theories which was born aggressively intolerant and insistent on its own complete correctness. Even Isaac Deutscher conceded a decline of intellectual standards as Marxism became ossified.[9] Marxism, moreover, is action oriented; when philosophers set out to change the world, they assume that they no longer have much thinking to do. It is a major attraction of Marxism that it relieves its adherents of any need to consider the shape of the new society; it suffices to destroy the old. As Rosa Luxemburg wrote, "And by the final goal I do not mean this or that conception of some future State, but that which must necessarily precede the establishment of any future socialist society, i.e., the conquest of political power by the proletariat." [10]

The challenge of the Russian Revolution and the Communist parties made it seem necessary for socialist parties also to claim the purity of Marxism.[11] Despite repugnance for the crudities of Leninism, they were unable to escape fascination with Soviet power and with the Communist movement which so bitterly attacked them, and confused themselves by insisting that the Soviet Union was somehow a workers' state. This inability to shed Marxist doctrines—or to apply them—led to intellectual paralysis.[12] It also caused political frustration, because Marxists were disqualified from real cooperation with "bourgeois" powers, which theoretically were class enemies. This most fatefully prevented socialists and moderates from effectively joining forces against extremists of the right in the 1930s.

FASCISM

MARXISM-LENINISM promised total liberation through the ruthless power of an elitist political party. It thereby stimulated political primitivism and an authoritarian reaction in the West wherever the democratic tradition was weakest and there was greatest insecurity, especially among the middle classes. The Marxist-Leninist example and the Communist parties reaccustomed the world to an intolerance, self-conceit, and ruthlessness which had seemingly been outgrown prior to World War I. They claimed legitimacy for violence and gave carte blanche to leftist goons; but they thereby legitimized rightist violence and gave carte blanche to rightist goons, who had more guns than the Marxists. Yet, as H. B. Acton wrote, "the introduction of violence into a society which has institutions which need peace if they are to flourish will almost certainly destroy those institutions." [13]

The Marxists also presented theoretical arguments that democracy was fakery from beginning to end, contended that only the naïve would take it seriously (despite the partial conversion of Engels to the democratic faith in his autumnal years), and hindered the democratic process insofar as they had power to do so. In Lenin's way, representative institutions were to be used only to sabotage and discredit them. It is not surprising that the faith of many in popular government should have been shaken, or that cynics might decide that since democracy was of no great value it might well be replaced. If democracy was really dictatorship anyway, why not let a strong hand take charge?

While undercutting democracy, the Communists offered a propagandistic promise of complete and true freedom and a real example of modernized autocracy. The principal Soviet or Communist institutions of control, including political police, concentration camps, state management of the economy, intensive indoctrination, and censorship, were not originated by Lenin but were much advanced by him; he made such effective use of the political party that he may justly be called the inventor of the party state and modern totalitarianism. The Marxist-Leninists not only provoked an anti-Marxist, antidemocratic reaction but gave it a model for organization which nationalists and militarists could use quite as effectively as "proletarian internationalists."

Communism consequently increased tensions and raised political tempers everywhere that it had the strength to do so. Reforms were often impeded by the cry that they implied socialism, which was taken to mean Communism and dictatorship. Conservatives, hearing threats of revolution, feared that concessions might show weakness and endanger the social fabric; some resolved to fight fire with fire. Not only was the left split into revolutionary, Soviet-oriented, and reformist sectors; the right was also split into conservative and semirevolutionary fascist sectors.

Many an anti-Marxist has acted more or less like a socialist in order to steal the fire of the leftists. Bismarck checked German radicalism by his social insurance program, which he recognized as socialistic. The originator of the term "fascism," Benito Mussolini, purposefully combined what he had learned as a radical socialist with militarism, nationalism, and anti-Communism. Perhaps the greatest cause of his triumph was the strength of Communism, or near-Communist socialism, in an Italy disorganized by World War I and disappointed in its results. In 1919 the radicals received 2 million out of 5 million votes; the Comintern looked on eagerly, and the air was thick with talk of revolution. Despite a split in the Socialist Party, tension was kept up by scattered violence and strikes. In August 1922 a general strike was attempted. Mussolini, who presented himself as restorer of order by armed squads, came to power in October.

Mussolini saw the Soviet state as proof of the practicality of the hierarchic principle.[14] He presented himself as a socialist, but he went back philosophically to Marx's teacher, Hegel, and took nation instead of class as the subject of history. His victory was facilitated by the internecine conflict of the left and by the Marxists' failure to perceive the fascists as anything but puppets of the bourgeoisie. The outstanding Italian Communist theorist, Antonio Gramsci, refused to collaborate with democratic socialists even after Mussolini came to power. Mussolini made himself useful to industrialists and was financed by them, but after he solidified his position he served himself and his party and fastened controls on the Italian economy which elsewhere would have been called socialism.

Hitler's party, a more extreme movement than Mussolini's, was still closer to the Leninist model. The unified, dedicated, disciplined, and ideologically tempered Nazi organization dedicated to total power was entirely in the image of Lenin's party. It was at first called the German Workers' Party. Its structure, from cells to auxiliaries, was kindred to that of the socialists or Communists, with the principal exception that Hitler discarded the democratic shams and formalized the de facto leadership principle of Leninist or Stalinist parties. The Nazis even had a red flag, distinguished by a swastika. Nazism appealed to many of the same déclassés as Communism, and in the years of its rise it was easy to pass from one to the other. Fascism and Nazism were younger, fresher, and more exciting than Marxism, and young people were more drawn to hypernationalist heroics, despite the doctrinal deficiency.

The Bolsheviks claimed that the party stood for the workers; the fascists with equal realism claimed that it and the leader represented the nation or race. Like the Communists, the Nazis promised to end class conflict and tried in practice to do so. The Communists blamed the capitalists; the Nazis blamed the Jews and promised to "smash international high finance." Hitler learned much about propaganda from his Communist rivals. The "big lie," about which Hitler and Goebbels were more candid than the Communists, was not their invention. The Marxist-Leninist language of class hatred was echoed in the Nazi language of racial and national hatred.

After they came to power as radical restorers of order, the Nazis continued to follow in the Leninist footsteps. They established a similar party monopoly, indoctrination, labor unions designed to control the workers, and the like. They did not nationalize the economy, but they did place it under an elaborate state organization which left little freedom to the entrepreneur. They carried out something of a social revolution for the benefit of nonaristocrats.[15] Aping Stalin's Five-Year Plans, the Nazis began Four-Year Plans. In Nazi wartime propaganda, the Third Reich became the true socialist country, fighting against Judeo-Bolshevik plutocracy. There was reverse influence, too. Hitler's successful use of patriotism and his "leadership principle" seem to have influenced Stalin to rehabilitate the Russian past and to regard himself more as a new tsar, while the success of Hitler's blood purge of June 1934 may have encouraged Stalin to initiate his great purges six months later.

Despite this kinship, Marxist analysts were so purblind to the nature of fascism or Nazism that they made the same error in Italy in the early 1920s and in Austria and Germany in the early 1930s, in each case weakening the democracy and helping to bring a fascistic reaction. Social Democrats shared with the Communists the basic error of applying economic class analysis to the Nazis. Since these had to be classified as agents of the "bourgeoisie," they could not be much worse than other "bourgeois" movements. Hence the Social Democrats saw the attack on fascism as linked with the attack on capitalism and held it futile to ally with "capitalist" parties against the fascists.[16]

The Communists carried this analysis further. Since the Nazis represented a desperate attempt of the ruling classes to save themselves, they could not last long. Meanwhile they would wreck the "compromisers" and bring about chaos, the outcome of which could only be "dictatorship of the proletariat." If the Social Democrats failed to cooperate with the centrists, the Communists declined to cooperate with the "social fascists," considered by Stalinists to be agents of bourgeois reaction and equal to Hitler and his crowd as enemies of the workers. An incidental result of painting the Social Democrats as fascist villains was to make the genuine fascists seem relatively harmless.

Yet Hitler's movement, like Lenin's, represented not an economic class but itself; it was political power run wild in a disturbed situation, not capitalist but nationalist-militarist, born of insecurity and injured pride. Hitler received financial support from the wealthy—as did Lenin to a degree—but National Socialism looked mostly to the support of the troubled middle classes, and it drew many of its servants from the unemployed or the lumpenproletariat.

For these reasons, the Communists must bear a large share of responsibility for Hitler's victory.[17] More directly, they contributed to paralyzing the German parliament, the Reichstag, opposing (along with the Nazis) any constructive measures. In the growing polarization of the deepening economic depression, with the extremist parties systematically in opposition, parliamentary government became unworkable: President Hindenburg was led to rule by emergency decree; German democracy was virtually destroyed before Hitler took power. The Communists helped Hitler morally even more. He claimed to be fighting bad Marxist violence with good German violence, and he presented Germany with the alternatives of Nazism or Bolshevism. Both were crude and violent, but Nazism was nationally oriented, purported to represent law and order, and seemed to most Germans much less threatening than Stalinist Communism. The armed forces in particular were prepared to swallow Nazism but not Communism. As Communist votes increased, Nazi votes increased still more, until it seemed good sense to name as chancellor the man who commanded the biggest party. The most virulent fascism came in the land targeted above all by the Comintern.

The Debt to Marx

After taking office, Hitler completed his dictatorship on the basis of fighting Communism and Marxism. He went on to diplomatic triumphs proclaiming that his regime was the alternative to a Communist dictatorship in Germany and the bulwark against Soviet penetration of Europe. He was able to confuse and divide; the issue of Communism and alliance with Stalin troubled and demoralized democratic resistance. More than Hitler's equal as a despot at home, Stalin could be neither brought into plans for collective security nor excluded from them. Together, Hitler and Stalin prepared Europe for barbarism and slaughter; and their joining of hands on August 23, 1939, was the signal for the beginning of World War II.

The German and Italian species of fascism were crushed and discredited by the war, but Russian Communism has continued to provide an example and excuse for the exercise of ruthless power under a variety of labels on several continents. Lenin was the inventor, Stalin the perfecter of the one-party state; and the Soviet Union has always been its most powerful proponent. Revolutionary, semirevolutionary, and pseudo-revolutionary regimes of Asia and Africa have availed themselves of the Soviet model and precedent. Similarly, conservative, militaristic, or semifascist dictatorships in Spain, Portugal, and many countries of Latin America have set themselves up as saviors from Communism, while profiting from the Soviet model and example. The lawlessness and violence of the left are the chief excuse for the lawlessness of the right. Even the Watergate conspirators felt justified in their illegalities by the way left-wing agitators, demonstrators, and rioters had defied the law.

MARXISM FOR THE LESS DEVELOPED

FOR those less developed countries acutely aware of their relations with the advanced industrial countries, Marxism is a salve for wounded pride. It tells them that their relative poverty is not a fault but a virtue, because it is the result of exploitation. Inferior in power and wealth, they are morally superior and can expect to be in the vanguard of the future socialist society. Nations, too, need to feel self-assurance, and those who lose faith in their own capacities may fall into a demoralization that leads to disorganization. Marxism helps the people, especially the intellectuals, to hold their heads high.

This balm, however, is applied at some cost. Marx's criticism of religion as a distraction from the material struggle for improvement because it promises a blissful future for the sufferers—salvation through moral purity—is applicable to Marxism also.[18] Marxism caters to impatience and tells the people of the poorer countries to rely on a will-o'-the-wisp of revolution—either in the industrial countries, which is not likely to occur, or in their own lands, which could not help them very much and would be contrary to the logic of the creed. Marxism promises a socialist utopia which is unattainable within a lifetime, if ever. Insofar as foreign exploitation is blamed for a country's difficulties, that country is relieved of the need to help itself. If world capitalism is responsible for the poverty of the street dwellers of Calcutta, it is easier to overlook the fact that Indian society has failed to make them useful. Instead of attacking problems, Marxism disposes the poor to denunciations of foreign villains, or to fatalistic resignation when the verbal attack on the rich powers produces no results.

For a whole series of problems, from land use to official corruption, Marxism offers bromides. For example, Marxists have usually rejected population control as some sort of imperialist scheme, although if the capitalists were really bent on maximum exploitation they would wish the poorer countries to reproduce as much as possible, in order to keep them poor and helpless and also to have the maximum work force to exploit. The problem is outside the Marxist field of view; to grant it importance would mean that there are causes other than capitalism for impoverishment. The Marxist remedy is simple and easy: the introduction of socialism. There is no need to please the Western leaders, whose interests must be selfish, by taking difficult, perhaps painful measures to check the birthrate. Likewise, there is no need to restrain wage demands. Poor countries cannot afford the socialist rhetoric which keeps them from facing real problems.[19]

Marxist attitudes hurt economic growth by distorting relations with non-Marxist industrial countries. A believer in class conflict and revolution must see almost any program they propose, be it economic, social, or cultural, as an instrument of capitalist domination, at best disguised and sugarcoated. Even though projects may be undertaken, they are poisoned by distrust. Yet it is difficult indeed for a technologically less advanced country to make its way without assistance; even the huge and relatively advanced Soviet Union seems to have given up the attempt.

More significantly, the application of socialist controls to backward economies is not promising. It is easy to see a need for planning in the use of scarce investment resources and in controlling powerful foreign interests; and it may be argued that, as Soviet Russia seemed to show, an authoritarian structure can force the early stages of industrialization. Unhappily, however, where private enterprise functions poorly, state enterprise is not likely to do much better and may do much worse. Inefficiently managed private concerns go bankrupt or are reorganized; incompetent state agencies receive subsidies or monopoly advantages. Resources are misdirected to heavy industry and prestige construction projects, to the neglect of agriculture and the consumer. Marxism encourages the vices of overcontrol with which most politicians are afflicted. Political objectives determine economic priorities; the economy is turned to serve the state and the elite in command. Incompetently administered controls invite all manner of cheating. If the poorer countries need socialism, they are less capable of making it work.

Whatever the theory, if Stalinist patterns of economic growth by decree were once valid, they seem no longer to be so. Castro's Cuba, Nkrumah's Ghana, Sékou Touré's Guinea, socialist Burma, and others have been gross failures in terms of production. State-managed agriculture has done poorly in African countries and in Cuba.[20] Allende's Chile, likewise, after a promising start, became bogged down in shortages, falling production, disorganization, strikes, and colossal inflation. The ruthless discipline and order of Stalinism seem necessary for full state control of the economy, and they cannot be conjured up by fiat. Much less is heard in recent years of the formerly favored argument that socialism is necessary for rapid growth; it is promoted instead as necessary for economic justice.

The countries which have displayed strong economic growth in recent years have been non-Marxist or anti-Marxist, generally regimes which keep a firm, perhaps harsh, grip while encouraging private enterprise, domestic and foreign—for example, Brazil, Iran, Singapore, and South Korea. Not only has Japan done much better than Communist China; both Taiwan and Hong Kong have also raised production levels much more spectacularly. The last is notable; as a colony, it is theoretically subject to maximum exploitation, and it has no resources whatever. Yet it has come into surprising affluence by Asian standards, and thousands of inhabitants of the People's Republic risk their lives yearly in the effort to become "slaves" of the capitalists of Hong Kong.

The best regime for economic growth seems to be one which promotes economic cooperation with the advanced countries, uses whatever advantages it may possess in materials or cheap labor to compete on the world market, welcomes controlled foreign investments, and invites entrepreneurs to produce for profit in areas considered desirable, while checking wage demands and refraining from forms of interference which discourage production or make it more costly—in short a pragmatic non-Marxist regime, although very likely not a democratic one. How far this is desirable is a question of values; it may be contended that the advances of the Castro government in Cuba in spreading education, building up the self-respect of ordinary workers, and giving them security are worth the sacrifice of a large part of total production. It is possible, however, that the relative equality of Castroite Cuba or Maoist China may be eroded by monopolistic political power.

The political effect of Marxist-Communist thought and action is stronger than the economic effect. With its stress on class conflict and its propensity to violence of word, if not deed, Marxism (or Marxism-Leninism) raises tensions and polarizes society, while relaxing moral-ethical restraints and leading proponents and opponents to excesses. Contrary to Fanon, violence does not humanize but brutalizes; if Debray, a cultured young man, called for public executions of police,[21] his enemies could be indifferent to beatings of radical students. Marxism permits a new despotism, usually of military men, to be labeled "socialism." If there should be a "socialist" revolution, it is inevitably elitist, and it is likely to be antipopular, as the vanguard theory suggests.

Marxism probably contributes to the political underdevelopment of countries which, above all, need sound government for economic and cultural progress. The Soviet example of arbitrary party rule is attractive, and Marxist theory discredits democracy and constitutional government as being either fraudulent or unimportant. By denying the reality and importance of political questions, Marxism makes it harder for the intellectuals—the most Marxist, who should take the lead in this regard—to devise means of checking power.

It is true that democratic government is not promising for the countries whose populations live on the edge of subsistence, but it is remarkable that few of the poor countries have a settled constitutional order of any kind. This is a unique situation in world history. Long before there was much democracy, most states had fairly reliable and orderly political systems; in the majority of countries today, as in China and the Soviet Union, power is fixed at the summit in an irregular, essentially anarchic fashion.

How much of this political backwardness in the non-Western world may be ascribed to the intromission of Marxist and Leninist motifs is a matter beyond human reckoning; but it can hardly be doubted that Marxist extremism has contributed to rightist reaction. Castro's campaign to repeat in the Andes his feats in the Sierra Maestra brought about no lusty popular rebirths but a spate of military coups.[22] In innumerable cases, where a democratic government has seemed to be breaking down amid the threat of class war, military leaders have stepped in to assume responsibility for order, either because of fear of socialism or because of loss of faith in the constitutional order. Thus, in 1964, when Brazil seemed to be taking a radical leftist turn under President João Goulart, a military group intervened, pledging to rid Brazil of Communism. Brazil had observed constitutional rule and had regular elections since 1890, except for the near-fascist rule of Getúlio Vargas between 1930 and 1945; after 1964, elections were almost of the Soviet, uncontested variety, and the regime dealt with opponents with a severity beyond Brazilian tradition. Somewhat similarly, in Uruguay, a country with a once highly respected democratic tradition dating from 1890, economic troubles in the latter 1960s brought a threat of Marxist violence. The Tupamaros strove to bring revolution by terrorism and succeeded in bringing a military semidictatorship to power in 1973. This proceeded to the usual repressions, even copying the Soviet Union by treating dissent psychiatrically.[23]

More dramatic was the experience of Chile. The election of Allende, an avowed Marxist socialist with Communist support, with a little over a third of the votes in a field of three in 1970, was accepted in good spirit and ratified by the non-Marxist majority of the Chilean Congress in return for his promise to respect civil liberties. The constitutional-democratic tradition of Chile, one of the firmest of Latin America, was thereby preserved. For a few months, support for Allende rose as he introduced programs favoring the needy. But Marxism was divisive, and gradualism proved impossible. Politics became class war, in which the CIA easily exerted a "destabilizing" influence. Allende stepped out of a democratic role, frankly invoking ideological reasons against whatever might be majority sentiments, saying, "I am not the President of all Chileans." [24] The extreme left sought and achieved confrontation. Acts of violence and counterviolence multiplied, with the discontent of the majority rising as inflation soared and production sank.

The military reaction in September 1973 was prompted by fears of the creation and arming of a leftist paramilitary force. Although Allende had prudently courted the generals, the reaction was stern and complete. Not only was the Allende government destroyed and its leadership arrested, but the governing junta also set aside the entire constitutional and democratic apparatus. To de-Marxify Chile, the military government of General Augusto Pinochet instituted censorship, purged the universities (requiring students to cut long hair and wear neckties), expelled large numbers of foreign adherents of the leftist government, banned not just leftist but all political parties, ended elections for an indefinite period, and promised "a constitution that will not give Marxism a chance to sink its claws again into the country." [25] All these were steps which three years earlier would have been inconceivable for the nonpolitical soldiery of Chile.

REVOLUTIONISM

MARXISM roils the politics of both industrialized and unindustrialized countries because its message is social revolution—that is, the overturning not only of a ruling group but of the established order of society. This is the core concept of Marx, who practically invented revolution as a goal in itself. Previously, men had begun revolutions by seeking redress of specific grievances or in anger against specific rulers. In Marxism, revolution came to be something unique and holy, the prime article of a semimystical faith, an answer for millennial yearnings, ennobling the crassest enterprise; the modern extortionist represents a revolutionary army.

It is difficult for Marxists to back away from the idea of revolution, although Marx in his later years qualified it and Engels at times sounded like a half-convert to democracy. The idea of sudden and total change is necessary because once it is admitted that prevailing institutions can be reformed and thus are not totally bad, the black-and-white Marxist picture of class-governed society is contradicted. It is also fatal to revolutionary morale to admit gradual change; a majority will prefer to work for amelioration rather than to venture the difficult and risky task of knocking the whole building down, and every little victory adds to the reformers' stake in the established institutions. If Marxist parties leave the ideal of revolution behind, they become practically equivalent to "bourgeois" parties. This has occurred with Western European socialist parties since World War II; they neither frighten nor greatly inspire anyone, and their goals are simply humanitarian.

If reform is the enemy of revolution, the image of revolution is the enemy of reform. Fascination with indefinite blessings from exciting revolution means neglect of small benefits from dull reformism. The idea of class struggle also stands in the way of cooperation between Marxists and other sectors of society, as each side is led to view the other as inherently evil. The idea is self-fulfilling. Because of it, the socialist parties before World War I and Communist parties thereafter have developed something of a separate subculture, set off from the rest of society. The dream and its supporting analysis cause alienation and impede realistic adjustment.[26] It was understandable for Kautsky and the German Social Democrats to cling to revolutionary rhetoric as a bond and inspiration for their party, but this erected an impassable barrier to their achieving power and was excuse enough for conservatives to veto democratization.

There is no logical reason that socialism should be burdened by association with class struggle and revolution. Socialism is not a particular interest of any one class—its chief proponents do not fit any Marxian class—and it may more easily be conceived as coming by evolution than by violence. If public control of economic enterprises works, it can always be extended. In the most capitalistic of states, there is some socialism, from the postal service onward. And if there is some popular control of government, this can be indefinitely increased, if the people are capable and desirous of ruling. Change can go as far as people are ready to push it.

Revolution, on the other hand, is a leap into the fire. It caters to emotions, exalting feeling over calculation, which usually counsels moderation; radicals understandably reject reason in principle as incapacitating for action. Revolution implausibly invokes violence to bring justice and harmony. It is the supreme billowing up of hatred. It means war; dominant classes often fade away, but when attacked they resist. The British, French, Russian, and Chinese revolutions were all sealed with much bloodshed. Civil war also means loss of skills and disruption of production, perhaps for many years. The Russian economy was thrust back to the level of a century earlier, and even primary education was practically in abeyance for several years. It is a price worth paying only if the old structures are very bad indeed. It is strong medicine, to be prescribed if one is certain of the expected cure—that is, if one has a clear and well-based conception of the new society to be built and the means of building it, elements strikingly lacking in Marxism. There are many varieties of economic organization; it is not easy to prove that the difference between one and another is worth the catastrophe (with doubtful outcome) of revolutionary collision.

There has been no real revolution in the Western world since 1789, except as a result of defeat in a major war. If modern societies are hard pressed, there may be a fascistic reaction; but this has been successful only by legal means, except in Spain, where foreign help was decisive. Mussolini and Hitler both received the insignia of office from the constituted authorities, and both pretended at first to govern in a legal fashion.

For the elastic, loose-jointed, nontraditional polity, the idea of revolution is inappropriate. It is unnecessary because there are legal procedures for change; although they may be denounced as fraudulent, they are probably as realistic as the cloudy promises of the revolution. Rulership is subject to renewal in any case; mores are perpetually changing; there is no need for revolution to set aside a cramping ideology when the state has no definite ideology. Marxist revolution is directed against an abstraction, "capitalism"; but in the pluralistic society power is shared by corporations, farmers, miners, labor leaders, and the like, together with the vast and many-branched apparatus of the government, with organs and bureaucracies that are local as well as central. Elections are substitutes for revolutions, whereby the people, if so minded, can theoretically bring about any change. When France in May 1968 seemed to face a revolutionary situation, thanks to an extraordinary ferment of mostly student protest, President de Gaulle had only to call for new elections to calm the country; the result was an increased majority for the governing party. There is not much for revolutionaries to promise that cannot be put up to the voters at the ballot box, and if a radical program shows signs of drawing mass support, an established party is likely to preempt it.

The Debt to Marx

There is more point to violence in undemocratic countries. Revolution is likely to be elitist, except where it is intended to restore traditional but temporarily lost democratic government. Neither in an advanced nor in a backward country can revolutionaries mobilize majority support for an upheaval, but there may be reason for a revolution to get rid of archaic elites opposing modernization in countries of relatively simple social structure. The firestorm that burns away the bad and leaves only the good is illusory; but revolution *is* relevant for countries with a closed ruling caste, where capable citizens, especially the intelligentsia, are unable to work for the betterment of the state and are condemned to frustration, and where there is no way to press for change from outside the ruling circles.

For a despotism, it does not much matter that the probable result of revolution is a new despotism. Revolution is most suitable for great absolutist empires, where the government is all-pervasive and all authority flows from the center of power, the ruler who is venerated as the source of blessings and chastisements. When such a state becomes rotten, thoroughly corrupt, and weak, as always happens sooner or later, the only reasonable hope for improving the state and escaping from intolerable burdens of taxation and official oppression is to smash the old center and replace it. Then a revolution may seem like a rebirth, a salvation and release of energies. New and vigorous talents take their place at the top and the people hope that good rulers mean a good life; and the more violent the overthrow, the more promising it seems.

Such have been the revolutions in great empires of the past, whereby outworn dynasties have been replaced by new ones. Such have also been the classic social revolutions of history, the English, French, Mexican, Russian, and Chinese, all mounted from a background of absolutism, all claiming to bring freedom and resulting in dictatorship. Such revolutions are mightily exciting, and they long impregnate the political atmosphere. The image of the French Revolution hovered over Europe for most of a century, inspiring successive attempts to repeat it until the fiasco of the Paris Commune in 1871. The idea of revolution was brought back into Western politics by the Russian Revolution. For the Russians it was a supreme inspiration. As Alexander Block wrote, in January 1918, "*Change everything.* Renew everything; let the falseness, the filth and the weariness of our life disappear and let it become free, just, pure, and beautiful." [27] This had a magnetic effect on many in the West, especially in times of troubles. But by now the example of the Russian Revolution is worn out for the Western world, if it ever was really pertinent.

Nowadays, the idea of revolution would seem most applicable to the states which exalt it, those of the Marxist-Leninist faith. There authority is integrated and centralized, so that change of leadership would mean change of society. The elite is closed and fixed in place, immune to pressures for renewal from outside. The ideology is closely tied to the rulership. There is no legal way for anyone outside the tiny group at the top to work for political change. In these conditions, only the powers of coercion and indoctrination stand in the way of a revolutionary movement.

AUTHORITARIANISM

MARXISM and Communism have raised tensions and created an atmosphere of violence by pursuing goals of class struggle and revolution; Marxism is a creed of combat. This has encouraged authoritarian politics, in which the command of the few becomes more important than the wishes of the many. But aside from its goals, Marxism (with Marxism-Leninism and its applied form, Communism) is authoritarian in method, as Lenin taught it to be.

This authoritarian aspect of Marxism may be ascribed to the fact that it was taken over by an imperious person, Lenin, put to use in an autocratic society, and later made the basis of consummate despotism by Stalin. Marxism in all its forms is so linked with and influenced by its political use in Russia—and more recently China—that the temper of more independent brands of Marxism, even of the rather anarchistic New Left, has been affected. The example is unavoidably contagious.

Many have tried to avoid it. People in a democratic society attracted by the goals of Marxism wish to see Marx as thoroughly democratic in outlook.[28] Anti-Soviet thinkers, Marxist or not, find love of democracy in Marx, hoping to separate him from Soviet misuse of his teachings and to deprive Leninism of its Marxist basis. For example, Ivan Svitak, an anti-Soviet Czech Communist, wrote, "Marx was one of the greatest democrats of history." [29]

But it is not easy to make the case. The evidence for a democratic Marx consists of little more than scattered nods to the prevailing democratic sentiments, such as the familiar claim of the *Communist Manifesto* to promote "the interests of the immense majority" and to bring about "an association, in which the free development of each is the condition of the free development of all." [30] But Marx did not dwell on such sentiments, elaborate any sort of democratic theory, or speculate how the will of the people was to be determined. It costs nothing to claim to have the popular interest at heart; Lenin always spoke as though his only concern was to serve the people and guard their welfare, acting on behalf of the long-term or future majority, if not the majority of the hour. Before the revolution, Lenin expressed himself more strongly and explicitly for a people's state (in *State and Revolution*) than Marx had ever done. Hitler, for that matter, claimed to be acting on behalf of the German people, whose will was allegedly better expressed through the leader than through corrupt parliaments; and he conducted plebiscites from time to time to demonstrate the near-unanimous support for his policies. Despots ancient and modern have regularly claimed to be good shepherds of their people.

Although it is easy and politic for radicals to speak of freedoms and the rights of the people, the founding fathers of Marxism made many antidemocratic utterances. For example, Engels in 1843 spoke of German socialism as superior to French because of the former's lack of "democratic prejudices," and favored a socialist society administered by an elite chosen not by elections but by examinations. [31] In his "Address to the Communist League" of March 1850, Marx saw democracy as the main obstacle, to be undermined and destroyed, no matter how progressive.[32] In a letter to Engels Marx characterized that address as "at bottom nothing but a plan of war against democracy." [33] Marx once wrote of the faithful Wilhelm Liebknecht, "That dumb ox believes in the future *democratic state*." [34] In his *Critique of the Gotha Program* Marx categorically rejected the call for a "free people's state" on the grounds that the state must repress its adversaries by force.[35] In the absence of signs of revolution, the aging Engels saw great possibilities in electoral action, but he did not cherish democracy as ordinarily understood. In his opinion, "the logical form of bourgeois domination is precisely the democratic republic . . . the bourgeois democratic republic always remains the last form of bourgeois domination, that in which it is broken to pieces." [36]

Imperious and unable to work with others, even to debate

amicably except with Engels, Marx was an absolutist who never sought the views of other people but believed in the unique rightness of his own truth, in a spirit of absolute noncompromise. Proudhon, it may be recalled, urged him, "let us not pose as the apostles of a new religion," but this is precisely what Marx proposed to do. As a newspaper editor, he argued eloquently against censorship, but his intolerance of conflicting views does not permit much doubt but that he was prepared to suppress views of which he disapproved if he had held the reins of power.

He contended that wisdom was to come not from the proletariat but from the philosophers, and he placed no value in popular opinion. In the words of his disciple, "Free from all conceit, Marx could not attribute any value to the applause of the masses. The masses were to him a brainless crowd whose thoughts and feelings were furnished by the ruling class." [37] The theories of Marx were about the worker, not for the workers. The few members of the Marxist group were not much better; Engels referred to them as "incorrigible blockheads." [38]

Marx's attitude toward "the scum of society" has been mentioned, as have been his haughty attitudes toward various peoples. For example, he saw the rule of Magyars over larger numbers of Slavs as justified and meritorious because of racial qualities.[39] He expressed his contempt for the Mexicans (whom Engels thought the United States should civilize) as follows: "The Spaniards are indeed degenerate. But a degenerate Spaniard, a Mexican, that is the ideal. All the vices of the Spaniards—boastfulness, grandiloquence, and quixoticism—are found in the Mexicans raised to the third power, but they no longer have the substance that the Spaniards possess." [40] He did not claim to stand for "human brotherhood."

Marx stood for violence, at least in his earlier and more sanguine years. For example, in his "Address to the Communist League," he said, "Far from opposing so-called excesses, instances of popular revenge against hated individuals or public buildings with hateful memories attached to them, it is necessary not merely to tolerate them but to take a leading part in them." [41] In the Marxian theory, conflict is of the essence, the importance of classes lying in their conflict; and those who wished to minimize violence and hatred were enemies for Marx. There was a strong militaristic bent in the thinking of the two philosophers who again and again hoped for war to generate communism. Engels approved of the Reign of

Terror in the French Revolution, speaking of it as a victory of the propertyless masses.[42] About the same time, in a speech of 1874, he characterized the goal toward which his life had been directed: "A revolution is certainly the most authoritarian thing there is: it is the act whereby one part of the population imposes its will upon the other part by means of rifles, bayonets, and cannon—authoritarian means. . . ." [43] Engels reproached the 1871 Paris Commune chiefly for failure to use force ruthlessly enough.[44]

The direction of Marxian political purposes can hardly be called democratic, quite aside from the unlikelihood that violent means, which are the possession of the strong few, could bring equality and respect for the will of the weak many. Marx frankly held that the state, in the proletarian revolution, was to repress class opposition; he did not suggest how repression was to be brought to a close. When he wrote of the dictatorship of the proletariat, he must have understood that in no real way could the mass of workers rule, and that dictatorship would be exercised by the leaders in the name of the proletariat. This is what Bakunin warned against in his remarkable exchange with Marx in 1875. "Under collective property," Marx said, "the so-called will of the people disappears to make way for the real will of the cooperative," a formulation with profoundly antidemocratic implications. Bakunin rejoined, "Result: rule of the great majority of the people by a privileged minority . . . of ex-workers, who, once they become only representatives or rulers of the people, cease to be workers." Marx's answer was a clever quibble—workers would no more cease to be workers in official positions than manufacturers did—ignoring the presumption that manufacturers and officials, not workers, were damned as a ruling and exploiting class. This discussion continued in the same vein, Bakunin pointing out that "from that time on they represent not the workers but themselves and their own claims to govern the people." Marx concluded, "He [Bakunin] should have asked himself: what form can administrative functions assume on the basis of the workers' state, if it pleases him to call it thus?" [45] This was a question Marx did not find necessary to ask himself.

It is logical to consider the immediate object of a leader to be more truly his object than some distant goal painted on the horizon to inspire his followers. To postpone freedom and democracy to a vague future is to deny them. The tendencies of Marxian ideas for the future, too, were undemocratic. Marx and Engels were fervent centralists and statists; they were hardly so naïve as not to know that centralization implies power for the rulers. The statement of aims in the *Communist Manifesto* included "establishment of industrial armies, especially for agriculture," [46] a demand unlikely to arouse much peasant enthusiasm. Engels in his *Anti-Dühring* looked to "a society which makes it possible for its productive forces to dovetail harmoniously into each other on the basis of one single vast plan." [47] Such total control would seem tacitly to assume permanent and complete dictatorship. In any case, the belief in a present society of pure conflict and a future of pure harmony makes democracy unnecessary.[48]

In the Marxist view, any state was class dictatorship, and civil rights and democratic institutions were of slight importance (except perhaps for the aged Engels). But to regard law and the state as normally tools of oppression is practically to invite their being used as such. Political inquiry is the enemy of tyranny, but Marx would have none of it for the socialist state, which was to be shielded a priori from criticism by its class character. Since the dictatorship of the proletariat remained undefined, it could be made anything—Engels's use of the Paris Commune as an example was inapt, since it was neither proletarian nor Marxist. Rights in Marxism are for abstract classes, not real people.

The theories of class conflict and its economic basis also destroy ideas of morality, without which there can be no respect for rights, no limited government, and no democracy. In Marxism there is no rule of law, since law is part of the class-based superstructure; the social process is struggle, with no holds barred. To allow the opposition rights is positively wrong. Since all morality is class bound, the new leaders are emancipated from "bourgeois morality" and invited to act as suits them. The "progress of society" justifies any ruthlessness, as Deutscher conceded in relation to his hero, the gifted, idealistic, and ruthless Leon Trotsky.[49] Messianism legitimates coercion; and, in the trite phrase, the end justifies the means. As the Yugoslav Communist Djilas more delicately put it, "with Communism as an ideal the important thing is not what is being done but why." [50] But democracy rests on civilized and agreed means of political action. Democracy consists of means whereby people can define changing ends.

The utopian end, too, has authoritarian implications. Equality of the (nonruling) citizens implies control over their activities; otherwise, in the give and take of persons of differing energy, ambition, and talent, some will rise above others. And if all are kept equal, none will be in a position to challenge the governing authority. The atomized society, the society of perfect tranquillity, is the despot's dream, in which he alone is perfectly free. It is also a static society; having been propelled for many generations by incessant struggle, society in the Marxian theory would come to rest, becalmed in the placid waters of conflictless socialism.

It is not surprising that Marxism has been put to authoritarian use; and it is no accident that it has become the official creed (with appropriate modification) of Russia and China, societies with autocratic traditions. In the years before World War I, Marxism was generally recognized as "state socialism," among the various branches of anarchist, Christian, ethical, and syndicalist socialism; the authoritarian use made of it after 1917 grew out of the theories and attitudes of the founders. Marxism does not of itself make authoritarianism but helps it, as in the Russia of Lenin, Stalin, and their successors, in the China of Mao, and even in the democratic countries, whose Communist parties are usually ruled by little dictators. Stalin was not mad but a quite successful dictator liberated by Marxism-Leninism from moral prejudices.

A paradoxical result of the authoritarianism inherent in Marxism is that the movement is peculiarly leader oriented, applying in political practice the leader principle exalted by the Nazis as political philosophy. The economic-historical theory downgrades individuals; the means of production, relations to them, and economically defined classes theoretically move history, not the character or will of exceptional men. If there had been no Napoleon, as Engels said, someone else would have taken his place. Yet from the beginning, Marxist parties (and subsequently states) have been strongly centered on outstanding individuals with their cults of personality, from Marx himself to Lenin, Stalin, Mao, Tito, Castro, Ho Chi Minh, Kim Il-song, Enver Hoxha, et al. Imitative one-party regimes, such as those of Sekou Touré and Kwame Nkrumah, have likewise been strongly focused on the great man. An ideological, ergo arbitrary, approach to politics requires a single head to give the truth.

Marxism is an ideology in the Marxian sense—that is, a cover for unconfessable interests. Under it, desires for equality and economic liberation can be manipulated for the benefit of a new ruling-owning class. Marxism gives autocracy a modern populist and equalitarian garb, under which it can act more freely. Marxism, with its apolitical analysis, absolutist mentality, superior but un-

217

defined goals, dialectical approach to facts, superior "class" right, and rejection of "bourgeois" morality can be an antidemocratic ideology for any society or group prepared to use the corresponding vocabulary.

THE INTOXICATION

IT MAY BE too much to call Marxism the opium of the intellectuals, as did Raymond Aron,[51] because it has stirred ample controversy and brainwork of a sort. But it has acted as a drug, leading its users to take abstractions for realities and to build theories which in another context would appear strange and unreal.

There is a theological density and turgidity in Marxist writings, especially those of Marx; one never knows just how much concrete meaning lies behind the words. The gray world is painted black-and-white and made comprehensible through verbal abstractions which can be made to behave as the writer wishes. Marx and Engels were quite unhampered by exactness of language, and their followers have taken equal liberties. Such basic concepts as "proletariat," "capitalism," and "class" shift radically in meaning according to the needs of the argument. "Bourgeois" comes to mean simply "enemy" or "non-Marxist," as in "bourgeois economics" or "bourgeois art." "Proletarian" is a less commonly used antithesis, meaning little more than "correct and proper," as in "proletarian outlook." In recent years many loaded neo-Marxist terms, such as "power elite," "American imperialism," "establishment," and "fascist pigs" have become infinitely repeated staples of semi-intellectual discourse in the United States. "Alienation" has been turned into an excuse for almost anything. "Imperialism" is used as reprobation for virtually any action of the powerful industrial countries in regard to the weaker nations, including giveaway programs, on the grounds that these impede progress toward "socialism." In this mode of thought, even human control of the environment is called "imperialistic." Many other words which Marxism has appropriated have been debased; for example, "feudal" has come to refer to almost any preindustrial structure which is not obviously primitive. The earlier meaning—a system of divided powers, personal obligations, and land tenure, as found in medieval Europe, premodern Japan, and a few other cases—is left to the scholars.

The Debt to Marx

In this flexible use of words, "socialist" and "capitalist" are generally accepted as descriptive of two groups of states on the world scene, with the implication that the one stands for the interests of the people, the other for those of the wealthy. It could be factually argued that the designation would be more appropriate if reversed. All manner of people speak of upper class versus lower class, as though these were useful analytical concepts; in fact, the distinction is as fuzzy as that of high clouds versus low clouds, since most are in middle altitudes. Such is the strength of usage that these terms—"capitalism," "bourgeoisie," "socialism," "workers," and so forth—have been often used in this book as though they had operational meanings; it hardly seems possible always to place them in quotation marks.

Marxism should be credited with having popularized more stereotypes than any other doctrine ever. But slithery use of words equals sloppy thinking, self-deception, or politically useful argumentation. In Marxism, right spirit or political correctness outweighs factuality. Words are repeated for emotive content, with little reference to the real world, in order to induce behavior patterns. "Revolution," for example, becomes a cherished symbol, with little thought of its likelihood or of what it would actually mean if it should come. It is a typical Marxist question to ask "What is the role of the lumpenproletariat?" although this "class" is undefinable and if definable would have no role; the millions of individual unfortunates have individual roles. Marxism abounds in reductionisms, the treatment of complex affairs as though they were simple, from the alleged economic causation of social and cultural institutions to the analysis of capitalism in terms of labor theory of value. Such concepts are an assault on reason, and not much is saved by saying that they are not to be taken literally.

The dialectic adds to confusion and muddles thinking. The concept of the sudden conversion of quantitative to qualitative change is verbal legerdemain, used to validate the logically shaky idea of revolution in a world where changes occur at all speeds, but mostly gradually, and where all quantitative change is to some degree qualitative, and all qualitative change, if well understood, can be described quantitatively. The idea that a thing implies its opposite is profound in paradox and very useful for sophistry; one can argue anything on this basis. It helped Marx contend that the workers got poorer the more they produced, and helped Engels claim that abundance causes poverty—not a feeling of poverty, but concrete poverty, and not future but present poverty.[52] It enabled Stalin to say that he had to strengthen the state for the sake of the withering away of the state. In similar fashion, John Strachey, conceding that Marxism and psychoanalytic theory were opposites but wishing to make the best of both, asked, "Do they, that is to say, by their very oppositeness, by means of their sharply contradictory character, not provide, when taken together, just the unity of opposites in which, Marx and Engels believed, reality can alone be adequately described?" [53] Such thinking is implied in many fatuities, such as, "If Malthus had not considered the matter so one-sidedly, he could not have failed to see that surplus population *or* labor power is invariably tied up with surplus wealth, surplus capital, and surplus landed property. The population is too large only where productive power as a whole is too large." [54]

In the confusing pretense of science, obfuscation comes into its own. Abstractions take over where reality fails to perform as directed. Thus, if the state obviously acts contrary to the desires of real capitalists, the answer is that a virtually Platonic "ideal capitalist" arranges things for the benefit of fleshly capitalists; if labor conditions are regulated, it is the better to exploit the workers; and social improvements are designed to maintain the rule of capital.[55] Opacity attains sublimity in such apologetics as those of Althusser, who argues that the Marxian masterwork, *Capital*, has not only an apparent but an invisible text not perceptible to the ordinary eye; thus, one must read the silences as well as the expressions, and Marx meant profound things he did not know he meant.[56] The meaning, like beauty, is in the mind of the beholder.

For the same reasons that Marxism brings violence and authoritarianism into politics, it promotes their intellectual equivalents of exaggeration and dogmatism. Lenin and Russian authoritarianism share responsibility, but Marx and Engels by their intolerance and arrogance, their vitriol and indifference to objectivity and fairness, gave the precedents for the harsh tone of their followers. Marxism is for revolution insofar as it is for anything, and revolution is practically by definition (Engels's especially) ruthless and contemptuous of received values. Facts per se are not important, just as Lenin and the Russian radicals of the late nineteenth century were scornful of knowledge unrelated to their cause.[57] Marxists take pride in being "committed," that is, nonobjective. In the class analysis there is no unbiased truth, just as law is held to be nothing but an expression of the power of one class over others. But since there is no real truth or law, anyone is authorized to proclaim his own prejudice or will as right. "Bourgeois objectivity" in Soviet parlance is infinitely inferior to "party spirit." The doctrine that ideas are to be judged by class origin amounts to raising the argument ad hominem to a philosophic principle.

That morality is class based is an equally destructive proposition. Science rests on a foundation of universal ethics; in the Marxist outlook, however, class power makes right and ethics. A class morality is a creed of violence. Marxism is moved much more by hatred of the possessors than love of the unfortunate, and it has excited or mediated some surprisingly violent sentiments in normally gentle people. Possibly with some exaggeration it was said that "the intellectuals did not merely accept violence: they liked it and asked for more." [58] The use of hatred and violence to bring peace and love suggests that the former may be the truer objective. Marx regarded ethical language as nonsense, and it is difficult to derive an ethic from his work.[59]

The Marxist fixation has its reward in will and concentration and its cost in rationality. Marxism suggests that man is basically a rather simple creature moved mostly and fundamentally by economic urges, and it is possible for anyone who has learned a few stereotypes and the requisite jargon to assume that he has mastered the big secrets. Often, the result is some very naïve views. For example, French students protested vocally in the early 1970s against technical training on the grounds that they were being made useful for the "establishment," without considering that they would thereby gain a potency to be used for good or ill at their own volition. It is still possible for intelligent people to hold that all ills are due to a confused complex of institutions called "capitalism" and are to be cured by something called "socialism" which humans inexplicably have never succeeded in fully implementing. Fantasy takes over economics; Daniel de Leon pictures the happy capitalist shoveling in his gains: ". . . out of the $7,000 that the cloth is worth my wage workers receive $2,000 in wages, and I receive the $5,000 as profits or dividends." [60]

The polemical-political nature of Marxism invites a feast of unreason. Marx and Engels carried on violent and utterly self-righteous polemics, the purpose of which was not to illuminate an issue but to destroy an adversary. One of the more moderate was Engels's famous *Anti-Dühring*, which gave the blind socialist leader the benefit of no doubt and credit for no good intention. Dühring's theories were outwardly quite as sensible as Engels's, and he had considerably more qualifications as a natural scientist, but Engels ends by blaming Dühring for *"mental incompetence due to megalomania."* [61] The masters fully sanctioned the truculence and loud wrath of the disciples; the clenched fist is aptly symbolic of the general Marxian movement. Debate between Marxists and non-Marxists tends to resemble a shouting match with more name-calling than enlightenment, with an advantage for the true believers. Such sciences as economics and sociology in many countries are separated into noncommunicating camps of pro- and anti-Marxists. Within the Marxist camp there is not much basis for agreement or even for genteel discussion, as each thinker of consequence (unless under political discipline) goes his own way. Controversies take on a scholastic tone, with more bandying of quotations than marshaling of evidence.

If Marxists agree on anything, it is on some sort of economic causation; but this assumption blinds them to the importance of psychological and political factors in this political universe. One purpose of Marxism in the Soviet system is to impede political thinking, and it does the same in Western societies. In theory, at least, Marxism seeks an economic solution for political problems, whereas the reverse approach (as applied in Marxist-Leninist countries) may be at least as realistic. It much overestimates the importance of ownership; monopoly or quasi monopoly is more a matter of power, no matter who holds formal title. Some Marxists welcome monopoly as hastening collectivism, or "socialism," which thus become only an exaggeration of capitalism. Marxist-influenced attitudes also lead to exaggeration of the political effects of economic change, as in the assumption that industrialization in the Soviet Union, China, or the developing nations must generate political institutions like those of the advanced industrial nations.

More serious has been the Marxist impediment to the understanding of the major political tides of our age. Marxist economic-social class approaches, shared to some degree by many non-Marxist observers, caused a fateful misunderstanding of fascism, as has been remarked. They also impeded understanding of Leninism, Stalinism, and what has happened to the Soviet Union since Stalin's death. Maoism in Marxist analysis is impossible; the forces of nationalism and racism make no sense; Western neocapitalism is not to be understood but to be explained away. [62] In a French view, "Marxist propaganda stands like a screen between society and understanding of society." [63]

The Debt to Marx

Because it makes democratic government more difficult, Marxism also impedes the reforms which should be a prime purpose of democracy. It attacks the state and social order as hopelessly rotten, thereby reducing their capacity to act, and gives a theory and rationale for their destruction without offering much positive to replace them. Looking to a mirage of revolution, it looks away from efforts to improve institutions and arouses fears and resistance to change. A leading American Marxist economist, Paul M. Sweezy, writes that "to speak of reforming capitalism is either naïveté or deceit." [64] Dogmatic and convinced of its answers, Marxism does not think in terms of problem solving. To be problem oriented is to be temperamentally non- or anti-Marxist. Obsession with capitalism is narrow; there is parasitic enrichment at the expense not only of factory workers but also of consumers, taxpayers, and many others, including capitalists victimized by bosses and manipulators. Overemphasis on one aspect, exploitation of labor, impedes consideration of many another ill, from boredom and pollution to unsound foreign policy. Perception is seriously distorted; the miserable of our day are not those who are exploited by producers but those who, for lack of skills or other reasons, have no useful role in society. Marxist perceptions of the war in Vietnam sidetracked much of the antiwar protest to a futile and counterproductive attack on the system as a whole, even against the universities which were alleged to have sold out to the evil forces but which in fact were the chief centers of the antiwar movement.

The ills of the present are too serious to be analyzed and confronted in terms of two semimythical classes. The Marxist-inclined view of economics is also unfortunate in that it concentrates entirely on the slicing of the pie, not its size or quality. Owners and managers of industry sin as much by their stupidity as by their cupidity; the biggest failure of American capitalism is not exploitation of people but failure to make better use of human capacities. To put the great debate in terms of transfer of ownership to the state is to invite unreason. There is a certain immorality, too, in making class relations a pillar of social philosophy. It deprives persons of individuality, making them theoretically (although not usually in practice) creatures of their situation. It raises the principle of guilt by association to the nth degree. It says, too, that society is at fault, not the partly autonomous people who comprise it. Marxism takes a naïve view of human nature in holding leisure, peace, and adequate materials sufficient for happiness; the idea that life is without

223

depth unless it has its share of suffering is totally outside the Marxist view.

Despite these weaknesses, Marxism has exercised a singular fascination for intellectuals wherever the political climate has been conducive; many have apparently seen in it a promise of power. Yet they have been ill served. Where Marxism-Leninism has taken power, intellectuals have found themselves downgraded unless they were able and willing to exchange free inquiry for a political vocation; there is no room for the free critic in "socialist" societies. In pluralistic societies, on the other hand, Marxism has seriously cramped the influence of the intellectual community by causing power elites to distrust the academics—not just those who speak in Marxist terms but, by association, the whole "class." Political and economic leaders are less prepared to seek or take the advice of the literati when many of these adopt attitudes which seem to the elite to be not only stupid but evil. Those left out, despite their superior knowledge, become even more receptive to Marxist views. Thus, Marxism is a wedge between groups whose full collaboration is most essential.

Against these demerits of Marxism must be weighed its merits, as frequently cited, of opening up new fields of inquiry and giving new insights, bringing out neglected economic factors in history and politics, and calling attention to the claims of the deprived. A German disciple of Marx put it this way: ". . . that gigantic brain, which embraced all the achievements of German philosophy, English economic science, and French revolutionary theory, has lavishly fructified millions of human intellects—not excepting those who were to oppose him as too extreme or too moderate." [65] Marxist concepts have been very important in the making of modern sociology. Karl Mannheim, Max Weber, Thorstein Veblen, Charles Beard, C. Wright Mills, and many others have been much influenced by Marx. All those who look to a radical reconstruction of society may be grateful to Marx for his debunking of respectable but outworn values and for his erosion of the foundations of the present order. Marx has above all been the great agitator.

How far the merits attributed to Marx in social philosophy are genuine and important is hard to assess because there is no agreement on what they really were. Marxist laws have been saved since Engels's day by being treated as conditional and qualified, matters of intuition and judgment, quite the opposite of what they were intended to be. Moreover, Marx's discoveries are stated in the broadest terms; he is rarely if ever credited with bringing out a specific truth. He pointed, in effect with a wave of the hand, to broad directions which subsequent thinkers have found important. One cannot say that Weber or Beard built on specific ideas of Marx, but to some extent they did conform to his outlook. There is no certainty, for that matter, that they were better off for the Marxist influence. The contrary is conceivable; for example, without Marx, Beard might have made a more balanced economic interpretation of the drawing up of the American Constitution.

In view of Marx's poor performance as a forecaster, there is a heavy burden of proof on those who see him as a major intellectual contributor to show that his was a vision, not a hallucination. Marxian economics being outdated and unrelated to the modern approach, one looks mostly to the interpretation of history for Marx's positive contribution. Whatever appraisal is made of this, the dogmatic and polemical way in which it was presented has detracted from its utility for understanding the past. The simple periodization of history which Marxism propagated has a religious tone and can hardly be deemed scientific. The fundamental idea that we should look to changes in ways of doing things (not merely making things) as a guide to understanding the development of institutions is excellent, although not entirely original with Marx. It is regrettable that this promising insight is burdened with the extraneous thesis of class struggle.

Nor is it clear that the idea of base and superstructure is helpful; the network of causation is far more complex and more interesting. It is neither useful nor inspiring to consider literature and philosophy as mere expressions of economic and class relations, and to say that art is "crucially determined in content and style" by the economic base [66] is at best only partially true, at worst degrading and misleading. The record of the past, too, is much less dismal than as seen under the Marxist lens, whereby all is moved by the self-seeking of the fortunate and the reaction of the less fortunate. An estimate of Marx's influence, although not of his originality, should take into account the fact that Marx's voice was hardly heard in intellectual circles until magnified by the Russian Revolution, by which time his innovations and criticisms were not much needed.

Marx as truth seeker stands against Marx as revolutionary advocate; Marxism, along with whatever positive ideas it may have offered, has insinuated elements of mythology into social science.[67] Catholic theology may believe in the literal reality of angels, but it has left science alone in modern times; Marxism asserts itself as doctrinal truth in whatever it touches. It permits or encourages ideology to overshadow empirical science.[68] In the view of Lipset, its gift is "fundamental anti-intellectualism." [69]

To Marxism belongs some, perhaps a large share, of the credit or responsibility for the fact that equalitarianism is a leading political passion of this age, contrary as it is in some ways to the demands of technological civilization. Whether Marxism has helped toward equality is another question. It made very little contribution to the successful labor movements in such countries as England, the United States, and Sweden. Its call has sometimes seemed to be "Workers of all lands, divide"; [70] nothing has done more to split labor and leftist movements. Marxism has made labor agitation more difficult by associating it less with humane justice for the economically weak than with the destruction of "bourgeois" society. The middle classes who might gain from juster distribution of wealth are pushed by Marxism to the side of the wealthy, and many who were of no mind to defend the profits of industry have become disturbed by talk of social revolution. It is unfortunate to put equalitarianism in a context of strife, and it is doubly unfortunate to link it with an attack on the middle classes, who have brought most of what we know of as social justice. Radical verbiage has ill served the cause of socialism.

Whatever the effects of Marxism, they are not entirely to be ascribed to the ideas of the master. In his theory, the good society of the future is to be built atop the present society; in practice the emphasis has been much more on tearing down. One may assume that an intelligent Marx would take changes of society better into account than many of his loyal followers. As one of the more open-minded wrote, "To try to apply the Marxist theory of the proletariat as the class which creates wealth to conditions in the twentieth century, in a highly developed world, is un-Marxist." [71] Marx stood on the threshold of modernity and looked backward and forward; Marxism is basically an effort to deal with the industrializing age and is consequently relevant for those who feel menaced by its disruptions. Nowhere is it creative of a new social order; it is a factor for dissent and disorganization in the West, for repression and authoritarianism where Marxist-speaking parties are in power.

The popularity of Marxism in the non-Communist world is a testimonial to exasperation with deep and growing (or at least increasingly irritating) inequalities and to the incapacity of social science to deal with the modern malaise. To resort to Marxist theories in this situation is something of a surrender, a renunciation of the effort to do better, a reversion to outdated approaches. Marxism in this view is more a symptom than a cause of the confusion which besets the modern mind. The frictions, divisions, and maladjustments were preexistent, and Marxism would have had small appeal without them. But Marxism has provided a channel, focus, and rationale for essentially negative approaches. In the same fashion, Marxism per se has not been responsible for authoritarian regimes in Russia and China; but it has done much to facilitate them and to add a stronger psychological dimension to political absolutism. Marxism has been an important contributor to the modern mind and the modern muddle.

CHAPTER
VII
──────

Prospects

THE END OF WARS

MARX was a political philosopher who wrote for and mostly about his own time. He became inactive a century ago, and every year the world has moved farther from the issues which exercised him. Yet the influence of Marxism has grown greatly down to the 1970s. While becoming less pertinent, Marxism has become more powerful.

How this has occurred has been the subject of this book: the development of Marxism as the ideology of a labor-socialist movement, its metamorphosis into the official doctrine of a great state, and its expansion in the wake of World War II. But it needs to be underlined how much Marxism has depended on war. The influence of Marxism has surged and subsided, and the great upsurges have come from wars and fears of war. Marxism, like fascism, millenarism, and ideology in general, thrives on violence and weakens in tranquillity. An age distorted and darkened by war, threats of war, or the aftermath of war seeks ideological, all-encompassing answers and the moral security of promised improvement; an age which feels secure goes about its business of living, working, and enjoying. War represents extremism, lawlessness, and crusading for a utopian goal, a sacred victory; it is the highest consecration of political over economic calculation. When violence recedes, politics turns from desperate hopes of remaking society to crasser, mundane, mostly economic issues, to coping with problems instead of planning total victory.

Thus Marxism became ideologically enfeebled after the death in 1895 of Engels, its most effective sponsor and the only person who could hold it together. There were electoral successes for some years, but within a decade its momentum seemed to have run out; revisionists were squabbling with the more orthodox, and few took revolution seriously as a near-term prospect. The biggest issue sustaining the Second International was fear of war growing out of the arms race and the alignment of Europe into two hostile blocs.

World War I brought European civilization into question, restored Marxism as a creed of action, and gave it revolutionary opportunities such as it had not known since 1848. Thanks to Lenin's stiffness of will and flexibility of doctrine, Marxism won a revolution. But after the Russian civil war was finished and Europe settled down, the apogee was past. The 1920s were a time of general decline. The hopes and fears of the first postwar days receded; Germany, the prime hope of the Comintern, became prosperous and evidently stable. The French Communist Party began with 130,000 members in 1920–1921 but through some fluctuations slipped to 20,000 by 1929.[1]

The economic depression which began in 1929 and worsened during the next three years was of a severity now nearly forgotten; world trade and stock exchange values both shrank to about a tenth of their previous high levels. It was the perfect confirmation of the Marxist critique of capitalism as wasteful and irrational; and it was the more persuasive because it coincided with the building up of industry in "socialist" Russia under the First Five-Year Plan, the successes of which loomed greater than life because of propaganda. Yet the depression brought no tidal wave of Marxism but a reaction more fascist than leftist. In the early 1930s both Communism and democratic socialism looked tired and unpromising. It could be stated categorically that "Marxism is no longer a power that seems destined to shape the course of future history," and "Marxism in all its forms is now old and spent."[2]

The resurgence of Marxism came from the fascist danger and the growing apprehension of war, which restored the attractions of the leftist-internationalist doctrine and gave it respectability in antifascist intellectual circles. Stalin took fright at Hitler and ordered the Communists to assume a Popular Front position; this meant sacrifice of revolutionary ideology in favor of a semidemocratic program, but it brought them new life. Still, the outlook for Marxism did not appear bright on the eve of World War II; the fascists, with their extraordinary foreign policy successes, seemed to be riding the bandwagon of history.

The boost which World War II gave to Marxism, now mostly identified with Marxism-Leninism, has already been mentioned. But again, the immediate aftermath of the war marked a high point. In Western Europe, Communist parties which had come out of the resistance movement with great strength shrank rapidly after 1947 and in the next decade became insignificant, except in France and Italy, where they made themselves a stable part of the political system. Even in France the Communists were never able to recover the 26 percent share of the vote they received in 1946. The 1950s saw steady economic recovery and declining tensions. The cold war became habitual and lost fervor, and people began to forget the menace that nuclear weapons posed to civilization. In the United States the years following the onset of the cold war in 1947 were marked by conformism and ideological indifference, qualified by general anti-Communism. The Korean war agitated some spirits, but it was brief enough—only a year from the invasion of South Korea to the beginning of truce talks—and successful enough so that it did not much roil the U.S. political atmosphere. After the Cuban crisis of October 1962, with the Western world showing remarkably stable prosperity and the Soviet Union losing spirit, one might well have predicted a lingering death for Marxism.

The fortunes of this creed, or collection of creeds, were again restored by the war in Vietnam, or at least as soon as it appeared that the war was not going well for the United States. The results of seven years of active American involvement, during which the great industrial nation bombed and pounded North and South Vietnam for reasons which seemed increasingly unconvincing, are a familiar story. Many laid more blame on the capitalists (who allegedly profited by the war and presumably were secretly able to make their will effective somewhere behind the scenes) than on the generals and politicians (who clearly had a stake in the war and who sat at the centers of decision) because there was a theory placing the real blame on the greed of the former. The old Leninist thesis of the responsibility of capitalism for imperialism and war flourished mightily. In the United States, liberals took Marxism as a rationale for their repugnance at the cruelty of the conflict, and students saw Marxism as a moralization of their reluctance to be drafted and their feelings of repugnance ("alienation") for the system which made the senseless war possible. Dissidence of many varieties, mingled with racial and generational protest tending increasingly to fall into Marxist patterns, reached its height with maximum American participation in the war in 1968. Denigrating the American "establishment" and "imperialism" became the fashion for a large sector of opinion makers, and the world accepted the self-denigration of America. The valiant and effective resistance of anti-American and more or less pro-Communist Vietnamese aroused admiration and encouraged leftists, Marxists, and Communists. The blood, dirt, and gore of war were laid out before the peoples of the world by television with incomparably more vividness than newspaper reports ever conveyed. Germans increasingly said, as did Americans, that the capitalist state was perpetrating mass horrors, that anti-Communism (or anti-Marxism) in action was wrong, and that the Communists, victors by virtue of the truths which inspired them, were morally right.

The influence of the war on opinion began to subside, however, as American forces began to be withdrawn in 1969, despite flare-ups when American involvement was temporarily heightened, as in the incursion into Cambodia in May 1970 and the intensive bombing of North Vietnam in December 1972. Wild language of revolution gradually ceased to be modish; campus activism faded along with the draft. Long hair and hippie garb were partly replaced by medium cuts and conventional dress; youths began to see some virtues in the older generation and turned from protest back to books and professional training. The radical Marxist Students for a Democratic Society disintegrated, and the revolutionary Black Panthers decided to work within the established order. By the time the American military intervention was officially over, with the ending of the bombing in Cambodia in August 1973, the upper-middle-class guilty conscience seemed to be healing and the younger generation was finding its way back to the "system" which it despised. There was no longer any moving and unambiguous cause; it was no longer sinful to live in and work for America. Ballots began to look more promising than bullets, and the fiery radicals scattered to sundry causes, from Oriental mysticism to women's rights, or to well-paying jobs. Soviet repressions came back into focus. By 1973 many of the scientists and sophisticates who had been most opposed to anti-Communism in Vietnam were critical of the Nixon administration for its indifference to Soviet oppressiveness.

With the end of the war in Vietnam, the threat of a major war also seemed less than at any time for nearly sixty years. From 1971, détente dominated relations between China and the United States, and between the Soviet Union and this country. The greatest tension between two major powers was, ironically, between the two Marxist-Leninist and "socialist" giants. Although nuclear stockpiles continued to mount, major war seemed to be regarded as inadmissible by everyone, while there appeared little likelihood that the United States or any other power would or could repeat the sad experience of intervention, à la Vietnam.

Thus, the world may have come near the end of an agitated period which began with the crumbling of the Turkish empire in Europe and the Balkan wars of 1912–1913. All major political quarrels thereafter arose out of the two world wars and from the breakup of the European colonial empires. The Korean and Vietnam wars were caused by the inability of Communist and non-Communist powers to agree on the demarcation between their respective spheres after the Allied victory in World War II; tensions in Europe arose over the same problem. Wars between India and Pakistan, plus civil wars in Africa, came out of the difficulty of fixing the boundaries of the new nations. The Arab-Israeli conflict began with the 1917 Balfour Declaration promising a Jewish homeland in Palestine. But as of 1975 these quarrels, if not all settled, seem to have too much subsided to become a casus belli. The superpowers, in any case, are reluctant to allow the lesser powers to fight, if only because they are afraid of becoming involved themselves; and no political or economic stake is worth a nuclear war. Although the arms race gives cause for concern in the United States, U.S. military expenditures are a slowly shrinking percentage of national product. Japan and Western Europe show that capitalist economies can prosper with slight to moderate arms budgets and without anything which can realistically be called imperialism.

If the role of war is reduced in the lives of nations, Marxism is the loser. Causes shed their character of desperation. The argument that capitalism makes war while socialism makes peace ceases to be stirring. Lenin's old thesis falls flat as the colonial empires, for the sake of which he thought the industrial countries had to go to war, break up into numerous small and weak countries that take pleasure in acting contrary to the wishes of the superpowers. Fascism and militaristic nationalism also fade from the scene; permanently discredited by defeat, they have no place in a world where war promises neither glory nor profit. And fascism was the best foil for Marxism.

RECEDING REVOLUTIONS

THE enduring importance of the great wars for Marxism lay in the revolutions they generated, which transformed the loose creed of the Social Democrats into the firm dogma of strong and prestigious Communist states. This book has stressed the central importance of that fact for Marxism since 1917; unique backing has given a unique place to an otherwise not very distinguished set of ideas. But all revolutions have worn out sooner or later, usually sooner, permitting a return to much of the mentality and many of the ways of the Old Regime. Revolutions are creative and exuberant, but they are exaltations from which nations return to worldly practicality or political sloth. One of their great strengths is precisely the newness of everything and the promise of the unattainable. The revolution becomes a victim of its success.

The marvel of the Russian Revolution is that it has lasted so well, that there is still something of its spirit in the well-indoctrinated Komsomol. No other social revolution has shown comparable staying power. In the English revolution, eleven years after Charles I was executed, Charles II mounted the throne. In the French, eighteen months after Louis XVI was executed, a reaction swept away Jacobin rule; ten years later, France had an emperor surrounded by a royal court in the style of the Bourbons. In this century, the equalitarian Mexican revolution which began in 1911 simmered down to moderate conservatism within a generation, although its symbols and traces of its ideals remain to this day. The very radical Turkish revolution of Kemal Atatürk, begun in 1920, did not much survive his demise in 1938. Marxism-Leninism must receive most of the credit for the fact that the Russian Revolution has so long maintained a stance (although since about 1940 hardly a reality) of social change, because Marxism-Leninism gives a framework for continuing struggle both domestically and on the world scene. But too many times and over too many years the results fail to correspond to the hopes and sacrifices. The organization ripens and ages, fighters become functionaries, the elite becomes selfish, and the ideology becomes wearisome repetition—a process which can be reversed only by upheaval and renewal of hope for new happiness from new sufferings.

The Soviet state has been retreating almost from the morrow of Lenin's seizure of power. The ideal of world revolution, only within which the Russian Revolution had proper Marxist meaning, was largely set aside by the decision to make formal peace with Germany in March 1918 and became hollow after the Red Army failed in Poland in 1920. Differences of reward were admitted, the state apparatus was accepted as necessary not just for a brief period (to assure power for the proletariat) but indefinitely, and the utopia was postponed to an ever vaguer future. The civil war brought radicalism and utopianism—it was in the civil war that the Soviet patterns were burned into Russia. But as soon as it was over, a large amount of private enterprise was reintroduced to restore the economy. The Soviets turned to foreign trade, hoping to gain from friendly commerce with the class-hostile forces what they failed to achieve by propagating revolution. Stalin, dedicating Russia to "Socialism in One Country," completed the nationalization of the universalist revolution and converted the international Communist movement to a tool of foreign policy.

Stalin could still revive the revolution by giving it grand new purposes, the collectivization of agriculture and the planned socialist industrialization of the backward but potentially rich country. He thereby kindled new hopes and raised a new elite. The Soviet Union seemed on the verge of something new and indefinitely promising. But the hopes were less generous and shallower than those of a dozen years earlier; Stalin's second revolution was less enthusiastic and more coercive than Lenin's had been. The sequel of the transformation from above was the purges, ideologically rationalized but cynical and at times sadistic. By 1940 the Russian Revolution was decadent, gripped by a despot and his courtiers, incompetently governed by fear. The degree to which bureaucratic stupidity had taken over was shown by the poor planning and weak waging of the war against Finland, 1939–1940.

Not surprisingly, the Russian Revolution was fairly well exhausted after a little over twenty years; Stalin was a reincarnation of the tsars whom he admired: Peter the Great and, more aptly, Ivan the Terrible. When the Nazis attacked in June 1941, they expected, like military experts around the world, that they could cut through the rotten structure in a few weeks. For several months it seemed that they were not far wrong; Stalinist Russia was beaten in 1941 much worse than tsarist Russia had been beaten in 1914–1917. But Soviet Russia had assets its predecessor lacked. Its elite was still fairly close to the people; it had a powerful organizational structure for mobilization and control; it still had some faith in its high destiny. German brutality inspired a common dedication to survival. Despite much incompetence and the burdens of a despotic form of government, Russia pulled itself together to win. In victory and subsequent expansion, with the new prestige of the Soviet state, ideology was vindicated and the revolution proved worthwhile.

The Soviet Union was consequently able to rebuild rapidly and to maintain itself as something of a model and a hope for those who found little inspiration in the older and less pretentious Western system. But in the last years of Stalin's reign, stagnation was again setting in; the dead hand of the centralized leadership was heavy, and isolation was oppressive. Khrushchev tried to revive something of the revolution with small doses of liberalization and equalitarianism; best of all, he raised hopes for worldwide Soviet victory by economic growth. But his espousal of peaceful coexistence was another step away from Leninism. Violent revolution was at least half renounced: socialism was to conquer the world by an unexciting, peaceful process, in ways unclear. Destalinization told the people that the dictator whom they had been taught to revere as the semidivine incarnation of Marxism-Leninism was a criminal and an incompetent. Faith so shaken cannot be rebuilt, and if the greatest leader of the workers' state could be so lacking, it was hard to expect uncritical acceptance for others. In 1961, when Khrushchev made his bid for a high place in the Marxist Valhalla by unveiling his plan for transition to Communism, it turned out to be bloodless verbosity, a promise of tranquil affluence little more inspiring than American political platforms.

Khrushchev failed in terms of his ambitions. The economic growth which was to carry the Soviet Union to world supremacy faltered, lagging behind that of many other states. Khrushchev could no more persuade large parts of the less developed world to join ranks with the Soviet Union than he could cure the ills of agriculture by planting corn nearly everywhere. After rocket-rattling bluster, he had to concede American strategic superiority; and he presided over the schism with by far the most populous member of the once formidable Sino-Soviet bloc.

Khrushchev's successors seem to have been alarmed that his efforts to revivify by a little slackening, experimentation, and updating of Soviet ideology might endanger the system—in other words, that some freer breezes might become a storm blowing the whole structure open. Since fear of loss of power is ample reason to cherish Marxism-Leninism, they began a determined campaign to sustain ideological fundamentalism, which has continued with waves of varying intensity to this day. Even in the aftermath of publicized détente with the chief imperialist, the United States, it was made clear to Soviet citizens that they should not draw political conclusions therefrom. Soviet propagandists by the hundreds of thousands were called upon to wage "aggressive, uncompromising battle" against such Western ideas as the preference for a "general human" over a "class" approach and the idea of technocratic rather than political solutions, warning that capitalism-imperialism had changed only some tactics, not its ingrained nature.

But while reemphasizing ideology, the post-Khrushchev leadership was unable either to modernize by realistic adaptation or to add anything which might rekindle a bit of enthusiasm. It could only hold to the well-worn dogmas, probably out of fear that to admit change of any part would call all into question. But the old answers were no longer satisfying. The new generation lacked experience not only of the revolution but also of the world war; the ideology and purpose were never burned into it. Very few true believers remained.[3] There was less and less change in Soviet society, and less promise that any change would bring elusive happiness. The simplest meaning of Marxism is the right of the poor against the rich, but inequality in Soviet society was growing. Despite occasional rejoicings over the troubles of the Western world, Soviet-Russian messianic feelings seemed to be drying up. Contradictory statements and actions, talk of struggle and confrontation mixed with friendly welcomes for foreign businessmen, may have reflected uncertainty in the Soviet leadership as to short- and long-term goals.

Worst of all was the contradiction between an ostensibly revolutionary creed and the growing fixity and conservatism of Soviet society. After the state settled down in the shape given it by Stalin, it tended increasingly to become the property of those in high positions, an elite the more fixed because it held economic as well as political power. Soviet society became inherently more conservative than American society because there were far fewer means— no means, so far as the rulership could arrange—by which dissatisfied elements could exert pressure for change.

The party-state elite, a self-perpetuating group controlling access to its own ranks, more like an aristocratic club than the looser elites of Western countries, inevitably became a privileged stratum—in effect, a closed governing nobility somewhat restrained by ideological commitment. To a large extent, privilege was kept inconspicuous, but the chauffeured limousine became a status symbol in the Soviet Union perhaps more than in any Western country. In no other army is the gap between ordinary soldiers and high officers so great as in the Soviet. This inevitably means that growing numbers of people with authority use their authority for their own purposes; a jungle of controls, with no checking from outside, is a mass of opportunities for private benefit. History shows that a tight, bureaucratic system, inevitably more or less self-serving, invariably loses effectiveness. And the Soviet system has no magic remedy.

An American scientist expressed the common view in the wake of the first Soviet sputnik: " 'When I really feel gloomy, I think that five years from now the Russians will be ahead of us in every area. But when I feel optimistic, I think it may take them ten.' " [4] But what he thought was an ongoing tide was only the crest of the wave. Around 1958 not only Soviet propagandists but also many Americans projected the Soviet economy as surpassing the American in a fairly short time; Soviet power in the world would presumably be overwhelming by 1970, or by 1975 at the latest. But by 1973, Japan, with only 43 percent of the Soviet population total and without the raw materials Russia possessed, had already exceeded the Soviet Union in nonmilitary goods produced. The Soviet Union sank from sixth place among trading nations in 1956 to tenth place in 1972. It was also becoming more dependent. After the big splurge of importation of Western machinery and technology in the 1930s, the Soviets moved toward industrial self-sufficiency; foreign trade (outside the Soviet bloc) was reduced to a trickle by Stalin's last years. But by the late 1960s the Soviet Union was again, as nearly forty years earlier, driven to purchasing abroad the industrial modernization it found difficult to engineer for itself, importing not only designs but entire factories and help in installing them, soliciting the participation of American, Japanese, and German capitalists in the exploitation of its resources. When an American bank opened a branch on Karl Marx Square in Moscow, and when Communist party leaders studied American managerial techniques at Karl Marx University in Budapest,[5] it was hard for a Marxist to doubt that something had gone wrong. Only in armaments did the Soviet economic system really excel.

A substantial part of the economy escapes into the gray and black markets. It is typical, for example, that fish taken by poachers approach in tonnage the legal catch from Soviet internal waters.[6] Laws may have little effect. For example, despite regulations severely limiting sales of vodka, it is said to be freely available at all hours; its widespread overuse is attributed to boredom.[7] The state can no longer control its citizens in the Stalinist way. A survey of Soviet tourists indicated that 70 percent of the population listened to foreign broadcasts.[8] The police strive to repress dissent—charging not ideological deviation but treason to the motherland—but they are far less effective than even a decade ago; dissidents now have higher morale. It has been found necessary to permit a stream of Jews to emigrate from the land of socialism, while authorities have increasingly applied the easy but somewhat craven remedy of exile for those they could not easily silence. Since the times of Khrushchev, who sometimes talked like a true believer, the Soviet state has done very little to advance the cause of Communism abroad and still less to promote revolutions in a world where the Soviets, like bourgeois gentlemen, seemed to prefer stability to agitation. The interests they have pursued are strategic, especially in the Near East, and are to be gained by dealing with governments, not ideological parties. Soviet foreign aid, which Khrushchev once boosted as a means of leading the world's majority to Soviet socialism, has shrunk to little more than a supplement to Soviet military aid to countries of special interest, such as India and Syria. No less disillusioning from the Marxist point of view has been détente with the United States, the great antagonist for Marxists. The Soviet press saw President Nixon, an erstwhile leading anti-Communist, as hounded from office by "reactionaries." When Nixon and Brezhnev embraced, leftists could only be critical of both.

Other Marxist-Leninist powers have likewise lost attractiveness as models. The hostility of the two Communist giants confused those who would be admirers of both, and it divided the Marxists of the world between the conformists to the Soviet line and the activist-idealists more charmed by the more spirited

Chinese. The faith of both was tried as each power branded the other as a dictatorship of the rankest order. The Chinese inspired many with their revolutionary zest in calling for guerrilla warfare in the early 1960s, but the chaos of the Great Proletarian Cultural Revolution caused bewilderment. Admirers had to overlook many foibles, from electrified statues of Mao that produced a glowing halo to the humiliations inflicted upon Chinese intellectuals, (compelled to learn true "socialism" by feeding pigs), the attack on culture, the closure of schools, and the proscription of art and literature except for a few propagandistic pieces.

Coming out of the Cultural Revolution, the Maoists disillusioned revolutionaries by reaching an understanding with the United States, less for economic reasons than from fear of possible Soviet aggression. The Chinese, like the Russians, settled down to rather realistic diplomacy, finding more to gain from dealing with states than with ideological movements. Drifting between a tendency to settle down, Maoist abhorrence of bureaucratization, and revolutionary rhetoric, China cannot be considered a major fountain of inspiration.

The lesser Communist states likewise, as the 1970s ripened, lacked inspirational glow. The Soviet satellites had fair to good records of economic growth, but the people showed more propensity for Western than Soviet culture. Except perhaps for Bulgaria and East Germany, they tended to drift away from the Soviet model, groped for what independence they might, and evinced little zeal for Marxism-Leninism or socialism in the abstract. Eastern Europe was far more influenced by the West than vice versa. It was only pathetic that the eighty-year-old Tito in 1971–1972 tried to put Marxism back into the universities and by fiat breathe new life into Marxist convictions.

Marxism as a philosophy can no more escape the implications of its failure as applied politics than it could excuse the failure of its predictions. In vain did a leading American Marxist economist protest that it was "naïveté or deception to cite the Soviet Union to prove anything about socialism." [9] It is about as fair to blame "socialism" for the sins of the Soviet Union as to judge "capitalism" by the United States. The Soviet Union remains the prime, self-proclaimed, and once much-touted example of the application of Marx to a big and potent state. Lenin presumably was in earnest in trying to establish a Marxist society; if his failure may be ascribed to especially unfavorable conditions in Russia (much less unfavorable than in China), none of the fourteen countries supposedly applying Marxist-Leninist principles has shown any substantial resemblance to Marx's utopia. Nor does any offer much guidance or inspiration for those who would build a better future atop the ruins of capitalism. A Marxist not only cannot point to the Soviet Union as proof of the liberating power of Marxism; he also has the burden of showing how one can be sure that Marxism applied elsewhere would have opposite results.

In view of the presence of such ostensibly Marxist but repressive, possibly decadent states, it is not easy for followers of Marx to see themselves in the vanguard of history. The uplift which Marxism received from the direct and indirect effects of the Russian and Chinese revolutions belongs to the past. It has become easier for the revolutionary-minded of the West to see in the Soviet state the evils they saw in America: alienation, bureaucracy, oppression, and exploitation. Marxism, it seemed, helped not the proletariat but a party manipulating and exploiting it; it was used, as Marx said of ideologies in general, to disguise reality. Ironically, protests against Soviet repression of dissident intellectuals in 1973–1974 came mostly from leftists and liberals, writers and scientists.

Marxism has a large admixture of charisma and hero worship, but the heroes are faded or discredited. The three exceptions are Lenin, who was fortunate enough to leave politics before he became outworn; Che Guevara, saved by martyrdom; and the reclusive Mao. But even Stalin was interesting and exciting, and he was doing new things. The latter-day Communist leaders suffer from the fact that they are capable of no innovation and of little that could be called leadership; hence they raise no passions among their followers, who badly want to be led out of the wilderness.

From an intellectual point of view, it has long been true, as remarked by De George, that association with Soviet power crippled Marxism-Leninism as a philosophical system.[10] It may become true, as Gurian wrote prematurely in the mid-1930s, that "it is Bolshevism more than anything else which has accelerated the decay of Marxism." [11] If one can project the trends of Soviet society, economics, and politics—a proposition by no means certain—corruption will become more prevalent, the ideology will become still more like a set of advertising slogans, the large majority which is excluded from political life will become more cynical, and the prostitutes in Red Square will rival those of Times Square, while the decadent Soviet state will continue to avow the name and doctrines of Marx.

THE FATIGUE OF IDEOLOGY

"IDEOLOGY" is another word whose meaning has been loosened by Marxist usage.[12] A pejorative term in Marx, it has been turned around in Communist usage to be an excellent thing, at least when it refers to the true ideology, scientific Marxism-Leninism. The term came into vogue in application to the totalitarian states of the 1930s. The original meaning, as indicated by etymology, was the science of ideas; from this it took the meaning of speculation or theorizing, especially in a visionary fashion. In Marxist language, it became the way of thinking of a class, especially as in "bourgeois ideology." From this it was taken as a description of the idea-system by which modern despotisms have sought to justify and rationalize their exercise of power.

Ideology was hence redefined to fit the totalitarianisms in the works of such writers as Carl Friedrich and Zbigniew Brzezinski. In this usage, ideology was an explicit belief system linking the leader with the movement, blaming an enemy, and defining a goal to be achieved; it was thus treated as a means of change. This applied to fascism, but fascist ideology was only a shallow mimicry of Marxism-Leninism; the real ideology was Marxism-Leninism-Stalinism. However, the official Soviet creed is no longer directed toward change or much political mobilization, and it has become more like a wall protecting the new established order than a battering ram for smashing the old. Ideology hence had to be redefined, and political scientists have since used the term freely for almost any kind of political rhetoric or nonreligious inspirational discourse, any attempt to involve people in a cause larger than themselves. In this sense, there are an indefinite number of ideologies.

There is something to be said for the narrower usage. A democratic state rests on certain ideas, but the government claims the right to govern on the basis of popular will in free elections, and this is so well understood that it needs no elaborate rationale and few people even talk about it. Very few indeed are aware of John Locke, compared with the multitude of those who claim familiarity with Karl Marx. If "ideology" is taken to mean an integrated world view and theory of history requiring definite commitment, it becomes almost equivalent to Marxism or some variant; there is little real competition. The question *Why Marxism?* is thus virtually an inquiry into the strength of ideology in the contemporary world. For such reasons, persons of Marxist inclination resist the thesis of the decline of ideology in general. But if ideology implies a dogmatic, combative, and utopian creed, one must admit decline in recent decades or loss of these qualities which were formerly considered its essence.

In the late 1930s the big issue in world politics seemed to be ideological confrontation of fascists and Communists, and the violence of their verbal duel was total. Some of this seemed to be revived in the cold war. At one time, the bipolar division of the world encouraged the belief that the essential fact about a state was its East-West orientation. But the postwar shouting match was never so unbridled, and there were recurrent efforts to reach understandings in the awareness that nuclear war must be avoided. Nationalism became conspicuous, especially in the new nations, and states increasingly broke away from the opposing camps, the "free world" and the Sino-Soviet bloc. Neutralism—that is, a nonideological posture—became acceptable and then fashionable.

By the early 1960s, the world had grown weary of the cold war, and the issues of Communism and anti-Communism seemed to lose significance. The Communist parties of the West had abandoned truculent Marxism in practice by committing themselves to a gradualist approach and working within the "bourgeois" system; all except the Italian and French had lost their wartime gains and became insignificant. At an international socialist conference in Hamburg in 1958, the name of Marx was only once mentioned, as delegates spoke of freedom and democracy.[13] The German Social Democratic Party, once the mainstay of Marxism in the world, by its 1959 Bad Bodesberg Program dropped proletarian revolution and effectively abandoned Marxism. European labor moved from semi-political to purely economic strikes, American-style. With the easing of the cold war, intellectuals felt freer to criticize both Communism and anti-Communism. World and social tensions were fading, and ideology seemed more and more to be an affair of the less developed countries,[14] irrelevant to the more technical problems of modernity.[15]

After 1965, however, the "decline of ideology" proclaimed by

242

such observers as Daniel Bell seemed an illusion.[16] The United States was swept by protest movements, beginning with students and running through organized demands for rights for blacks, Amerindians, Mexican-Americans, women, homosexuals, and others.[17] There was a strong upsurge of Marxist writing and of extreme criticism of American institutions as a backdrop for agitation against the war in Vietnam. In a sharply ideological spirit abroad, many proclaimed the conviction that right thinking was more important than clear thinking, that passion took precedence over reason. Social and intellectual disorder was sufficient to inspire some predictions that the breakup of civilization was imminent. The Western world followed the American example; protest was the order of the day. In the Soviet bloc, too, Khrushchev's successors, who seemed for the first months to take a more relaxed and pragmatic attitude, reemphasized ideological drive and discipline.

But this appearance of reideologization was illusory. The New Left and the whole wave of protest and discontent were diffuse, disorderly, and incoherent. It was visceral protest; it knew a few things it hated but very little in which it positively believed. It demanded conformity in hairstyles but intellectually embraced anything which seemed antiestablishment, from Oriental mysticism to hard-line Marxism. Marxism for the New Left was mostly a code word for radicalism. It had no utopia but peace and perhaps a commune. It was more hysteria than theory. It was practically innocent of any idea—indeed, of any thought—as to what was to be done positively to reconstruct the world which was angrily to be torn down. It was not doctrine but revulsion.

The tumult of these years, which included everything from academicians' semi-Marxist writing to arson and riot, was closely linked with a single, somewhat anachronistic, cause, American military intervention in Vietnam. Calm began returning as soon as it appeared that America was disengaging. This was a long process, from the restriction of the bombing over North Vietnam (March 31, 1968) to the cessation of the bombing of Cambodia (August 15, 1973); and protest resurged when withdrawal was temporarily interrupted. But already in 1969, President Nixon in his State of the World report could say, "isms have lost their vitality"; and when disengagement was completed, America and the world were prepared to look at themselves in a more sober light.

Violent revolution, the most engrossing subject for ideology, is a dead issue in the West. Few hold nationalization of the economy to be a cure-all, in the light of the experience of Western as well as Marxist-Leninist states. British coal miners go on strike as though the bosses were private capitalists instead of the public. The antithesis of "socialist" and "capitalist" states has diminished. The former desire investment from the latter, and the latter agree fairly well on socialized welfare programs. Business and propertied interests have accepted many "socialistic" measures which in Marx's day seemed possible only by violence. Even in the United States, respectable and fairly conservative politicians call for nationalization where special circumstances may require it, as of the railroads or, during fuel shortages, of the petroleum industry. In the first part of this century socialists thought abolition of private property would make men into supermen in body or intellect or both,[18] while conservatives thought the opposite. But the extent of public ownership is no longer an issue to raise tempers very much.

The exploitation of labor has likewise cooled as an issue. Most factory operatives and many other laborers, such as construction workers, have obtained quite satisfactory pay scales in industrialized countries. Others are left behind, but there is no more feeling that social justice is simply a matter of a battle between labor and capital or between any clearly defined groups. No simple formulas are believable. The whole idea of right versus left, which has run through politics since its invention in the French Revolution, is outmoded. Ideology bespeaks simplicity and certainty, but this is an age of complexity and uncertainty of directions.

Ideology derives its force from the we-they opposition. But the world picture is blurred when the Marxist-Leninist Russians and Chinese denounce each other more bitterly than either denounces the United States, and when an American administration sometimes seems more concerned over relations with the Soviet Union than with its major allies. A complicated world of multifaceted diplomacy is emerging, and the issues which preoccupy statesmen and fill the media are much less questions of power, prestige, and national survival than of economics, trade conditions, and monetary management. These are dull, not adventurous; concrete, not symbolic. They involve means more than ends; they are ordinarily adjustable by bargaining; and they arouse relatively little exhilaration.

But there is not much point in being a Marxist or a devotee of any ideology unless one can be passionate about it. Ideology is primarily a cry of holy war, and this age does not encourage faith in violent solutions. The idea of the people rising in the style of the

French storming the Bastille has only faded further since Engels sensibly found it outmoded eighty years ago. International violence has lost allure; the glorification of military heroics is a specialty of the Marxist-Leninist world. Fear of nuclear war is general, and it tends to inhibit ideas of taking up conventional arms; even hijackings and the terrorism of "liberation armies" may be passing somewhat out of fashion. But without large-scale violence abroad, it becomes difficult to dream of an indignant people mobilizing to reorder society. There may be coups, but ideological agitation is not necessary for these.

The problems of this age—preventing nuclear war, reducing the gap between rich and poor nations, safeguarding the planetary environment, controlling population increase and feeding the masses of humanity, management of natural resources, directing economic growth in salutary directions, among others—are complicated, technical, and amenable to no quick and easy solutions. There are a medley of issues and a medley of ideas regarding them, with numerous overlapping divisions of society on both the world and domestic stages. Far from becoming ever simpler, as Marx believed, the social order becomes ever more complex. It is hard even to pretend to put forward a solution framed in stereotypes; the world needs problem solvers more than prophets. But ideology, in the older sense of the word, is faith and prophecy, the religious and not the engineering approach.

It may be that the period of modernization and industrialization, which became conspicuous toward the end of the eighteenth century and which formed the backdrop for the thought of Marx and Engels, may be coming to a close or a change of direction. If the world is in fact moving into a postindustrial society, it will frame its political notions differently than the industrializing societies did. Ideology, in the sense in which it was brought forward by the French Revolution, will then be replaced by new modes of thought.

THE MARXIST-COMMUNIST MOVEMENT

ORGANIZED MARXISM is largely represented by the Communist parties (or those of other names which subscribe to Marxism-Leninism), a large majority of which are affiliated with and depend on the Soviet party. They incorporate the principal hope of Marxism for expansion of its political sphere; and they are, in effect, a set of chimneys through which Marxism is belched into the intellectual air. The parties also serve as organizational foci for Marxist thought, at least in the countries where they are strong. Without them, Marxism would be much more subject to disintegration, everyone taking something different from the Marxist mass and adapting it to his taste.

The nonruling parties' future is problematic. They are troubled, when times are relatively tranquil, with the old dilemma of the pre–World War I Social Democratic parties and of the Soviet Union (and other Marxist-Leninist countries): the necessity of reconciling revolutionary ideology with nonrevolutionary practice, the old dichotomy of rhetoric and reality. There is no revolution in sight, and people tire of waiting for it; there is not even an overwhelming conviction that it is desirable. In 1968 the French party showed how little stomach it had for real-life revolution by rejecting the best opportunity for bringing down the government it had ever seen or was likely to see for many years. Yet the parties cannot give up radical goals because these are their badge of distinctiveness and the chief bond of the membership, without which they could not call for the wholehearted and uncritical commitment that gives the Communist Party its special strength. The course adopted is the same as that of the Social Democrats toward the end of the last century, to maintain an ideological-revolutionary posture but to act like a reformist party.[19] If there is no prospect of revolution, the sensible course is to work toward power by the means available, through elections and parliaments. But the Communist Party cannot hope to win power in any Western country unless it becomes acceptable to the middle classes; this is impossible unless the party sheds its militant essence.

Unable to square this circle, the Communist parties of Western Europe have in most countries shrunk to insignificance. Only in France and Italy have they kept a hold on a substantial fraction of the electorate, about one-fifth in France and about one-third in Italy; only in these countries do they have hopes of sharing national power by democratic process in the foreseeable future. But the nearer the party grows to staking out a claim to power, the stronger the pressure to adapt to the system. Since a Communist party cannot hope for a majority alone, it must seek alliances with rival parties; but to recognize them as legitimate is a serious ideological backstep. To make itself acceptable as a partner, moreover, it must persuade others that it subscribes to the rules of the constitutional game, that it respects freedoms and elections, and that if it obtained a grip on power it would, like other parties, be prepared to release it if the voters and the law so ordained. Thus, the French Communist Party, entering an electoral alliance with the socialists in June 1972, formally undertook to observe democratic processes. In December the Communist leader Georges Marchais assured the world that his was "no longer the party of the clenched fist but of the outstretched hand," and claimed that their socialism was wholly French.[20] In 1973 the Communists supported a presidential candidate, François Mitterrand, who claimed not to be a Marxist. In the election the Socialists outpolled the Communists for the first time in postwar history.

In seeking to make use of the electoral process, a Communist party, like any other, accommodates to it and acquires a stake in it, becomes more opportunistic, and sees more to gain by broadening its appeal than by purity of doctrine.[21] The process may be cumulative; the more the party gains by adaptation, the easier it becomes to adapt further for additional gains. The Italian Communist Party, with a larger following than the French, has gone still further in this direction. Since shortly after the death of Stalin, the Italians have been making themselves nationally respectable by separating themselves from the Soviet party, taking an independent position and reserving a right of criticism of Soviet actions, such as the repressions of independence movements in Hungary in 1956 and Czechoslovakia in 1968. They have many times called for greater freedoms in the Soviet Union; whereas the French Communists followed faithfully the Moscow line regarding the exile of Aleksandr Solzhenitsyn, the Italians were moderately indignant. They no longer recognize the CPSU as a "guiding party." [22] They have long accepted the European Economic Community, detested by Moscow; since 1968 they have participated in the European Parliament (the French followed in 1973). The Italian Communists have practically put the United States and the Soviet Union on the same level, calling officially for a Europe neither anti-Soviet nor anti-American.[23] The party claims to accept NATO and gets along well with the Catholic Church, to please which it opposes abortion. It deals more freely and easily with other parties than does the French CP. It takes a more populist than class approach; in any case, the attack on Italian capitalism is somewhat inhibited because most really big firms are government controlled—and the Communist Party, like other Italian parties, is officially subsidized.

The only other party in the industrialized world with a reasonable chance of securing a share of national political power is the Japanese. It is quite independent of the two ruling parties which seek its adherence, the Soviet and the Chinese; and it has gone far to shed the old revolutionary image. It makes capital of sundry grievances, such as pollution and the high cost of living, and proposes nothing radical. It would keep the emperor, the Japanese defense forces, and possibly the U.S.-Japanese Security Treaty. It would not even nationalize most industry.

It is easier for small parties than for large ones to be dogmatic and extremist. The former have less reason to bend doctrines or to seek accommodations with other parties. They rely more on their place in the world movement. They are constrained by dependence on Soviet aid, which involves not just subventions but many other forms of organizational and political support, without which many or most of them would probably degenerate to the merest splinters or go out of business entirely. Their future thus depends to a large extent on the evolution of the Soviet Union; as the Soviet party becomes less revolutionary, it may be expected both to pay less attention to the foreign parties and to become less attractive as a guide and model. Some may well decide, as the Norwegian party proposed in May 1974, that Communists no longer have a special role and can function better in a broader leftist coalition.

The future would seem more hopeful for the Communist and near-Communist parties of the less developed world. The differences between rich and poor countries do not decrease, and population growth makes it difficult to narrow the chasm. On one side of the gulf stand countries which can reasonably be called "capitalist"; on the other are countries which may well see themselves as exploited victims of capitalism and neo-imperialism. Even if inequality does not grow, awareness of it does. There is no satisfactory answer as to why some countries enjoy so much more wealth and potency than others, but Marxism more than any other creed addresses itself to the problem.

Yet it appears that in the less developed world also Marxism may have passed a zenith with the end of American involvement in Vietnam. The war offered a noble cause with which poor and dark-skinned peoples could easily identify, the better because the intellectual world of Europe and America gave the example of damning

American interventionism. Not only did Marxism fit many emotional needs of the Third World; it was also the intellectual fashion of the advanced countries, to which the inevitably imitative poorer ones look up. But for this same reason, if the intellectual communities of the United States and Europe turn away and discover that Marx is boring and unpromising, many in the developing countries will discover the same thing.

The idea of proletariat versus capitalists is grotesquely unsuited to the Third World and requires such reinterpretation as to deprive it of meaning; and to use the ideology of revolution in industrial societies to industrialize preindustrial nations is confusing. Lenin could at least lean on the notion of an urban proletariat taking over a bourgeois revolution as part of the world movement, but no such logic (or illogic) pertains to the less developed countries of today. Consequently, their Marxism rests upon the idea of imperialism, and Marxists have to keep shouting as though imperialism were a terror stalking the world. But the hundred-odd governments of the Third World do not themselves admit to being dominated by anyone. All claim to be very independent, and many of them enjoy flouting the superpowers on occasion. Oil-producing nations with no military strength jeopardize the economic well-being of the biggest "imperialist" powers, and not a gunboat appears on the horizon. It seems in some non-Marxist way that the new "imperialists" are the oil-rich countries which suck huge sums from the "capitalist" countries in return for little or no labor of their own. The problem of access to materials, which Marxism-Leninism omitted, looms larger than access to markets.

Anti-imperialism also suffers by the relative decline of the United States, the natural target of resentments. The ebbing of American economic and political predominance at once eases guilt feelings (and Marxist sentiments) among American intellectuals, reduces the resentment of Europeans at the American presence (which no longer threatens but guards their independence), and relieves the fears of weaker countries that America might take over their world. Several different competitive foreign interests are by no means so overbearing as a single big one. It can hardly be contended that the Japanese, European, and American interests conspire together; Leninist Marxism itself firmly contradicts this possibility. The more power is divided in the world, the less any state can coerce another and the less realistic becomes a theory based on imperialism or neo-imperialism.

Marxism also loses much of its appeal because leaders of less developed countries usually want economic progress and are realistic enough to see that the Soviet model is not the best way to get it. The Soviet pattern of industrialization, impressive in 1960, is no longer so. Governments which encourage and reward entrepreneurship have shown much better results than the so-called socialist regimes. So far as planning is desirable, it is more effective in the style of Western modified market economies, with governmental guidance instead of direct administration of production. The trend is exemplified by Egypt, which a dozen years ago was nationalizing and moving as rapidly as it reasonably could toward socialism, bringing nearly all industry and most other enterprises under government control. In recent years it has turned back to capitalistic institutions and offered many inducements to foreign capital. An Egyptian official was quoted as saying, "We have been asleep for twenty years. It is now time to wake up." [24]

For such reasons, Marxism may already have lost ground in the Third World or at least become more diffuse, more philosophical, and less political. The mood in the mid-1970s is one of increasing sobriety. The threat of "wars of liberation," which were regarded as a major danger by the United States around 1960, has practically vanished. Fidel Castro no longer talks of raising Latin America to fight the Yankees, only of joining other Latin American governments to oppose the United States diplomatically. Revolutionary Cuba was one of the very few countries in the world actually to go downhill economically in the fifteen years under Castroism. Communist parties in Latin America have made little progress, have generally ceased to be revolutionary, and in most places have lost influence. In 1973, Juan Perón's purge of radicals disappointed the Argentinian leftists who had helped him return in triumph. The 1970 victory of Allende in Chile elated Marxists everywhere, and his overthrow in 1973 gave them a minor martyr, but Marxist power had been unable to win a majority of the people and had brought economic breakdown. After Allende, only Peru in Latin America had a leftist government.

Elsewhere, socialist patterns have lost much of their enchantment. Various countries, including Ghana and Indonesia, have turned decisively away from socialism. In 1956 all major parties in Burma were more or less Marxist,[25] but afterward Marxist influence waned. As countries become accustomed to independence, the zest of change disappears, the Paris- or London-trained students become senior bureaucrats, and traditional values seem more attractive. Marx was best for the anticolonial struggle; countries which were never colonized (such as Ethiopia, Liberia, and Thailand) have shown much less Marxist influence than those which were. Independent Algeria renounced the semi-Marxism of Fanon in favor of Arabism and nationalism,[26] and Libya's strongman Muammar al-Qaddafi turned back to Muslim fundamentalism and berated Soviet Communism as fiercely as American imperialism. Zaïre went for Africanization, including the requirement that everyone take an African name. A token of the decline of Marxism in the developing world is the decreased popularity of single-party regimes, which have been replaced in many countries, especially those of Africa, by oligarchies or military dictatorships, which have little care or need for ideology.

Nevertheless, the outlook for Marxism as a faith remains best in the less developed countries. There is a belief abroad, propagated by the missionaries of Western capitalism, that technology can do whatever is necessary and that there should be abundance for all, the peoples of the earth being alike in native endowment. But when abundance fails to come, the supposedly equal peoples wait in poverty and humiliation. Countries, like India, which feel much more important than the world treats them languish in injured pride, for which there is no better salve than Marxism. Yet Marxism is much less potent than might be expected, in part because the truly desperate are powerless, while the powerful elite is tolerably satisfied with its situation. And if it becomes apparent that Marxism is peculiarly the ideology of the poorer, less educated, and less sophisticated, this will not raise it in the esteem of the intellectuals of the affluent industrial world.

THE FUTURE

THE near-term future of Marxism seems reasonably secure. If there is large-scale violence, Marxism would probably be the beneficiary; the Russians have contended that World War III would carry on the good work of the preceding wars and swell Marxist-Leninist power to cover the globe. A fairly tranquil world, on the other hand, may still expect to see Marxism in its official and unofficial forms live tranquilly on for a good many years. It has the great advantage of a tradition and a history of struggle, with its own prophets and apostles. It is a creed that has worked; it has profited from the psychology of success ever since it was taken up by the German Social Democrats. Even if its ideas are not taken seriously, its forms and vocabulary can be retained as the readiest means to express discontent. Form has outlasted content, as in all religions.

One may expect that Marxist-Leninist ideas will continue to lose relevance in the Soviet Union, as they have done with little remission since the day of the revolution. But they may long continue to be useful, if only in upholding the venerable authority of the party, a holy institution because it maintains the ideology of Lenin and the revolution. The theme of the new man may be as outworn as the idea of the battling proletariat, but in the normal course of affairs there would be no stimulus to cast it all overboard. It would be shattering to the Soviet state to discard the faith for which so much has been suffered and to admit that it was all a colossal mistake. One may consequently suppose that the Soviet Union will most likely continue long to venerate the name of Lenin without much using his or Marx's thought. Future historians may well debate over which year, perhaps which decade, could be said to mark the end of the Russian commitment to Marxism-Leninism. Something of the same might be said of other Marxist-Leninist countries, which have less to lose by abandoning the apotheosis of a Russian.

The Communist parties abroad, unless they are reenergized by unforeseeable events, can only become gradually less revolutionary. But they continue to exist and, in the French and Italian cases, fill a role in the political system; they may well be as permanent as any other party. They continue also to maintain some of the rhetoric of ideological radicalism, which they cannot officially renounce without renouncing their special title to existence. But the French Socialist Party also calls itself radical and retains radical symbols from the days of the Second International, while proposing nothing frightening to the schoolteachers and petty bureaucrats who support it. Only in Portugal, embittered by long dictatorship and a failed colonial war, has the Communist Party retained the old-time dogmatism; and there it drew strength, ironically for Marxists, primarily from the military.

Marxism is well-rooted in the intellectual world, especially in Western Europe and Japan but also around some institutions in the

United States. Those trained in Marxism have a vested interest in Marxist thought and approaches, and they may raise a new generation of Marxist-inclined scholars; many of the professors instructing the next generation will come from the youth formed during the years of most passionate radicalism. With their convictions of correct thought, Marxists in universities have tended to push forward other Marxists, and they do not propose that anti-Marxists be brought in for balance.[27] Even if specific articles of Marxist doctrine are dropped as inconsonant with reality, the neo-Marxists or post-neo-Marxists are likely to keep up as much as they can of the language and general approach ("creative Marxism") and pass them on to their successors.

It is rather common in the scholarly world that a certain thinker is set up as an authority beyond the depth or real creativity of his thought; he becomes a culture hero and is respected and discussed without being much read. Some scholars become specialists in studying, elaborating, and applying his ideas; and these scholars bring in students who, in turn, become specialists with a vested interest in maintaining special respect for this authority, whose work may have lost relevance except as commented on and interpreted by succeeding generations. Something of this occurred with such men as Plato and Aristotle, and in our day possibly with Weber and Durkheim, whose theories do not have to be taken very literally to be widely used. So too with Marx. The very specialness of the Marxist cast of thought helps give it academic permanence, since the mind molded to its semi-Hegelian conceptualizations finds empirical modes difficult. Marxists can become anti-Marxists more easily than they can become non-Marxists.

The shell of Marxism is thus likely to outlast the substance, in the ordinary way that radical movements are deradicalized. Parties of discontent will go on using Marxist language, which is applicable to a broad spectrum of discontents. But Marxism has lost novelty and charm. In 1917, or even in 1945, it was a fulsome promise, but now it has in too many places failed to produce anything conforming to the promises. The mystique is dulled in the repetition of formulas.

For real vitality, Marxism needs to be reshaped, and it may still be possible to read new "true meanings" into Marx. But this is difficult. In the past generation, Marxism has been very weak in theoretical development even when most loudly and fervently sustained; there are no new outstanding names or stimulating perspectives within the Marxist framework. The New Left was an intellectual failure, a melancholy confession of lack of forward-looking ideas. Perhaps Marxism is too backward-looking for more than routinized radicalism, just as its utopia is too primitive. Its basic ideas are incongruent with modern social theory, and Marxian economics offers nothing for such problems as optimal resource use, business cycle management, inflation, and monetary disequilibria. "Capitalism," a dirty word for successful self-seeking, potentially covering everything from a Cro-Magnon bully taking more than his share of the slain mammoth to investment by American firms in Russia, is not a persuasive analytical concept, and "exploitation" has become too complex for Marxist stereotypes. The division of society is more credibly between those who have power of some kind and those who do not, but Marxism is not elastic enough to handle this. The real problem is that the modern economy is too complicated to be guided effectively, and modern society is too complicated to be well governed.

Human beings are emotional, anxiety-ridden, and often lost in the complexities of a society and a universe beyond comprehension. But this is an age of ferment, not of faith. In the nineteenth century, it was too late to start a new religion; only sects arose. Now it seems too late to start a new ideology; ironically, fascism, exalting brawn over brain, was the last. The dream of socialism, the aspiration to bring happiness by restructuring social relations, is not easily given up. Too many articulate people feel unjustly treated, and others are pained by the injustices inflicted upon the inarticulate. But socialists, unable to cope with modern complexities or to generate new answers for problems, go back to inappropriate mid-nineteenth century texts to order their thoughts and find a ground of authority on which to stand.

Why they have done so has been the subject of this book. The answer can never be fully known because it is as complex and multifaceted as the political and psychological situations to which Marxism has been fitted. "Marx does not explain history; history explains Marx." [28] Science is permanent; later scientists add on, tearing down very little. Marxism is not a science, hardly even a theory, but rather a phenomenon, a tool, always adapted to the contemporary scene.

Arising from the impact of the new monetary-industrial society and the pangs of change from an agricultural way of life, Marxism belongs to the era of uneasy transition from a fairly stable preindustrial existence to a new, perhaps postindustrial adjustment.[29] Utopianisms and radicalisms commonly arise in the early stages of industrialization,[30] and Marx raised the most effective voice, mingling promise and protest. But the transition for the West is over; the land-based people can be uprooted and urbanized only once, and the great problems are no longer of production but management. Marxism, an unhappy, disturbing creed, has been part of the malaise of modernization, with its two great revolutions, the French and the Russian. It wears out as this era gives way to a new one, the outlines of which are beginning to emerge.

NOTES

___

CHAPTER I

1. Karl Marx and Friedrich Engels, *Manifesto of the Communist Party*, in *Basic Writings on Politics and Philosophy*, ed. Lewis S. Feuer (Garden City, N.Y.: Doubleday Anchor, 1959), pp. 9, 10.

2. As suggested by Carl Landauer, *European Socialism* (Berkeley: University of California Press, 1959), vol. 1, p. 18.

3. Discussed as the source of socialist thinking by George Lichtheim, *Marxism* (New York: Praeger, 1961), chap. 3.

4. David McLellan, *The Thought of Karl Marx* (London: Macmillan, 1971), p. 197.

5. Henry De Man, *The Psychology of Socialism* (London: George Allen & Unwin, 1928), p. 143.

6. Quoted in William R. Kintner, *The Front Is Everywhere* (Norman, Okla.: University of Oklahoma Press, 1950), p. 16.

7. For the antecedents of Marx, see Alexander Gray, *The Socialist Tradition: Moses to Lenin* (London: Longmans, Green, 1946).

8. A. James Gregor, *A Survey of Marxism* (New York: Random House, 1965), pp. 146–147.

9. George Lichtheim, *The Origins of Socialism* (New York: Praeger, 1969), p. 57.

10. Lichtheim, *Marxism*, p. 127.

11. Gregor, *Survey of Marxism*, p. 149.

12. Adam B. Ulam, *The Unfinished Revolution* (New York: Random House, 1960), pp. 74–80.

13. Marx, "Toward the Critique of Hegel's Philosophy of Right," in *Basic Writings*, ed. Feuer, p. 263.

14. Marx, *Economic and Philosophical Manuscripts*, quoted in Lichtheim, *Marxism*, pp. 49–50.

Notes

15. Marx, *Selected Writings in Sociology and Social Philosophy*, trans. T. B. Bottomore, ed. T. B. Bottomore and Maximilien Rubel (New York: McGraw-Hill, 1964), p. 97.

16. For example, see H. Langford, "The Imagery of Alienation," in *Marxism and Alienation*, ed. Herbert Aptheker (New York: Humanities Press, 1965), pp. 58ff.

17. Robert C. Tucker, *The Marxian Revolutionary Idea* (New York: Norton, 1968).

18. Ibid. Cf. Engels, *Anti-Dühring* (New York: International Publishers, 1939), p. 324.

19. Marx, *Selected Works* (Moscow, 1936), vol. 1, pp. 16–18.

20. Marx, preface to *A Contribution to the Critique of Political Economy*, in *Selected Writings*, ed. Bottomore and Rubel, p. 51.

21. M. I. Finley, "Between Slavery and Freedom," in *Economic Development and Social Change*, ed. George Dalton (Garden City, N.Y.: Natural History Press, 1971), p. 128.

22. McLellan, *Thought of Karl Marx*, p. 123.

23. For Marx's wrestling with the origins of feudalism, see Lichtheim, *Marxism*, pp. 145–146.

24. Engels to P. Ernst, June 5, 1890, in Marx and Engels, *Selected Correspondence* (Moscow: Foreign Languages Publishing House, 1953), p. 494.

25. Marx, *Poverty of Philosophy* (Chicago: Chas. H. Kerr, n.d.), p. 119.

26. Marx, *Capital* (New York: Modern Library, 1907), vol. 1, p. 712.

27. Marx, "Preface to the Critique of Political Economy," in Marx and Engels, *Selected Works* (Moscow, 1968), p. 183.

28. Engels to Bebel, March 18–28, 1875, in Marx and Engels, *Selected Correspondence* (Moscow, 1968), p. 338.

29. Engels, *The Origin of the Family, Private Property, and the State*, quoted in Gray, *Socialist Tradition*, p. 327.

30. Marx, *A Contribution to the Critique of Political Economy*, in *Basic Writings*, ed. Feuer, p. 44.

31. Marx, *Capital*, in *Basic Writings*, ed. Feuer, p. 135.

32. Marx, *Essential Writings of Karl Marx*, ed. David Caute (New York: Macmillan, 1967), p. 137.

33. Marx, *Economic and Political Manuscripts*, in *Karl Marx: Scientist? Revolutionary? Humanist?*, ed. V. Stanley Vardys (Lexington, Mass.: D. C. Heath, 1971), p. 51. Italics in original.

34. Marx and Engels, *Manifesto*, in *Basic Writings*, ed. Feuer, p. 14.

35. Leopold Schwarzschild, *The Red Prussian* (New York: Scribner's, 1947), pp. 328–329.

36. Marx to Engels, April 2, 1858, in Marx and Engels, *Selected Correspondence* (New York: International Publishers, 1942), p. 105.

37. Max Nomad, *Apostles of Revolution* (New York: Collier, 1961), p. 106.

38. Marx, *Poverty of Philosophy* (New York: International Publishers, 1973), p. 175.

39. Lewis S. Feuer, *Marx and the Intellectuals* (Garden City, N.Y.: Doubleday Anchor, 1969), p. 11.

40. Marx, *Karl Marx on Colonialism and Modernization*, ed. Shlomo Avineri (Garden City, N.Y.: Doubleday, 1968), p. 19.

41. Marx, *Critique of Hegel's Philosophy of Law*, quoted in Lichtheim, *Origins of Socialism*, p. 53. Italics in original.

42. Marx, *Wage Labor and Capital*, quoted in Gregor, *Survey of Marxism*, p. 277.

43. Richard T. De George, *Patterns of Soviet Thought* (Ann Arbor: University of Michigan Press, 1966), p. 10; Gray, *Socialist Tradition*, p. 330.

44. De Man, *Psychology of Socialism*, p. 164.

45. Sidney Hook, *Towards the Understanding of Karl Marx* (New York: John Day, 1933), p. 10.

46. Marx to Weydemeyer, March 5, 1852, in *Selected Correspondence* (1953), p. 86. Italics in original.

47. Lichtheim, *Marxism*, p. 240.

48. Marx, *Early Writings*, trans. and ed. T. B. Bottomore (New York: McGraw-Hill, 1964), p. 166.

49. George F. Kennan, *Democracy and the Student Left* (Boston: Little, Brown, 1968), p. 8.

50. Howard Sherman, *Radical Political Economy* (New York: Basic Books, 1972), pp. 5, 6.

51. György Lukács, *History and Class Consciousness* (London: Merlin, 1971), p. 1.

52. Engels recognized the religious character of the socialist movement. See *On the History of Early Christianity*, in *Basic Writings*, ed. Feuer, pp. 168–194.

53. Robert C. Tucker, *Philosophy and Myth in Karl Marx* (Cambridge: Cambridge University Press, 1961), pp. 14, 233.

54. Quoted in David Flakser, *Marxism: Ideology and Myths* (New York: Philosophical Library, 1971), p. 209.

55. Konrad Farnen, *Theologie des Kommunismus* (Frankfurt: Stimme Verlag, 1969).

56. Marx, *Theses on Feuerbach*, in *Basic Writings*, ed. Feuer, p. 245. Italics in original.

57. E. H. Carr, *Karl Marx: A Study in Fanaticism* (London: J. M. Dent, 1938), pp. 266–267.

58. Arnold Künzli, *Karl Marx, eine Psychographie* (Vienna: Europa Verlag, 1966), p. 805.

59. Richard T. De George, *The New Marxism* (New York: Pegasus, 1968), p. 248.

CHAPTER II

1. Isaiah Berlin, *Karl Marx: His Life and Environment* (New York: Oxford University Press, 1963).

2. Bernard Voyenne, "De Marx à Staline," in *De Marx au marxisme*, ed. Robert Aron (Paris: Éditions de Flore, 1948), p. 29.

3. Franz Mehring, *Karl Marx* (New York: Covici, Friede, 1935), p. 533.

4. Ibid., p. 536.

5. Engels to E. Papritz, June 26, 1884, in Marx and Engels, *Selected Correspondence* (Moscow: Foreign Languages Publishing House, 1953), pp. 450, 451.

6. Engels to Florence Wischnewetzky, February 1886, quoted by Daniel Bell, "A Critique of Alienation," in *Marxism*, ed. Michael Curtis (New York: Atherton Press, 1970), p. 139.

7. Voyenne, "De Marx à Staline," p. 30.

8. Alexander Gray, *The Socialist Tradition: Moses to Lenin* (London: Longmans, Green, 1946), p. 300.

9. Karl Marx and Friedrich Engels, *Manifesto of the Communist Party*, in *Basic Writings on Politics and Philosophy*, ed. Lewis S. Feuer (Garden City, N.Y.: Doubleday Anchor, 1959), p. 18.

10. Wilhelm Liebknecht, *Karl Marx* (1901; reprint ed., New York: Greenwood Press, 1968), p. 83.

11. Edmund Wilson, *To the Finland Station* (Garden City, N.Y.: Doubleday, 1941), p. 171.

12. Oscar J. Hammen, *The Red '48ers: Karl Marx and Friedrich Engels* (New York: Scribner's, 1969), p. 152.

13. Michael Harrington, *Socialism* (New York: Saturday Review Press, 1972), p. 60.

14. Marx, *Critique of the Gotha Program*, in Marx and Engels, *Selected Works* (Moscow: Progress Publishers, 1955), p. 36.

15. Marx, *Herr Vogt*, cited in George Lichtheim, *The Concept of Ideology and Other Essays* (New York: Random House, 1967), p. 89.

16. Engels to Marx, February 13, 1851, quoted in Arthur Rosenberg, *A History of Bolshevism* (London: Oxford University Press, 1934), p. 14.

17. Cited by Harrington, *Socialism*, p. 64.

18. Marx, *Capital* (Chicago: Chas. H. Kerr, 1909), pp. 454–455.

19. Tibor Szamuely, "The Birth of Russian Marxism," *Survey* 18 (Summer 1972): 59.

20. H. Collins and C. Abramsky, *Karl Marx and the British Labour Movement* (London: Macmillan, 1965), p. 297.

21. Marx and Engels, *Selected Correspondence* (New York: International Publishers, 1968), p. 412.

22. Marx to F. Domela-Nieuwenhuis, February 22, 1881, in Marx and Engels, *Selected Correspondence* (1953), p. 410.

23. A. Zévaès, quoted in Voyenne, "De Marx à Staline," p. 37.

24. Engels to C. Schmidt, August 5, 1890, in Marx and Engels, *Selected Correspondence* (Moscow: Foreign Languages Publishing House, 1953), p. 496.

25. Lewis S. Feuer, *Marx and the Intellectuals* (Garden City, N.Y.: Doubleday Anchor, 1969), p. 31.

26. Gustav Mayer, *Friedrich Engels* (New York: Howard Fertig, 1969), pp. 149, 155.

27. Engels to A. Bebel, March 18–28, 1875, in Marx and Engels, *Selected Correspondence* (1968), p. 338.

28. A. James Gregor, *A Survey of Marxism* (New York: Random House, 1965), p. 171; Engels to Marx, December 8, 1882, in Marx and Engels, *Selected Correspondence* (New York: International Publishers, 1942), p. 403.

29. Engels to C. Schmidt, October 27, 1890, in Marx and Engels, *Selected Correspondence* (1968), p. 507.

30. Engels to J. Bloch, September 21, 1890, in Marx and Engels, *Selected Correspondence* (1942), p. 475.

31. Engels to I. P. Becker, June 15, 1885, in Marx and Engels, *Selected Correspondence* (1942), p. 439.

32. Engels's preface to the 1895 rev. ed. of Marx's *Class War in France*, in Marx and Engels, *Selected Works* (Moscow: Progress Publishers, 1969), vol. 1, pp. 186–204.

33. *Times* (London), August 10, 1895, p. 10.

34. Louis Boudin, *The Theoretical System of Karl Marx* (New York: Monthly Review Press, 1967), p. 20.

35. Engels, *The Origin of the Family, Private Property and the State*, in Marx and Engels, *Selected Works* (1969), vol. 3, pp. 204–334.

36. Alfred G. Meyer, *Communism* (New York: Random House, 1967), p. 26.

37. Engels to H. Starkenburg, January 25, 1894, in Marx and Engels, *Selected Correspondence* (1953), pp. 548–549, 550.

38. G. R. S. Taylor, *Socialism Past and Present* (1910; reprint ed., Freeport, N.Y.: Books for Libraries, 1968), p. 10.

39. George Lichtheim, *The Origins of Socialism* (New York: Praeger, 1967), p. 86.

40. *Times* (London), August 12, 1895, p. 10.

41. Werner Sombart, *Socialism and the Social Movement*, trans. M. Epstein, 6th ed. (1909; reprint ed., New York: August M. Kelley, 1968), p. 169.

42. "Present Position and Future Prospects of Socialism," *Quarterly Review* (London) 213 (July 1910):164.

43. Quoted in David McLellan, *The Thought of Karl Marx* (London: Macmillan, 1971), p. 211.

44. Marx to F. A. Sorge, September 27, 1877, in Marx and Engels, *Selected Correspondence* (1953), p. 374.

45. Engels to Vera Zasulich, April 23, 1885. Marx and Engels, *Selected Correspondence* (New York: International Publishers, 1942), p. 437.

46. Paul Miliukov, *Russia and Its Crisis* (New York: Collier Books, 1962), p. 336.

47. Quoted in Donald W. Treadgold, *The West in Russia and China* (New York: Cambridge University Press, 1973), vol. 1, p. 180.

48. Quoted in Robert C. Tucker, *The Marxian Revolutionary Idea* (New York: W. W. Norton, 1968), p. 121.

49. On equalitarianism in empires, see Robert G. Wesson, *The Imperial Order* (Berkeley: University of California Press, 1967), pp. 145–152.

50. Szamuely, "Birth of Russian Marxism," p. 58.

51. Treadgold, *The West in Russia and China*, vol. 1, p. 219.

52. Quoted in Szamuely, "Birth of Russian Marxism," p. 69.

53. I. N. Steinberg, *In the Workshop of the Revolution* (London: Victor Gollancz, 1955), p. 11.

54. E. H. Carr, *Karl Marx: A Study in Fanaticism* (London: J. M. Dent, 1938), p. 30.

55. J. L. H. Keep, *The Rise of Social Democracy in Russia* (Oxford: Clarendon Press, 1963), p. 12.

56. V. I. Lenin, *What Is to Be Done?*, in *Selected Works in Three Volumes* (Moscow, 1967), vol. 1, p. 110.

57. Adam B. Ulam, *Stalin: The Man and His Era* (New York: Viking Press, 1973), p. 31.

58. Ibid., pp. 42–43.

59. Gregor, *Survey of Marxism*, p. 223.

60. Richard Pipes, *Struve: Liberal on the Left* (Cambridge: Harvard University Press, 1970), p. 49.

61. Quoted in Gilles Martinet, *Marxism of Our Time* (New York: Monthly Review Press, 1965), pp. 85–86.

62. Pipes, *Struve*, p. 134.

63. Lenin, "Our Program," quoted in Donald M. Lowe, *The Function of "China" in Marx, Lenin, and Mao* (Berkeley: University of California Press, 1966), p. 60.

64. Marx and Engels, *Selected Works* (Moscow: Progress Publishers, 1969), p. 120.

65. As noted by Lenin, *What Is to Be Done?*, in *Selected Works* (Moscow: Progress Publishers, 1970), p. 150.

66. Hammen, *Red '48ers*, p. 166.

67. Marx to Weydemeyer, March 5, 1852, in Marx and Engels, *Selected Correspondence* (1953), p. 86.

68. Keep, *Rise of Social Democracy in Russia*, pp. 95–96.

69. Quoted in Adam B. Ulam, *The Bolsheviks* (New York: Macmillan, 1965), p. 181.

70. C. Gneuss, "The Precursor: Eduard Bernstein," in *Revisionism: Essays on the History of Marxist Ideas*, ed. Leopold Labedz (New York: Praeger, 1962), p. 35.

71. Quoted in Peter Gay, *The Dilemma of Democratic Socialism* (New York: Columbia University Press, 1952), p. 61.

Notes

72. Quoted in Henry Somerville, "Disintegration of Marxism," *Catholic World*, 98 (November 1913):176.

73. As noted by Henry De Man, *The Psychology of Socialism* (London: George Allen & Unwin, 1928), p. 165.

74. Gay, *Dilemma of Democratic Socialism*, p. 267.

75. Lenin, "The Urgent Tasks of Our Movement," in *Selected Works* (1970), p. 114. It first appeared as the lead article of the first issue of *Iskra*.

76. Nicholas Berdyaev, *The Origin of Russian Communism*, trans. R. M. French (1937; reprint ed., Ann Arbor: University of Michigan Press, 1960), pp. 108–110.

77. Nicholas V. Riazanovsky, *A History of Russia* (New York: Oxford University Press, 1963), p. 501.

78. Keep, *Rise of Social Democracy in Russia*, pp. 74–75.

79. Ibid., p. 289.

80. Lenin, *Selected Works in Three Volumes*, vol. 1, p. 584.

81. Quoted in Ulam, *Stalin*, p. 100.

82. Lenin, *Collected Works* (Moscow: Foreign Languages Publishing House, 1960–1970), vol. 17, p. 578; vol. 18, p. 21.

83. Sidney Hook, *Toward an Understanding of Karl Marx* (New York: John Day, 1933), p. 23.

84. Gerhart Niemeyer, "The Second International: 1889–1914," in *The Revolutionary Internationals, 1864–1943*, ed. Milorad M. Drachkovitch (Stanford, Calif.: Stanford University Press for the Hoover Institution, 1966), p. 105.

85. George Lichtheim, *Marxism in Modern France* (New York: Columbia University Press, 1966), p. 35.

86. Georges Haupt, *Socialism and the Great War* (Oxford: Clarendon Press, 1972), p. 122.

87. These all received nearly equal space in G. R. S. Taylor, *Leaders of Socialism, Past and Present* (1910; reprint ed., Freeport, N.Y.: Books for Libraries, 1968).

88. Waldemar Gurian, *The Rise and Decline of Marxism* (London: Burns, Oates, and Washbourne, 1938), p. 6; Harold J. Laski, *Communism* (London: Thornton Butterworth, 1927), p. 30.

89. Sombart, *Socialism and the Social Movement*, p. 91.

90. "The Mystery of Socialism," *The Independent* 73 (October 1912):850–852.

91. Tucker, *Marxian Revolutionary Idea*, p. 33.

92. H. G. Wells, *New Worlds for Old* (New York: Macmillan, 1913), pp. 223–224.

93. W. H. Mallock, "The Intellectual Bankruptcy of Socialism," *The Living Age*, 274 (September 21, 1912):772.

94. Sombart, *Socialism and the Social Movement*, p. 64.

95. Paul Weisengrün, "Is the Death of Marxism at Hand?" *The American Review of Reviews* 43 (March 1911):375.

CHAPTER III

1. Adam B. Ulam, *Stalin: The Man and His Era* (New York: Viking Press, 1973), p. 126.

2. Milorad M. Drachkovitch and Branko Lazitch, "The Third International," in *The Revolutionary Internationals, 1864–1943*, ed. Milorad M. Drachkovitch (Stanford, Calif.: Stanford University Press for the Hoover Institution, 1966), p. 160.

3. Lenin, *Collected Works* (Moscow: Progress Publishers, 1964), vol. 21, p. 18.

4. Lenin, *Imperialism, the Highest Stage of Capitalism*, in *Selected Works in Three Volumes* (Moscow: Progress Publishers, 1970), vol. 1, pp. 725, 743.

5. Leonid Brezhnev, *On the Policy of the Soviet Union and the International Situation* (Garden City, N.Y.: Doubleday, 1973), p. 18.

6. Robert C. Tucker, *Stalin as a Revolutionary* (New York: W. W. Norton, 1973), p. 416.

7. Lenin, *Selected Works in Three Volumes* (Moscow: Progress Publishers, 1967), vol. 2, p. 363.

8. Tucker, *Stalin as a Revolutionary*, p. 35.

9. William R. Kintner, *The Front Is Everywhere* (Norman, Okla.: University of Oklahoma Press, 1950), pp. 30–36.

10. Lenin, *Selected Works* (New York: International Publishers, 1943), vol. 10, p. 281.

11. Leopold Schwarzschild, *The Red Prussian* (New York: Scribner's, 1947), p. 142.

12. Quoted in Michael Harrington, *Socialism* (New York: Saturday Review Press, 1972), p. 25.

13. Lenin, *Selected Works* (New York: International Publishers, 1943), vol. 7, p. 341.

14. Drachkovitch and Lazitch, "Third International," p. 173; Ulam, *Stalin*, p. 229.

15. George Lichtheim, "On the Interpretation of Marx's Thought," in *Marxism*, ed. Michael Curtis, p. 78.

16. "A Lenin Litany," excerpted in *Stalin*, ed. T. H. Rigby (Englewood Cliffs, N.J.: Prentice-Hall, 1966), pp. 40–41.

17. John Scott, *Behind the Urals* (1942; reprint ed., New York: Arno Press, 1971), passim, esp. p. 47.

18. *New York Times*, December 31, 1973, p. 1.

19. Drachkovitch and Lazitch, "Third International," p. 188.

20. Quoted in Josef Korbel, *The Communist Subversion of Czechoslovakia* (Cambridge: Harvard University Press, 1950), p. 84.

21. I. V. Stalin, *Problems of Socialist Economy*, in *Works* (Stanford, Calif.: Hoover Institution, 1967), vol. 3, p. 206.

22. A. Mednikov, in *Oktiabr*, no. 4 (April 1972); *Current Digest of the Soviet Press* 24 (May 31, 1972):18.

23. W. W. Kulski, *The Soviet Union in World Affairs* (Syracuse, N.Y.: Syracuse University Press, 1973), p. 6.

24. I. Soloviev, in *Pravda*, March 2, 1970, p. 2.

25. Kulski, *Soviet Union in World Affairs*, pp. 171, 172.

26. Brezhnev, quoted in *Pravda*, December 22, 1972, p. 2.

27. Brezhnev, *Policy of the Soviet Union*, p. 12.

28. V. Shevtsov, in *Pravda*, October 23, 1973, p. 2.

29. A. Yegorov, *Kommunist*, no. 2 (January 1973):36; *Current Digest of the Soviet Press* 15 (April 25, 1973):11.

30. *Pravda*, December 5, 1973, p. 3.

31. I. Foniakov, in *Pravda*, December 8, 1973, p. 3. Versified in original.

32. *Krasnaia zvezda*, November 4, 1970, p. 2.

33. E. Malcolm Carroll, *Soviet Communism and Western Opinion, 1919–1921* (Chapel Hill, N.C.: University of North Carolina Press, 1965), p. 7.

34. James W. Hulse, *The Formation of the Communist International* (Stanford, Calif.: Stanford University Press, 1964), p. 35.

35. Drachkovitch and Lazitch, "Third International," p. 162.

36. Ibid.; Richard E. Cornell, "Youthful Radicalism and the Formation of Communist Youth Organizations," in *Students in Revolt*, ed. S. M. Lipset and P. G. Altbach (Boston: Houghton Mifflin, 1969), p. 475.

37. Drachkovitch and Lazitch, "Third International," p. 193.

38. Milovan Djilas, *Conversations with Stalin* (New York: Harcourt, Brace & World, 1962), pp. 11–12, 57.

CHAPTER IV

1. John S. Kautsky, *Communism and the Politics of Development* (New York: John Wiley, 1966), p. 1.

2. *New York Tribune*, June 24, 1853; quoted in L. H. Gann and Peter Duignan, *Burden of Empire* (New York: Praeger, 1967), p. 17.

3. *Northern Star*, January 22, 1848, p. 7; reprinted in Karl Marx and Friedrich Engels, *Basic Writings on Politics and Philosophy*, ed. Lewis S. Feuer (Garden City, N.Y.: Doubleday Anchor, 1959), p. 451.

4. Engels to Kautsky, February 16, 1884, in Marx and Engels, *Selected Correspondence* (Moscow: Foreign Languages Publishing House, 1953), p. 441.

5. Henry De Man, *The Psychology of Socialism* (London: George Allen & Unwin, 1928), p. 39.

6. Engels to Kautsky, September 12, 1882, in Marx and Engels, *Selected Correspondence* (1953), p. 423.

7. Engels to Bebel, December 11, 1884; ibid., pp. 454–455, 457.

8. Engels to "Social-Democrat," June 9, 1893; ibid., p. 539.

9. Loren Baritz, ed., *The American Left: Radical Political Thought in the Twenties* (New York: Basic Books, 1971), p. 46.

10. Donald M. Lowe, *The Function of "China" in Marx, Lenin and Mao* (Berkeley: University of California Press, 1966), p. 69.

11. Lenin, "The Awakening of Asia" (May 1913), in *Collected Works*, vol. 19, p. 86.

12. Donald M. Lowe, *Function of "China,"* p. 71.

13. Robert C. North, *Moscow and the Chinese Communists* (Stanford, Calif.: Stanford University Press, 1953), p. 19.

14. Lenin, "Report on the National and Colonial Questions," in *Selected Works in Three Volumes* (Moscow: Progress Publishers, 1967), vol. 3, pp. 458–459.

15. Quoted in Adam B. Ulam, *Stalin: The Man and His Era* (New York: Viking Press, 1973), p. 193.

16. Lenin, *Selected Works in Three Volumes*, vol. 3, pp. 784–785.

17. George Lichtheim, *Imperialism* (New York: Praeger, 1971), p. 113.

18. North, *Moscow and the Chinese Communists*, p. 28.

19. Treadgold, *The West in Russia and China* (Cambridge: Cambridge University Press, 1973), vol. 2, p. 163.

20. Quoted in Milorad M. Drachkovitch and Branko Lazitch, "The Third International," in *The Revolutionary Internationals, 1864–1943*, ed. Milorad M. Drachkovitch (Stanford, Calif.: Stanford University Press for the Hoover Institution, 1966), p. 183.

21. Karl A. Wittfogel, "The Legend of Maoism," *China Quarterly* 1 (January–March 1960):76.

22. Richard C. Thornton, "The Emergence of a New Comintern Policy for China: 1928," in *The Comintern: Historical Highlights*, ed. Milorad M. Drachkovitch and Branko Lazitch (New York: Praeger, 1966), pp. 95–109.

23. Stuart R. Schram, *The Political Thought of Mao Tse-tung* (New York: Praeger, 1969), p. 48.

24. Ibid., p. 32.

25. Mao Tse-tung, *Quotations from Mao Tse-tung* (Peking: Foreign Languages Press, 1967), p. 13.

26. Ibid., p. 47.

27. Ibid., pp. 56–57.

28. Arthur A. Cohen, *The Communism of Mao* (Chicago: University of Chicago Press, 1964), p. 8.

29. North, *Moscow and the Chinese Communists*, p. 11.

30. Parris H. Chang, *Radicals and Radical Ideology in China's Cultural Revolution* (New York: Research Institute on Communist Affairs, 1973), pp. 8–9.

31. Lowe, *Function of "China,"* p. 109; Franz Michael, "Ideology and the Cult of Mao," in *Communist China, 1949–1969: A Twenty-Year Appraisal*, ed. Frank N. Trager and William Henderson (New York: New York University Press, 1970), p. 29.

32. Mao, *Quotations*, p. 35.

33. Ibid., p. 36.

34. "1963 Draft Resolution of the Central Committee," quoted in Klaus Mehnert, *China Returns* (New York: E. P. Dutton, 1972), p. 260. This resolution was drafted by Mao.

35. Ibid., pp. 259–260.

36. Mao, *Quotations*, p. 62.

37. Ibid., p. 61.

38. Lowe, *Function of "China,"* p. 119.

39. *People's Daily*, November 7, 1973; *Peking Informers* 27 (December 1, 1973).

40. Schram, *Political Thought of Mao*, p. 72.

41. Mehnert, *China Returns*, p. 198.

42. Mao, *Quotations*, p. 72.

43. Robert Scalapino, "China and the Road Ahead," *Survey* (Autumn 1973):7.

44. Leslie Palmier, *Communists in Indonesia* (Garden City, N.Y.: Doubleday Anchor, 1973), pp. 95–98.

45. Kwame Nkrumah, *Consciencism: Philosophy and Ideology of De-Colonization* (New York: Monthly Review Press, 1970), p. 74.

46. Peter Worsley, *The Third World* (London: Weidenfeld and Nicolson, 1964), p. 93.

47. Kautsky, *Communism and the Politics of Development*, p. 176.

48. Edward Shils, "The Intellectuals and the Political Development of the New State," in *Political Change in Underdeveloped Countries*, ed. John H. Kautsky (New York: John Wiley, 1962), p. 199.

49. Milovan Djilas, *Conversations with Stalin* (New York: Harcourt, Brace & World, 1962), pp. 58–59.

50. Mao, *Quotations*, p. 215.

51. C. G. Shak, *Marxism, Gandhism, Stalinism* (Bombay: Popular Prakashan, 1963), p. 23.

52. D. A. Rustow, "The Politics of the Near East," in *The Politics of the Developing Areas*, ed. Gabriel S. Almond and James S. Coleman (Princeton: Princeton University Press, 1960), p. 419.

53. Tom Fawthrop, "Toward an Extraparliamentary Opposition," in *The New Revolutionaries*, ed. Tariq Ali (New York: William Morrow, 1969), p. 59.

54. Max Nomad, *Apostles of Revolution* (New York: Collier, 1961), pp. 102–103.

55. Quoted in Luis E. Aguilar, *Marxism in Latin America* (New York: Alfred A. Knopf, 1968), pp. 66–67.

56. Juan Luis Segundo, "Has Latin America a Choice?" in *Development: An Introductory Reader*, ed., Hélène Castel (New York: Macmillan, 1971), pp. 122–123.

57. Marx, *The Poverty of Philosophy*, in *Karl Marx on Colonialism and Modernization*, ed. Shlomo Avineri (Garden City, N.Y.: Doubleday, 1968), p. 31.

58. Quoted in Leonid Brezhnev, *On the Policy of the Soviet Union and the International Situation* (New York: Doubleday, 1973), pp. 44–45.

Notes

59. For a critique, see Gann and Duignan, *Burden of Empire*, esp. chap. 6.

60. P. T. Bauer, *Dissent on Development* (London: Weidenfeld and Nicolson, 1971), p. 151.

61. Cf. Fred R. von der Mehden, *Politics of the Developing Nations*, 2d ed. (Englewood Cliffs, N.J.: Prentice-Hall, 1969), pp. 11–14.

62. Marx, *Marx on Colonialism and Modernization*, ed. Shlomo Avineri (Garden City, N.Y.: Doubleday, 1968), pp. 16–17.

63. Kwame Nkrumah, *I Speak of Freedom* (New York: Praeger, 1961), p. 217.

64. George C. Lodge, *Engines of Change: United States Interests and Revolution in Latin America* (New York: Alfred A. Knopf, 1970), p. 247.

65. As contended by Ronald Muller, "Poverty Is the Product," *Foreign Policy*, no. 13 (Winter 1973–1974):71–103.

66. Lodge, *Engines of Change*, p. 262.

67. Worsley, *Third World*, p. 30.

68. See Shils, "The Intellectuals and the Political Development of the New State," pp. 203–204.

69. Andrew Feenberg, "Marxist Theory and Socialist Society: A Dilemma," *Newsletter on Comparative Studies of Communism* 6 (May 1973):14.

70. D. C. Beller and M. Rejai, "Communism in Sub-Saharan Africa," in *The New Communisms*, ed. Dan N. Jacobs (New York: Harper & Row, 1969), p. 232.

71. Ruth McVey, "Communism in Southeast Asia," ibid., p. 260.

72. Reprinted in *Marxism and Communism: Essential Readings*, ed. Robert V. Daniels (New York: Random House, 1965), p. 161.

73. Marx and Engels, *Manifesto of the Communist Party*, in *Basic Writings*, ed. Feuer, p. 12.

74. J. H. Clapham, *The Economic Development of France and Germany, 1815–1914* (Cambridge: Cambridge University Press, 1963), p. 87; A. Sartorius von Waltershausen, *Deutsche Wirtschaftsgeschichte, 1815–1914* (Jena: Gustav Fischer, 1920), pp. 46–48.

75. George Lichtheim, *The Origins of Socialism* (New York: Praeger, 1969), p. 53.

76. N. K. Krupskaya, *Reminiscences of Lenin* (New York: International Publishers, 1960), p. 71.

77. Engels to F. A. Sorge, December 31, 1892, in Marx and Engels, *Selected Correspondence* (1953), p. 535.

78. Shils, "The Intellectuals and the Political Development of the New State," pp. 195ff.

79. *New York Times*, March 3, 1973, p. 11.

80. D. C. Beller and M. Rejai, "Communism in Sub-Saharan Africa," p. 237.

81. Kwame Nkrumah, *Africa Must Unite* (New York: International Publishers, 1972), p. 101.

82. Jean-Paul Sartre, preface to *The Wretched of the Earth*, by Frantz Fanon; trans. Constance Farrington (New York: Grove Press, 1963), p. 10.

83. Frank N. Trager, ed., *Marxism in Southeast Asia* (Stanford, Calif.: Stanford University Press, 1959), p. 11.

84. *New York Times*, May 19, 1973, p. 11.

85. Quoted in Worsley, *Third World*, p. 244.

86. Kautsky, *Communism and the Politics of Development*, p. 178.

87. Lewis S. Feuer, *Marx and the Intellectuals* (Garden City, N.Y.: Doubleday Anchor, 1969), pp. 217–219.

88. David Caute, *Fanon* (London: Collin, 1970), pp. 33–34.

89. Fanon, *Wretched of the Earth*, p. 32.

90. Irene L. Gendzier, *Frantz Fanon* (New York: Pantheon Books, 1973), pp. 20–21, 199.

91. Ernesto Guevara, *Guerrilla Warfare* (New York: Monthly Review Press, 1961), p. 5.

92. Ibid., pp. 17, 18.

93. Ernesto Guevara, *The Diary of Che Guevara* (New York: Bantam Books, 1968), p. 105.

94. Régis Debray, *Revolution in the Revolution?* trans. Bobbye Oritz (New York: Monthly Review Press, 1967), pp. 68–69.

95. Ibid., p. 67.

96. Ibid., p. 106.

97. Quoted in Clea Silva, "The Errors of the Foco Theory," in *Régis Debray and the Latin American Revolution*, ed. Leo Huberman and Paul M. Sweezy (New York: Monthly Review Press, 1968), p. 23.

98. Debray, *Revolution in the Revolution?*, p. 72.

99. *Newsweek*, March 5, 1973, p. 43.

CHAPTER V

1. Jean-Jacques Servan-Schreiber, *The American Challenge* (New York: Atheneum, 1968).

2. David Caute, *Communism and the French Intellectuals* (London: André Deutsch, 1964), pp. 213–214.

3. As seen, for example, by Raymond Aron. See Victor Brombert, *The Intellectual Hero: Studies in the French Novel* (Philadelphia: J. B. Lippincott, 1961), p. 140.

4. W. E. B. Du Bois, "Marxism and the Negro Problem," in *The American Left: Radical Political Thought in the Twentieth Century*, ed. Loren Baritz (New York: Basic Books, 1971), p. 279.

5. See Robert L. Allen, *Black Awakening in Capitalist America* (Garden City, N.Y.: Doubleday, 1969).

6. Robert L. Allen, "Toward a Transitional Program," in *Readings in American Ideologies*, ed. Kenneth M. Dolbeare et al. (Chicago: Markham, 1973), p. 161.

7. Dick Howard and Karl E. Klare, eds., *The Unknown Dimension: European Marxism since Lenin* (New York: Basic Books, 1972), p. 21.

8. Friedrich Engels, *The Origin of the Family, Private Property and the State* (New York: International Publishers, 1942), p. 51.

9. *Readings in American Ideologies*, ed. Dolbeare, pp. 197, 199.

10. Naomi Jaffe and Bernadine Dohrn, "The Look Is You: Toward a Strategy for Radical Women," in *The American Left*, ed. Baritz, p. 477.

11. Howard and Klare, eds., *Unknown Dimension*, p. 20.

12. Henry De Man, *The Psychology of Socialism* (London: George Allen & Unwin, 1928), p. 97.

13. Howard and Klare, eds., *Unknown Dimension*, p. viii.

14. Frank S. Meyer, *The Moulding of Communists* (New York: Harcourt, Brace & World, 1961), p. xxi.

15. Charles Frankel, "The Nature and Sources of Irrationalism," *Science* 180 (June 1, 1973):927–931.

16. Immanuel Velikovsky, *Worlds in Collision* (Garden City, N.Y.: Doubleday, 1950).

17. Alfred De Grazia, ed., *The Velikovsky Affair* (New Hyde Park, N.Y.: University Books, 1966).

18. Gabriel A. Almond, *The Appeals of Communism* (Princeton: Princeton University Press, 1954), p. 246.

19. Werner Blumenberg, *Portrait of Marx* (New York: Herder and Herder, 1972), p. 174.

266

20. Tom Fawthrop, "Toward an Extraparliamentary Opposition," in *The New Revolutionaries*, ed. Tariq Ali (New York: William Morrow, 1969), p. 58.

21. Kurt Sontheimer, "Marx als Allheilmittel," *Die Zeit*, April 20, 1973, p. 11.

22. Meyer, *Moulding of Communists*, pp. 53–54.

23. Edmund Wilson, *To the Finland Station* (London: Secker and Warburg, 1941), p. 156.

24. Karl Mannheim, *Ideology and Utopia* (New York: Harcourt, Brace & World, 1936), p. 130.

25. Arthur Koestler, in *The God that Failed*, ed. Richard Crossman (New York: Harper, 1949), p. 23.

26. Louis Boudin, *The Theoretical System of Karl Marx* (1907; reprint ed., New York: Monthly Review Press, 1967), p. 11.

27. Herbert Marcuse, *New York Times*, June 27, 1973, p. 39.

28. Al Weinrub, *SSRS Newsletter*, no. 232 (June 1973):4.

29. John Strachey, introduction to *Marxism and Psychoanalysis*, by Reuben Osborn (London: Barrie and Rockliff, 1965), p. xiv.

30. Maurice Comforth, *Marxism and the Linguistic Philosophy* (London: Lawrence and Wishart, 1971), p. 369.

31. Lewis S. Feuer, ed., *Basic Writings on Politics and Philosophy*, by Karl Marx and Friedrich Engels (Garden City, N.Y.: Doubleday Anchor, 1959), p. x.

32. Marx, preface to *A Contribution to the Critique of Political Economy*, in Marx and Engels, *Selected Works* (Moscow: Progress Publishers, 1969), vol. 1, p. 504.

33. Tom Wolfe, in foreword to Arnold Beichman, *Nine Lies About America* (New York: Library Press, 1972), p. xiv.

34. Isaac Deutscher, *Marxism in Our Time*, ed. Tamara Deutscher (Berkeley: Ramparts Press, 1971), p. 16.

35. Milorad M. Drachkovitch and Branko Lazitch, "The Third International," *The Revolutionary Internationals*, ed. Milorad M. Drachkovitch (Stanford, Calif.: Stanford University Press for the Hoover Institution, 1966), pp. 191–192.

36. S. M. Lipset, *Political Man: The Social Bases of Politics* (Garden City, N.Y.: Doubleday, 1960), p. 119.

37. Engels to C. Schmidt, August 5, 1890, in Marx and Engels, *Selected Correspondence* (Moscow: Foreign Languages Publishing House, 1953), p. 497.

38. Max Nomad, *Rebels and Renegades* (1932; reprint ed., Freeport, N.Y.: Books for Libraries, 1968), pp. 206–7, 239.

39. Wilson, *Finland Station*, p. 328.

40. Marx, "Theses on Feuerbach," in Karl Marx, *Selected Writings in Sociology and Social Philosophy* trans. T. B. Bottomore, ed. T. B. Bottomore and Maximilien Rubel (New York: McGraw-Hill, 1964), p. 69.

41. Marx, "Critique of Hegel's Philosophy of Right," in *Selected Writings*, ed. Bottomore and Rubel, p. 59.

42. Marx, "Statement of National Caucus for Labor Committees," in *Readings in American Ideologies*, ed. Dolbeare et al., p. 305.

43. Quoted in Lewis S. Feuer, *Marx and the Intellectuals* (Garden City, N.Y.: Doubleday Anchor, 1969), p. 101.

44. Ibid., p. 52.

45. George Watson, "Were the Intellectuals Duped?" *Encounter* 41 (December 1973):29.

46. John Plamenatz, *Ideology* (New York: Praeger, 1970), p. 139.

47. Eugen Loebl, *Conversations with the Bewildered* (London: George Allen & Unwin, 1972), p. 88.

48. See Erich Fromm, *Beyond the Chain of Illusion* (New York: Simon and Schuster, 1962), p. 8.

49. *Business Week,* June 17, 1972, pp. 100–102.

50. Herbert Marcuse, *Five Lectures* (Boston: Beacon Press, 1970), p. 73.

51. For example, by Sidney Lens, *The Forging of the American Empire* (New York: Crowell, 1971); William A. Williams, ed., *From Colony to Empire* (New York: John Wiley, 1972); David Horowitz, *The Free World Colossus* (New York: Hill and Wang, 1971); Gabriel Kolko, *The Roots of American Foreign Policy* (Boston: Beacon Press, 1969).

52. Howard L. Parsons, *Humanism and Marx's Thought* (Springfield, Ill.: Charles C. Thomas, 1971), p. 270. For a discussion of radical expressions around 1970, see Beichman, *Nine Lies about America.*

53. See Clinton Rossiter, *Marxism: The View from America* (New York: Harcourt, Brace, 1960), p. 6.

54. Concerning student extremism, see Zbigniew Brzezinski, *Between Two Ages: America's Role in the Technetronic Era* (New York: Viking, 1970), pp. 94–110.

55. Lewis S. Feuer, *The Conflict of Generations* (New York: Basic Books, 1969), p. 511.

56. Guido Martinotti, "The Positive Marginality: Notes on Italian Students in Periods of Political Mobilization," in *Students in Revolt,* ed. S. M. Lipset and P. G. Altbach (Boston: Houghton Mifflin, 1969), p. 173.

57. Feuer, *Conflict of Generations,* p. 262.

58. Irving L. Horowitz, *The Struggle Is the Message: The Organization and Ideology of the Anti-War Movement* (Berkeley: Glendessary Press, 1970), p. 98.

59. Quoted in Lewis S. Feuer, "Alienation: The Marxism of Contemporary Student Movements," in *Marxist Ideology in the Contemporary World,* ed. Milorad Drachkovitch (New York: Praeger, 1966), pp. 43–44.

60. Kirkpatrick Sale, *SDS* (New York: Random House, 1973), p. 390.

61. Ibid., pp. 663–664.

62. Ibid., p. 628.

63. Robert C. Tucker, *Philosophy and Myth in Karl Marx* (Cambridge: Cambridge University Press, 1961), p. 233.

64. As observed by Sidney Hook, "Marxism in the Western World: From 'Scientific Socialism' to Mythology," in *Marxist Ideology,* ed. Drachkovitch, p. 2.

65. J. A. Banks, *Marxist Sociology in Action* (Harrisburg, Pa.: Stackpole, 1970), p. 11.

66. C. Wright Mills, *The Marxists* (New York: Dell, 1962), p. 30.

67. As noted by Harold J. Laski, *Communism* (London: Thornton Butterworth, 1927), p. 31.

68. Du Bois, "Marxism and the Negro Problem," p. 276.

69. Quoted in Marcel Liebman, "The Webbs and the New Civilization," *Survey,* no. 41 (April 1962):73.

70. For examples, see Feuer, *Marx and the Intellectuals,* pp. 100–140.

71. Ibid., p. 3.

72. David Caute, *The Fellow-Travellers* (New York: Macmillan, 1973), p. 3.

73. G. D. H. Cole, *A History of Socialist Thought,* vol. 5: *Socialism and Fascism, 1931–1939* (London: Macmillan, 1960), p. 29.

74. Caute, *Fellow-Travellers,* p. 4.

75. C. Day Lewis (1934), quoted in Watson, "Were the Intellectuals Duped?" p. 25.

76. Sidney Webb and Beatrice Webb, *The Soviet Union: A New Civilization* (London: Gollancz, 1937).

77. Caute, *Communism and the French Intellectuals,* p. 220.

78. *Partisan Review,* 4 (December 1937); reprinted in *American Left,* ed. Baritz, p. 230.

79. K. A. Jelenski, "The Literature of Disenchantment," *Survey*, no. 41 (April 1962):101.

80. Paul Sweezy, quoted in Lewis A. Coser, "USA: Marxists at Bay," in *Revisionism: Essays on the History of Marxist Ideas*, ed. Leopold Labedz (New York: Praeger, 1962), p. 352.

81. Jules Monnerot, *Sociologie de la révolution* (Paris: Fayard, 1969), p. 278.

82. Howard and Klare, *Unknown Dimension*, p. 65.

83. As noted by R. N. Carew Hunt, *Marxism Past and Present* (New York: Macmillan, 1959), p. 165.

84. John C. Clews, *Communist Propaganda Techniques* (New York: Praeger, 1964), pp. 279–280.

85. L. I. Brezhnev, *On the Policy of the Soviet Union and the International Situation* (Garden City, N.Y.: Doubleday, 1973), p. 19.

86. Frederick C. Barghoorn, *Soviet Foreign Propaganda* (Princeton: Princeton University Press, 1964), p. 261.

87. Ibid., p. 306; Clews, *Communist Propaganda Techniques*, p. 23.

88. Lyman B. Kirkpatrick, Jr., and Howland H. Sargeant, *Soviet Political Warfare Techniques* (New York: National Strategy Information Center, 1972), p. 70.

89. Quoted in Caute, *Fellow-Travellers*, p. 4.

90. As noted by Sidney Hook, *Towards the Understanding of Karl Marx* (New York: John Day, 1933), p. 36.

91. Jorge I. Dominguez, "Is Castro's Cuba Good?" *Intellectual Digest* 4 (November 1973):52.

92. Mills, *Marxists*, pp. 105–131.

93. Caute, *Fellow-Travellers*, p. 228.

94. Horowitz, *Struggle Is the Message*, p. 87.

95. Brzezinski, *Between Two Ages*, p. 72.

96. Alfred G. Meyer, comment in *Marx and the Western World*, ed. Nicholas Lobkowicz (Notre Dame, Ind.: University of Notre Dame Press, 1967), pp. 99–100.

97. Caute, *Communism and the French Intellectuals*, p. 265.

98. Paul Baran and Paul Sweezy, *Monopoly Capital* (New York: Monthly Review Press, 1966), pp. 263, 363.

99. Jeremy Shapiro, "The Dialectic of Theory and Practice in the Age of Technological Rationality: Herbert Marcuse and Jürgen Habermas," in Howard and Klare, eds., *Unknown Dimension*, p. 277; Beichman, *Nine Lies about America*, chap. 4.

100. Feuer, "Alienation," p. 58.

101. Labedz, ed., *Revisionism*, p. 21.

102. Irving Howe, ed., *Beyond the New Left* (New York: McCall, 1970), p. 5; Richard Lowenthal, "Unreason and Revolution," ibid., p. 70.

103. Howe, "New Styles in 'Leftism,'" ibid., pp. 23–24.

104. Horowitz, *Struggle Is the Message*, p. 97.

105. D. Howard, "The Historical Context," in Howard and Klare, *Unknown Dimension*, p. 72.

106. Paul Goodman, "The New Reformation," in *Beyond the New Left*, ed. Howe, p. 86.

107. Feuer, *Marx and the Intellectuals*, p. 5.

108. Tariq Ali, "The Age of Permanent Revolution," in *New Revolutionaries*, ed. Ali, p. 309.

109. Feuer, *Conflict of Generations*, p. 503.

110. Sidney Hook, "Marxism in the Western World," p. 16.

111. *For Marx*, trans. Ben Brewster (London: Penguin Books, 1969); Maurice Cranston, "The Ideology of Althusser," *Problems of Communism* 22 (March–April 1973):53–60.

112. Klare, "The Critique of Everyday Life, the New Left, and the Unrecognizable Marxism," in Howard and Klare, eds., *Unknown Dimension*, p. 7.

113. *New York Times,* April 19, 1973.

114. See Lee Baxandall, *Radical Perspectives in the Arts* (Harmondsworth: Penguin Books, 1972).

115. See Osborn, *Marxism and Psychoanalysis.*

116. As argued by Michel Schneider, *Neurose und Klassenkampf* (Reinbek: Rowohlt Verlag, 1973).

117. Jack Lindsay, *The Anatomy of Spirit* (London: Methuen, 1937).

CHAPTER VI

1. Adam B. Ulam, *Stalin: The Man and His Era* (New York: Viking Press, 1973), p. 740.

2. According to the socialist G. D. H. Cole. Cited by Judith N. Shklar, *After Utopia* (Princeton: Princeton University Press, 1957), p. 266.

3. Robert Conquest, *The Great Terror* (New York: Macmillan, 1968), has given the most complete account.

4. According to a *samizdat* writer in *Survey*, no. 19 (Autumn 1973):60.

5. See A. James Gregor, *A Survey of Marxism: Problems in Philosophy and the Theory of History* (New York: Random House, 1965), pp. 261–273.

6. Richard Crossman, ed., *The God that Failed* (New York: Harper, 1949), p. 10.

7. McInnes, "The Labour Movement," in *The Impact of the Russian Revolution*, ed. Arnold Toynbee et al. (London: Oxford University Press, 1967), p. 109.

8. P. Samuelson, "Marxian Economics as Economics" in *Marxism, 1917–1967,* ed. Michael Curtis (New York: Atherton, 1970), p. 239.

9. Isaac Deutscher, *Marxism in Our Time*, ed. Tamara Deutscher (Berkeley: Ramparts Press, 1971), p. 16.

10. Quoted by C. F. Elliott, "Problems of Marxist Revisionism," in *Marxism*, ed. Curtis, p. 51.

11. Henry De Man, *The Psychology of Socialism* (London: George Allen & Unwin, 1928), p. 20.

12. Stanley Pierson, *Marxism and the Origins of British Socialism* (Ithaca, N.Y.: Cornell University Press, 1973), p. 278.

13. H. B. Acton, *The Illusion of the Epoch: Marxism-Leninism as a Philosophical Creed* (Boston: Beacon Press, 1955), p. 264.

14. R. Lowenthal, "The Model of the Totalitarian States," in Toynbee et al., *Impact of the Russian Revolution*, p. 337.

15. See David Schoenbaum, *Hitler's Social Revolution* (Garden City, N.Y.: Doubleday, 1966).

16. Carl Landauer, "Social Democracy," in *The Revolutionary Internationals, 1864–1943*, ed. Milorad M. Drachkovitch (Stanford, Calif.: Stanford University Press for the Hoover Institution, 1966), p. 144.

17. G.D.H. Cole, *A History of Socialist Thought*, vol. 5: *Socialism and Fascism, 1931–1939* (London: Macmillan, 1960), p. 81.

18. As observed by Acton, *Illusion of the Epoch*, p. 269.

19. As noted by the socialist Michael Harrington, *Socialism* (New York: Saturday Review Press, 1972), p. 242.

20. Paul E. Sigmund, ed., *The Ideologies of the Developing Nations* (New York: Praeger, 1972), p. 51.

21. Régis Debray, *Revolution in the Revolution?* trans. Bobbye Ortiz (New York: Monthly Review Press, 1967), p. 53.

Notes

22. Luis Aguilar, *Marxism in Latin America* (New York: Alfred A. Knopf, 1968), p. 51.

23. *New York Times*, March 13, 1974, p. 2.

24. David J. Morris, *We Must Make Haste Slowly* (New York: Random House, 1973), p. 149.

25. *New York Times*, September 28, 1973, p. 6.

26. Gerhart Niemeyer, "The Second International: 1889–1914," in *The Revolutionary Internationals*, ed. Drachkovitch, p. 126.

27. Quoted in I. N. Steinberg, *In the Workshop of the Revolution* (London: Victor Gollancz, 1955), p. 12.

28. Harrington, *Socialism*, chap. 3, is dedicated to this proposition.

29. Ivan Svitak, "The Genius and the Apparatus," *Soviet Communism and the Socialist Vision*, ed. Julius Jacobson (New Brunswick, N.J.: Transaction Books, 1972), p. 303.

30. Karl Marx and Friedrich Engels, *Manifesto of the Communist Party*, in *Selected Works* (Moscow: Progress Publishers, 1969), vol. 1, p. 127.

31. Lewis S. Feuer, *Marx and the Intellectuals* (Garden City, N.Y.: Doubleday Anchor, 1969), p. 69.

32. Hammen, *The Red '48ers: Karl Marx and Friedrich Engels* (New York: Scribner's, 1969), p. 408.

33. Marx to Engels, July 13, 1851, in Marx and Engels, *Briefwechsel* (Berlin: Dietz, 1949–1950), vol. 1, p. 196.

34. Marx to Engels, August 10, 1869, in Marx and Engels, *Selected Correspondence* (Moscow: Foreign Languages Publishing House, 1953), p. 268.

35. Cited by Robert C. Tucker, "Ambivalence about Gradual Change," in *Marxism*, ed. Curtis, p. 299.

36. Engels to Bernstein, March 24, 1884, in Marx and Engels, *Selected Correspondence* (New York: International Publishers, 1942), p. 435.

37. Wilhelm Liebknecht, *Karl Marx* (1901; reprint ed., New York: Greenwood Press, 1968), p. 82.

38. Engels to Marx, February 13, 1851, quoted in Hammen, *Red '48ers*, p. 172.

39. Marx and Engels, *The Russian Menace to Europe*, ed. Paul W. Blockstock and Bert K. Hoselitz (Glencoe, Ill.: Free Press, 1952), pp. 75–76.

40. Marx to Engels, December 2, 1847, quoted in Aguilar, *Marxism in Latin America*, p. 67.

41. Quoted in Max Nomad, *Apostles of Revolution* (New York: Collier, 1961), p. 106.

42. Engels, *Anti-Dühring* (New York: Collier, 1961), pp. 281, 282.

43. Tucker, "Ambivalence about Radical Change," p. 281.

44. "On Authority," Marx and Engels, *Selected Works* (Moscow: Foreign Languages Publishing House, 1950), vol. 1, p. 638.

45. Cited by David McLellan, *The Thought of Karl Marx* (London: Macmillan, 1971), p. 222.

46. Marx and Engels, *Manifesto*, in *Basic Writings on Politics and Philosophy*, ed. Lewis S. Feuer (Garden City, N.Y.: Doubleday Anchor, 1959), p. 28.

47. Quoted in Gregor, *Survey of Marxism*, p. 198.

48. As observed by S. M. Lipset, *Political Man: The Social Bases of Politics* (Garden City, N.Y.: Doubleday, 1960), p. 26.

49. Deutscher, *Marxism in Our Time*, p. 45.

50. Milovan Djilas, *Conversations with Stalin* (New York: Harcourt, Brace & World, 1962), p. 58.

51. Raymond Aron, *The Opium of the Intellectuals* (Garden City, N.Y.: Doubleday, 1957).

52. Engels, *Anti-Dühring*, p. 285.

53. John Strachey, introduction to *Marxism and Psychoanalysis*, by Reuben Osborn (London: Barrie and Rockliff, 1965), pp. viii, ix.

54. Engels, "A Critique of Political Economy," in *Karl Marx: Economic and Political Manuscripts of 1844*, ed. Dirk J. Struik (New York: International Publishers, 1964), p. 219.

55. As observed by Kurt Sontheimer, *Die Zeit*, April 20, 1973, p. 11.

56. R. Blackburn and G. S. Jones, "Louis Althusser and the Struggle for Marxism," in *Unknown Dimension*, ed. Howard and Klare, p. 367.

57. Pipes, *Struve: Liberal on the Left* (Cambridge: Harvard University Press, 1970), p. 126.

58. George Watson, "Were the Intellectuals Duped?" *Encounter* 41 (December 1973):24.

59. See Eugen Kamenka, *The Ethical Foundations of Marxism* (New York: Praeger, 1962).

60. Daniel de Leon, "What Means This Strike?" in *The American Left*, ed. Loren Baritz (New York: Basic Books, 1971), p. 9.

61. Engels, *Herr Eugen Dührings Revolution (Anti-Dühring)* (New York: International Publishers, 1939), p. 354.

62. Alasdair MacIntyre, *Marxism and Christianity* (New York: Schocken Books, 1968), p. 139.

63. Jules Monnerot, *Sociologie de la révolution* (Paris: Fayard, 1969), p. 118.

64. *New York Times*, June 20, 1973, p. 57.

65. Quoted in Nomad, *Apostles of Revolution*, p. 83.

66. Berel Lang and Forrest Williams, *Marxism and the Arts* (New York: David McKay, 1972), p. 7.

67. As observed by Jules Monnerot, *Démarxiser l'université* (Paris: La table ronde, 1970), p. 22.

68. J. A. Banks, *Marxist Sociology* (Harrisburg: Stackpole, 1970), p. 14.

69. Lipset, *Political Man*, p. 119.

70. Georges Izard, "Marxisme et U.R.S.S.," in Robert Aron et al., *De Marx au marxisme* (Paris: Editions de Flore, 1948), p. 227.

71. Eugen Loebl, *Conversations with the Bewildered* (London: George Allen & Unwin, 1972), p. 89.

CHAPTER VII

1. David Caute, *Communism and the French Intellectuals* (London: André Deutsch, 1964), p. 14.

2. Waldemar Gurian, *The Rise and Decline of Marxism* (London: Burns, Oates, and Washbourne, 1938), pp. v, 148.

3. Karel van het Reve, "Unofficial Russia: The Dissenters and the West," *Encounter* 42 (February 1974):12–19.

4. Quoted in Albert Parry, *The Russian Scientist* (New York: Macmillan, 1973), p. 7.

5. *New York Times*, June 11, 1973, p. 55.

6. *Ekonomicheskaia gazeta*, no. 41 (1973), p. 22.

7. *New York Times*, February 11, 1974, p. 11.

8. Radio Liberty, *Annual Report, 1973*, p. 31.

9. Paul Sweezy, *New York Times*, June 20, 1973, p. 57.

10. Richard T. De George, *Patterns of Soviet Thought* (Ann Arbor: University of Michigan Press, 1966), p. 247.

Notes

11. Gurian, *Rise and Decline of Marxism,* p. 128.

12. For definitions see *The End of Ideology Debate,* ed. Chaim J. Waxman (New York: Funk and Wagnalls, 1968).

13. S. M. Lipset, in *Decline of Ideology?* ed. M. Rejai (Chicago: Aldine-Atherton, 1971), p. 81.

14. Ibid., p. 34.

15. W. Delaney, "The Role of Ideology: A Summation," in *The End of Ideology Debate,* ed. Waxman, p. 302.

16. Daniel Bell, *The End of Ideology* (New York: Free Press, 1961).

17. Some of the student radicalism is described in Zbigniew Brzezinski, *Between Two Ages: America's Role in the Technetronic Era* (New York: Viking, 1970), pp. 94–110.

18. Bell, *End of Ideology,* p. 275.

19. Robert C. Tucker, *The Marxist Revolutionary Idea* (New York: W. W. Norton, 1968), p. 192.

20. Quoted in Maurice Cranston, "Althusser's Ideology," *Problems of Communism* 22 (March–April, 1973):53.

21. P. Uliassi, "Communism in Western Europe," in *The New Communisms,* ed. Dan N. Jacobs (New York: Harper & Row, 1969), pp. 288–289.

22. Norman Kogan, "The French Communists and Their Italian Comrades," in *Studies in Comparative Communism* 4 (Spring–Summer 1973):187.

23. *New York Times,* September 14, 1973, p. 12.

24. *Business Week,* February 16, 1974, p. 72.

25. F. S. V. Donnison, *Burma* (New York: Praeger, 1970), pp. 169–170.

26. Irene L. Gendzier, *Frantz Fanon* (New York: Pantheon Books, 1973), chap. 5.

27. Jules Monnerot, *Démarxiser l'université,* (Paris: La table ronde, 1970), p. 89.

28. Jules Monnerot, *Sociologie de la révolution* (Paris: Fayard, 1969), p. 111.

29. See Daniel Bell, *The Coming of Post-Industrial Society: A Venture in Social Forecasting* (New York: Basic Books, 1973).

30. W. Delaney, "The Role of Ideology: A Summation," in *End of Ideology Debate,* ed. Waxman, p. 303.

INDEX

Index

Index

Index

Index

Sukarno, 137
Sun Yat-sen, 105
Superstructure, infrastructure (base) and, 17–18, 87, 225
Surplus value, 23
Svitak, Ivan, 212
Sweezy, Paul, 183, 223
Syndicalism, 42

Taiping Rebellion, 26, 101
Taiwan, 110, 205–206
TASS, 176
Thales, 141
Theses on Feuerbach (Marx), 32
Third International, 62, 91–93; *see also* Comintern
Third World, 85, 116, 117, 120–123, 125, 128–131, 135, 137, 139, 140, 187, 249; *see also* Less developed countries
Tito, Marshal (Josip Broz), 239
Tolstoy, Leo, 56
Totalitarianism, *see* Authoritarianism
Trotsky, Leon, 49, 67, 73–74, 80, 110, 111, 123, 171, 184, 216
Trotskyites, 95, 184
Tucker, Robert C., 16
Tupamaros, 207
Turcios, Luis, 129
Turkey, 101
Turkish revolution, 233

Ulam, Adam B., vi, 66n
Underdeveloped countries, *see* Less developed countries
United States, 4, 26, 80, 96, 109, 145–146, 149–150, 179, 230–232; cold war and, 164, 165, 230; 1960s radical movements in, 148, 185, 231, 243; Third World countries and, 122, 125, 126, 128–130; war and peace issues and, 164–169
"Unity of opposites," 115
Uruguay, 125, 138, 207
U.S.S.R., *see* Soviet Union

Varga, E., 94
Vargas, Getulio, 139, 207
Vatican, the, 187
Veblen, Thorstein, 224
Vekhi (manifesto), 56
Venezuela, 125, 139
Venus, 153–154
Vietcong, 187

Vietnam, 138; *see also* North Vietnam; South Vietnam
Vietnam war, 147, 165–169, 185, 223, 230–232, 243, 248
Violence (violent change or revolution), 25, 184–185, 209–211, 214, 220, 221, 235, 243–244

War: Marxism and, 161–169, 228–233; revolution and, 209, 210, 214
War Communism, 73
"Wars of liberation," 81, 84, 250
Weathermen, 168
Webb, Beatrice, 171–173
Webb, Sidney, 171–173
Weber, Max, 224, 225, 253
Weisengrün, Paul, 59
Weitling, Wilhelm, 34
Wells, H. G., 58
West Germany, 147
Weydemeyer, J., 53
What Is to Be Done? (Lenin), 50, 54
Wittgenstein, Ludwig, 141
Women's Liberation, 148–149, 185
Woodcock, Leonard, 183n
Workers (factory workers; proletariat; working class), 5–7, 10–13, 20, 54, 99, 142; dictatorship of the, *see* Dictatorship of the proletariat; intellectuals and, 158–161, 183–184; Marx and Engels' attitude toward, 214; in Russia (pre-revolutionary), 46, 47, 51–52, 55, 71–72; in Soviet Union, 84; *see also* Class struggle
Workers' Opposition (Russia), 73
World revolution, 73–75, 102, 174, 234
World War I, 90, 229; Soviet Marxism and, 60–63, 66
World War II, 96–97, 173, 230
World Youth Festival (1975), 176
Wretched of the Earth, The (Fanon), 141–142

Young Hegelians, 13–14
Youth: American, 167; *see also* Student movements
Yugoslavia, 96–98, 138, 139, 181

Zaire, 251
Zasulich, Vera, 35
Zhdanovschina, 173
Zinoviev, G., 73–74, 94

281